GLOBAL NOMAD

GLOBAL NOMAD

MY TRAVELS THROUGH DIVING, TRAGEDY, AND REBIRTH

• • • • • • • • • • •

TOM HAIG

BASALT
BOOKS

Basalt Books
P.O. Box 645910
Pullman, WA 99164-5910
Basaltbooks.wsu.edu
Basalt.books@wsu.edu

Library of Congress Cataloging-in-Publication Data

Names: Haig, Tom, 1961- author.
Title: Global nomad : my travels through diving, tragedy, and rebirth / Tom
   Haig.
Description: Pullman, WA : Basalt Books, [2022]
Identifiers: LCCN 2022033517 | ISBN 9781638640035 (paperback)
Subjects: LCSH: Haig, Tom, 1961- | Divers--United States--Biography. |
   Cliff diving. | Diving accidents. | Athletes with disabilities--United
   States--Biography. | Wheelchair road racing.
Classification: LCC GV838.H35 A3 2022 | DDC 797.2/4092
   [B]--dc23/eng/20220811
LC record available at https://lccn.loc.gov/2022033517

Basalt Books is an imprint of Washington State University Press.
The Washington State University Pullman campus is located on the homelands of the Niimíipuu (Nez Perce) Tribe and the Palus people. We acknowledge their presence here since time immemorial and recognize their continuing connection to the land, to the water, and to their ancestors. WSU Press is committed to publishing works that foster a deeper understanding of the Pacific Northwest and the contributions of its Native peoples.

On the cover: The author in Paharganj, India, in 2010.
Cover design by Jeffry E. Hipp

CONTENTS

Waking to a New Reality

Coming out of surgery, I saw a cloudy blue light vaguely illuminating a pale green room. It was the same dull, putrid green of the high-rise apartment buildings I'd once seen in East Berlin. In the dream, I was strapped down, resigned to live in this hell forever.

When I awoke, I was in a hospital room, cemented in by nothing. For the next three months, I had nightmares every night, followed by a worse reality when I woke. The pain overwhelmed the army of endorphins recruited to soothe my brain. I'd been through some pressure cookers before, but this one wasn't a crack from a diving board or a fastball crushed into my temple. This wasn't the smash of a windshield against my back or the scrape of pavement ripping open my knee.

Since birth, my skull had been commissioned to hold my consciousness in place. But for the first time, I asked my skull to take a rest and let my consciousness float out of my body. I could see my time here was over. There was no coming back from this. No cast or ACE bandage was going to heal this. I was begging the powers that be to let me check out. But the docs were doing too good a job on me. I could have fought for death, but I didn't have the guts. I complacently let my soul back into my body. As much as I wanted to end it, I didn't even have the power to off myself.

• • • • • • • • • • • • • •

Before the nightmares, I had lived in Dubai, Holland, Taiwan, and Les Avenières in the French Alps. I'd performed eight-story high dives into 10 feet of water to audiences all over the world. I'd competed in the Acapulco cliff diving championships. And just three weeks earlier I had been diving off cliffs in Hawaii with my brother Bagus. But everything about my old life changed on that sunny Sunday morning in September 1996. While the rest of the world kept spinning, I lay broken on a Portland, Oregon intersection near my bicycle and the 24-foot delivery truck I'd just hit.

The scene around me was chaotic as some people tried to move me and others pulled them off. People asked me questions, but I couldn't respond. I hadn't passed out, and I wasn't feeling pain. I was watching the first 35 years of my life vanish with every passing second.

I reached down and touched my right thigh to see if I could feel it. I could feel my thigh, but the sensation was odd. It was only when I tried to unclip my cleats that I noticed something was wrong. There was no response. I reached down for my thigh and realized my fingers were feeling skin, but my leg wasn't feeling anything back. I slowly dragged my fingers up my body until I got a response—just above my waist. I was in for something bigger than I'd ever imagined. I looked down at my fingers and started playing air guitar scales. They worked fine. I was still a musician but not much else. I'd become a cripple.

I've always been a competitor, but surviving and recovering from a spinal cord injury is an ugly and complicated game that nobody wants or deserves to play. The object is to get back everything you've just lost—and you will not win this game. It's you versus your new body. Your new body makes and changes the rules without notice. There are no timeouts. You always play in pain. You can no longer urinate or defecate by yourself, yet the new body has the option of discharging anything at any time. You no longer have a car, and you can't get into your house (or anyone else's for that matter). You are out of work and out of money. There is very little reason to carry on.

• • • • • • • • • • • • •

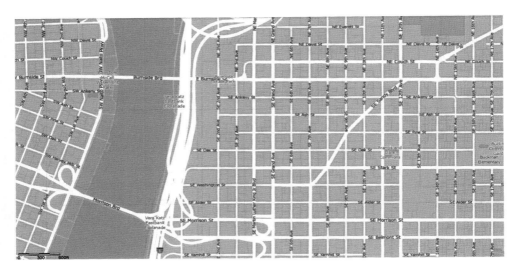

Sandy Boulevard in Portland, Oregon

Let's Go to the Pool!

It's absurd to say I grew up in a rough neighborhood in an idyllic north shore suburb of Milwaukee, but it's true. Ever since the first day my mom let me out of the door to play with the neighborhood kids, odds were that we were going to get in trouble. Lots of it.

Our neighborhood barely existed when we moved in, just a reclaimed wetland ten miles north of downtown Milwaukee. In 1966 my father was the first to buy property in the Lower Clovernook section of Glendale. He still lives there. Every year the 40-acre open field we grew up next to was taken over by more and more new houses. Not knowing the intricacies of the real-estate market or anything about property values, we assumed the field surrounding our houses was ours and anyone taking any part of it was our enemy. Our Schwinn banana-seat cavalry protected the field with a vengeance, destroying dozens of half-built homes and smashing the windows of those just getting ready to show. We didn't see ourselves as vandals. We thought we were protecting what was ours.

Football was our passion, second only to our adventurous forays into the developing suburb of Glendale. The southern border of Lower Clovernook was a raised railroad track that served as our link to the outside world. Our rock-war enemies lived on Bender Road, south of the tracks. As we ventured west, we came across a long bridge that spanned the Milwaukee River to Kletzsch Park. One of the rites of passage into our gang was to climb a 50-foot steel trestle that led to a clubhouse on a cement pillar above one of the last chunks of farmland left in Milwaukee County. The penalty for slipping was a 50-foot drop onto a concrete slab. Once on the trestle you walked along four-inch girders under the tracks until you came to our clubhouse on a pillar. The older guys, including my brother Dan, could hold onto the girder over their heads. The little guys had to balance on the lower girder and pray they didn't slip. But getting to the clubhouse was just the start. In order to be a member of "Bridge Club" you had to wait for an oncoming train, climb up to the tracks, and moon the conductor while the gazillion-ton locomotive sped by, inches from your ass.

Whether it be football or adventures, we arrived home filthy. Instead of making us take baths, my mom would give us a quarter and send us up to the Nicolet High School swimming pool for freeswim. It was tricky for us, as we had to dodge the few adequate enemies we had in the wimpy gentrified neighborhood of Upper Clovernook. It was best we got to the pool unnoticed so we could lock our Stingray bikes without them interfering. Once at the pool we asserted our dominance by taking over the diving board at the deep end. While the dweebs from the established neighborhoods of Glendale did small hops and nose-plugged jumps, we assaulted the plank with a vengeance. Having just felt a train rumble by inches from your butt, how afraid could we be of a front flip? We leapt high into the air to catch nerf-ball passes thrown by the lifeguards. We tried anything they asked us. I can't really put a finger on when it happened, but eventually the lessons learned from Bridge Club matched up better with the diving board than the football field.

When I was older and a professional, I would feel, deep in my soul, that I was a diver. I liked to jump, I loved the sensation of spinning, and, more than anything else, I loved the way water could fool gravity. I could drop nine stories and, if I kept tight and lined myself up, I could enter the water without feeling a thing. I could enter forward, backward, on my head, or on my feet. I had the sensation that I was fooling Isaac Newton.

In high school, the main event at swim meets, and the one that brought the senior cheerleaders over from the varsity basketball games, was the one-meter diving. In 1975 the swimmers at Nicolet High School were overshadowed by a pair of divers ranked first and second in the state. Mark Rosandich was a good spinner and had cat-like quickness, but Keith Potter had all the school records and the flair of a champion.

When Potter stepped up to the board, the crowd turned dead silent. All eyes were on the sandy-haired athlete as he approached the end of the board and snapped his iron-tight physique into a high graceful hurdle. His big trick was the front 1½ with 2 twists. With a 2.7 degree of difficulty, it was the toughest dive in the state, and he knew how to put that thing in the water. He soared in the air, spun into his twists, and then neatly squared out just above the board. As he dropped in vertically, the crowd's silence morphed into manic caterwauling that wouldn't stop until the referee blew his whistle, like a judge ordering silence in the courtroom. Potter would climb out of the pool, smile at his coach, Don Osborne, and then calmly return to his seat with another victory.

The State Meet in 1975 was held at the Natatorium on the campus of the University of Wisconsin in Madison, about 90 minutes away. I wasn't allowed to go, as I was only in seventh grade, but the final competition was televised on a local station. Of my seven siblings, four were at the meet and the three youngest were at home watching it on TV. We were a Nicolet swimming family and watching one of our guys go for the gold medal in Madison was as big as life got.

The final three dives of the eleven-dive contest were televised. Potter's first dive was a front dive with a half-twist. He confidently took it up in the air, pointed down towards the water then gently made the half turn and sliced the water. Next up was his front 2½ tuck. It wasn't the most difficult dive in his list, but it was one he knew he could hit. He stood it up, spun like a top and kicked out vertically, again collecting 7s and 8s. I shot off the couch and screamed with my two little brothers.

Finally, it was time for the big double twister. Up in the air he went, spinning as tight as a pencil. He squared out, looked at the water, and disappeared below the surface without a trace. The three of us burst off the couch and shook our fists. He'd done it. He capped off an unbeaten season with a state championship and an All-American qualifying score.

Along with my dreams of playing for the Brewers at County Stadium, the Bucks at the MECCA, the Packers at Lambeau Field, and winning the Olympic marathon (I wanted to be Frank Shorter for a while, too), I wanted to win that damn meet in Madison. Whereas the other sports dreams were the same dreams that every kid in my school had, diving seemed to be particularly suited to me. Diving was an adventure into the unknown and untested. Ever since I took my first hike along the railroad tracks, that's what I was all about. Every day I had to go a little farther—see a little more, climb another tree, scale a different building. Diving was the same way. Every day I wanted to add another flip, do a different position, or try a trick on a higher board or platform. There was always something out there I hadn't done. As much as I loved the other sports, none of them had that adventurous appeal. When the team came back from Madison, I got to know Coach Osborne. I had to belong to this.

Two years later I ended a comfortable stay at St. Monica's Catholic elementary school and enrolled at Nicolet. My class at St. Monica's consisted of 60 close-knit friends, only a handful of whom joined me in the new uncontrollable mob of 1,600 at Nicolet. Even though my two older sisters Barb and Nari were at Nicolet, I was petrified to step onto the campus. I barely said a word to anyone for three months. But in November, I strapped on my tight black Mike Pepe diving suit and went to my first practice for the Nicolet Knights. Potter was long gone, diving in the Big Ten at the University of Illinois, but Nicolet still had two state contenders, Dave Worth and Andy Klapperich. It was a painful year as I was pushed to take my single somersault dives and add another half-flip so I would go in headfirst. We had a good crop of freshmen and if one of us went for a dive, the other ones couldn't back off. If we'd been born 20 years later, we would have been skateboarders or snowboarders. But in the cold, flat, nerdy Midwest we became springboard divers.

I was competing all year with Dan Ullsperger, a big kid from neighboring Fox Point. I could twist better, but he could jump higher and spin better. Just like Coach Osborne said, whoever hit their required dives did better. Nicolet would send four divers to all the big meets, so with Worth and Klapperich taking up the first two varsity spots, that left the final two spots to either Ullsperger, me, or Frank Clark, a junior who was just growing into his body. When the big invitational meets came in January, I was determined to make my spot on the varsity a permanent one.

I won half of the freshman and junior varsity (JV) dual meets, so I was picked for the Nicolet Invitational, our big varsity home meet. In a dual meet, a diver only does six dives, but in the big invitational meets everyone does eleven. Diving has five categories: front, back, reverse (walking forward and spinning backwards), inward (standing backwards and spinning forward) and twist. For the big meets, everyone does one simple dive from each category and one difficult dive from each category. The eleventh dive was a high difficulty dive from the diver's best category. Looking at the dive lists for the divers coming into the meet, I had my work cut out to make the final cut of 12. They were throwing a lot of difficulty. I was worried I didn't have a big eleventh dive. But, if I made the final and scored some points for the team, I might qualify for my varsity letter as a freshman.

A freshman wearing a varsity letter was beyond what I could ever imagine. A varsity letter was for a starting senior football player or the point guard of the basketball team. Getting a varsity letter meant I could go to church on Sunday wearing a letterman's jacket with a real varsity letter on it, not just the shoulder numerals you got for being on JV. None of my old St. Monica classmates would ever believe it.

Once the warm-ups started, I saw some scared divers and felt my chances improving. We dove into a nine-foot pool that freaked out divers who were used to diving into twelve-foot pools. As the meet started, I rode the board well and only missed one of eight dives, putting me in the finals in eighth place. If I had a decent couple of final dives I could make it into the top five, which meant a medal.

My first dive in the final round was a half-twist. By now the judges liked seeing a freshman doing well and paid me off with the first 7s of my life. Next came my front double tuck. I wasn't a strong front spinner, but I skyed it, grabbed a tight tuck, and stepped out of it for 6s.

My last dive was a back somersault with 1½ twists. I'd just learned it the week before, but it was an easy trick for me. I jumped up in the air, twisted it up, and finished looking straight at the starting blocks on the opposite end of the pool. I collected a bunch of 6s and 6½s so I was sure I'd moved up to fifth place. I looked into the stands for my father, a professional math wiz, who kept score for all the meets (not just for me but everyone in the meet). He was grinning, and my mother, who had taken time from her weekend shift as an X-ray technician, was on her feet waving three fingers in the air.

I almost passed out. I'd moved all the way up to third place, right behind Worth and Klapperich. I didn't just score a couple of points for the varsity; I'd scored a shitload of points for the varsity. When I was in grade school, I used to go to track meets at Nicolet and look at the top five sprinters in the 100 meters as if they were gods who walked among us. And I just got third at the same level meet. That can't be right, can it?

The big senior swimmers who led the cheers and dated senior timettes (swimming equivalent of cheerleaders: they dressed in cheerleader uniforms and helped out the swim coach with everything from stopwatches to calculating diving scores) threw me around and slapped me upside the head. Two minutes later, I was kissing the most beautiful woman I'd ever seen (first kiss ever…at an award presentation. I wonder what her name was?), accepting the bronze medal and stepping up to the third place podium.

When Worth grabbed his gold medal and kissed his award presenter he motioned for Klapperich and me to join him on the first-place victory block. The swimmers led the standing-room-only crowd of parents and students in a deafening cheer of "One-Two-Three! One-Two-Three! One-Two-Three!" It was the highest level cheer a Nicolet athlete could ever receive. I didn't even make third string on my grade-school basketball team and 12 months later I was receiving a crowd roar at a big-time varsity invitational. It changed me forever.

But it also overwhelmed me with responsibility. Now I was expected to score points all the time. And that didn't happen for a long time. It was a good enough moment for me to get my varsity letter, but I didn't topple my freshman score my entire sophomore year. I placed well enough in the meets and managed a fourth place at the Nicolet Invitational, but Ullsperger beat me regularly.

I asked my high school guidance counselor if she could connect me with Indiana University and Hobie Billingsley, but she didn't have the answer. I went to the high school library and looked up "Indiana University Diving." The library had a book called *Diving Illustrated* by Hobie Billingsley. On the last page of the book was contact information about Indiana University diving. I wrote down the address, penned a letter, and five months later I was in Bloomington.

When I showed up at the IU pool at 7:00 a.m., a semi-bald, mustachioed man with thick glasses walked on to the deck and spoke to the group of college divers who were camp counselors. I thought he was one of the Indiana janitors talking about turning off the lights, but he turned out to be Hobie Billingsley. As unassuming as his exterior was, his interior was just as focused and unwavering. Hobie wasn't interested in developing good one-meter springboard divers. He wanted to develop three-meter springboard and ten-meter tower champions. The camp had a bunch of elementary school kids who had already learned college-level three-meter dives. These dives were some of the scariest ones to learn. This is when most divers quit the sport. At that point I was afraid to bounce on the three-meter board, let alone do simple required dives. But Hobie didn't push divers like a drill sergeant. He just showed you the proper mechanics, taught you the tricks on a trampoline, then said you were ready to do the trick. If you didn't do the tricks, he sent you home.

It was that simple. He was there to train divers, not baby-sit rich kids on vacation. You did your tricks, or he asked you to call your parents and have them pick you up. No malice or pressure was involved. If you weren't into it by yourself, for yourself, well this just wasn't the place for you. There were plenty of other diving camps in the country, but in order to put on this camp's T-shirt, you had to toss some tricks.

Hobie was at poolside every morning to give us a pep talk and make sure we were ready to toss those big tricks. At night he either gave us a physics lecture or showed us movies of past Olympians, all of whom were his closest friends. I'd never been in the company of such greatness.

The more time I spent with Hobie, the more I knew I was a diver. It felt like I was cheating gravity. I should be getting crushed doing these head-first, multi-somersault, twisting tricks, but instead I was emerging from a cool inviting element to the amazement of most of the people around me. The other sports dreams I had before meeting Hobie Billingsley disappeared. All I wanted to do was dive—and win that damn State meet.

I returned from Hobie's Heroes with a mission. Dan Ullsperger was my friend, but I was going further. He continued to beat me at the beginning of our junior year, but as soon as I learned to put my tougher tricks into the water, I paced by him. I won the Braveland Conference championship as well as the Whitefish Bay state sectional meet, even though I hit the board on my back 1½. I was ranked third in the state but finished an embarrassing (for me) fourth place in Madison.

Back to Hobie's Heroes: The baseball team I'd played with since I was 10 was now playing varsity for Nicolet. I was one of their catchers, but now I was a diver. It was a traumatic decision, but I had to go back to Bloomington. I had to learn all the hard three-meter dives. Instead of donning the tools of ignorance, I spent all summer in Bloomington, soaking up the wisdom of Hobie Billingsley. At the end of the summer I won the Hobie's Heroes meet, which was arguably harder than the Wisconsin state meet.

I started off my senior season by breaking Keith Potter's school record for six dives at my second dual meet. By the time the big meets came around in January, I'd set the pool record at every pool I entered. That streak came to a halt when I cracked my head on the board doing a reverse 2½ in the warm-ups at Menomonee Falls East high school. It was the same kind of dive Greg Louganis did when he cracked his head during the Seoul Olympics. I still won the meet, but I can't remember a thing from it. Practice the next two weeks was brutal—not from the concussion, but from a dislocated jaw and a couple of bruised ribs that came from crashing my chin into my chest.

By the time the Whitefish Bay sectional came along, I'd almost made good on my promise to rewrite the record books. I'd broken all but one pool record, with the most gut-wrenching exception being the Nicolet 11-dive pool record. I had my worst meet of the year during my home invitational and Keith Potter kept his name on the record board. I was furious with myself after the meet, but when I went to practice the next Monday and saw his name still on the pool record board, it brought a smile to my face. Any self-esteem I had came from his example. It was best that his name still hung around that pool.

Milwaukee Journal photo from an article naming me the odds-on favorite to win the 1980 State diving title.

Everything came together during the Whitefish Bay sectional meet. I cracked the magical 500-point mark, crushing the Sectional record as well as the historic Whitefish Bay pool record. I went through to Madison as the prohibitive favorite.

The state meet started early on Saturday morning with only a few parents and coaches in the stands. I started out hot and nailed my first five dives, opening a commanding lead. As we got to the semi-final round, I missed the finish on my inward 1½ but put the two required dives away for 8s. I'd saved my three highest scoring dives for the finals. It was pretty much in the bag, but I still had to dive out the set.

It was then that I started to do what no athlete should ever do. I stopped thinking of diving and started to think of the state record. It was in reach if I zipped my last three dives. "I'm really going to have to go for it on these hurdles if I'm going to get the son of a bitch!" I thought. One of Hobie's rules was to dive practice like it was a meet and dive the meet like it was practice. In other words, make each dive count in workout—and dive normally in the meet. I was going for big dives, and it almost cost me.

My first dive was the front dive with a half-twist. Ever since Potter used that dive in the final, every Nicolet diver used it in the final. It was my highest scoring required dive, and I'd collected 9s on it a couple of times during the season. I went for a big hurdle but didn't get my arms above my head on takeoff. I was late initiating the dive and had to pull like hell just to get vertical. Some of the less experienced judges still gave me 7s but I also collected some 5½s—not what the guy leading the state meet is supposed to do.

My next dive was a front 2½ pike. I didn't do this one very well in practice, but it always seemed to come around in meets. I went for another big dive, but I got stuck in the spin. Luckily, I'd been in this position hundreds of times before. I just squished my face between my knees and stayed in the pike as long as I could. I sprung open just before the water and managed to get my hands together and stretch my legs high into the air. Two dives—two horrible takeoffs. At least I got 7s on the front 2½.

Now I had the damn thing won. To lose at this point, I would have to land flat on my butt on my best dive. That wasn't going to happen. I'd learned my lesson on going for the big hurdle. I had a reverse 1½ with 1½ twists left. I'd nailed it for 8s in the sectional meet and hadn't missed it all week long. All I had to do was go for a normal hurdle and I was going to walk away with everything. I relaxed before my approach, went for a normal hurdle then rode the board high into the air. It ended up being the best hurdle of the day. I tossed my arms above my head, began twisting, and the toughest dive in my list was floating through the air as if I were on a pulley. I squared out of the twist and looked at the board only to discover I'd never gotten that good of a top on a reverse twister in my life. I was done with the dive with two meters to fall. I wasn't going to blow it, but I was going to have to put on the brakes and go for a big underwater save.

While I was underwater, I could hear the roar of the crowd. I'd actually missed the dive—just not that badly. I needed to nail that last trick to get to 500 points, but I didn't. Nonetheless, I was the undefeated Wisconsin State Champion and a lock to be named High School All-American.

I came out of the water to a deafening scream. I looked up at my family in the stands and then over at Coach Osborne. Osborne came over; we hugged each other, and the tears started to flow. The next thing I knew there was a TV camera on us and reporters were asking questions. I felt like I'd just won the Olympics. A few minutes later they announced the results and presented the medals at the awards podium. Before the meet, Osborne had been selected to hand out the diving awards. He didn't want to tell me because he thought it might put extra pressure on me. I climbed the podium, he put the medal around my neck, and I said, "This could have really backfired on you!"

"Not a chance," Osborne said. "You weren't gonna lose this thing."

I looked into the cavernous stands and the University of Wisconsin Natatorium. The the Nicolet contingent was screaming and waving old political yard signs from my dad's school board campaign: "Haig for Nicolet Board."

I walked towards the stands but was mobbed before I could get there. Nearly everyone I knew was in Madison forming a circle around me in a big group hug. I was so overwhelmed I almost passed out. It was the first time in my life I completed what I thought to be an impossible dream. It would not be the last...

But while I was getting mobbed, Ox was getting ready to swim. Ox qualified for the finals of the 500-yard freestyle, and I always counted laps for Ox.

Ox and his brother, Toys, are my oldest friends in the world. We shared a backyard growing up and they're charter members of Bridge Club. On most swim teams, counting laps (sitting at the end of a swimmer's lane with large plastic number cards you stick into the pool, showing the swimmer how many laps they've done) for the 500 free is designated to an inconsequential freshman. But I never looked at it like that. Ox was my brother, so I counted for him even though I was captain of the varsity and not even a swimmer. I first counted his laps when I was a sophomore and he was a freshman. I counted every 500 free he ever swam up until the day I was State Champion and he made All-State. And, as of this writing, I'm going on my fourth decade of playing music with Toys.

● ● ● ● ● ● ● ● ● ● ● ● ●

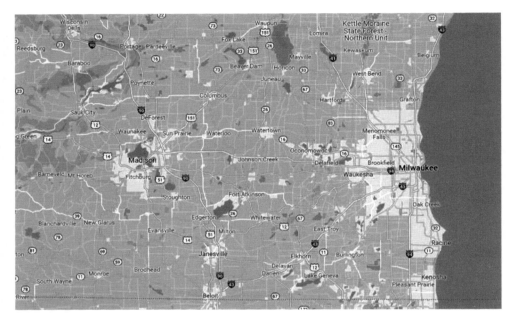

Milwaukee-Madison

The Bridge to Venice

I had a state title in my pocket and a dozen schools recruiting me, but somehow it felt a bit fraudulent. I wasn't sure why diving worked so well when in all the other sports I tried, I was anywhere from decent to downright bad. After my thighs exploded and I put on 50 pounds my sophomore year, I couldn't keep up with any of my classmates on the cross-country team. After my state championship diving season, I went back to baseball and my Glendale Little League teammates, now the full Nicolet varsity, made it to the State quarterfinals. I was the State champ in one sport; the backup catcher in another.

But any time I got on a diving board, everyone in the pool stopped and watched what I was doing. I worked hard at becoming a good diver, but I put in nearly as much work trying to be a great catcher. Somewhere in the back of my head there was a nagging sense of insecurity and once I got to college it really began to show.

Coach Fred Newport gave me a tuition scholarship to the University of Illinois, but I quickly realized that being a state champ doesn't mean anything in the Big Ten. In the 1980s Big Ten diving, you needed to be an Olympian just to make the final five competitors. I continued to work hard, waking up at 6 a.m. for practice and spending three hours after class at the pool. But I just wasn't cutting it in the big leagues. After two years at Illinois, I transferred to a lower division school, but soon after I got there, I realized I was just quitting on myself. I begged Coach Newport for my scholarship back at Illinois and, eventually, I made it back on to the team. Two weeks into my senior season, after a great summer of training where I thought I was becoming a solid Big Ten diver, I got all big in my head over a team policy and walked out of the pool.

It was a huge mistake. I remember having a lot of existential and psychological crap running around my brain and for some reason I wigged out. I was finished. I was done with diving, and I'd only just begun to grow into my mature body. I couldn't have picked a worse time to be headstrong.

I got a job waiting tables but, without diving practice, I didn't know what to do with all the free time. I'd come home from class and wonder what

13

the hell regular students did with all the extra time. And then it occurred to me—some of them play music.

I started playing guitar during the summer after my freshman year. I was home in Wisconsin picking notes on my sister Sue's cheapo Spanish cat-gut guitar that only had three strings. The noise must have been godawful, I would watch TV and noodle while anyone else in the room cringed. I swore I would only play during commercials, but that never worked. I kept playing. Eventually, my mom told me if I wanted to keep picking, I had to buy new strings and learn how to play.

A year later, I went to a music store and picked up a Gibson SG copy I could turn upside down and string left-handed. Playing left-handed is a curse that has cost me thousands of dollars over my lifetime. When you are right-handed you can walk into any party, any music shop anywhere in the world, and play any guitar or bass. When you are left-handed you have to haul your guitar everywhere and also learn to play a right-handed guitar upside down. I saw a Jimi Hendrix documentary in which the other players in Greenwich Village raved at how dedicated he was because he always carried his axe around with him. As it turns out EVERY left-handed player carries their axe around with them or we don't get to play. I could have just learned how to play right-handed from the start, but that wasn't going to work. My brother Bagus is left-handed. He tried playing righty for a year and had to switch back. The Townshend windmills didn't work for Bagus playing the right-handed axe. You have to play what's natural or you're gonna quit or suck.

Both my younger brothers were playing music and most of our old high school swim team friends were either playing music or smoking weed all day and listening to Grateful Dead bootlegs. I was listening to those bootlegs too, which led to a 12-year odyssey of catching Dead shows all over the country. I am an old-school Deadhead with 50+ shows on my resume. The lessons I learned on the Grateful Dead tour were crucial to my success traveling the globe

If you see me play now, you'll hear that I'm a Garcia disciple. Hopefully I'm not too stuck in that style. The Grateful Dead came into my musical journey late in the game as I'd already been a big music junkie before I started playing. My sister Nari got me started on The Beatles at a very young age and, to this day, it's that Beatles diversity and depth I strive for. Later on in grade school, our neighborhood football savant, Burns, turned us on to Pink Floyd's album *The Dark Side of the Moon*. That idea of pure tone and lyrical efficiency set a song-writing standard I constantly strive for.

Then there's The Who. My friend Gary turned me on to The Who my freshman year at Illinois and it was as if I'd never heard music before in my life. The band was a four-headed monster of virtuosity. They blew my skull apart. They demanded I pick up a guitar, respect it as sacred, and learn how to play the snot out of it. Music became my religion, and it remains that to this day. When I fill out airline disembarkation forms and they ask "what religion," I always write "musician."

Playing music is a calling, just like what the Catholic priests and nuns explained to us in grade school about turning to God. Every year St. Monica's held "Vocation Day," in which a group of clergy would speak to us about the profound effect their calling had on their lives. How it changed everything, rearranged their priorities and set the path for their future. They described it as deeply personal, difficult to explain, yet impossible to ignore. This is exactly what happened to me after just a few dorm sessions listening to Quadrophenia. The Catholic Church, which I had dumped a year earlier, was replaced. I became a Townshend seeker. Pete wasn't a proselytizer. He didn't care if you paid attention to his message or not (although his record company did!). So I listened...

My roommate Charlie had a copy of the Grateful Dead's "Black Book," which contained the sheet music for most of the classic Dead material. I had no idea how to read music, but I could figure out the chord charts above the words and get the song to flow. It took a while, but eventually I could sit in with a group and play rhythm guitar without screwing everything up.

Playing music is as mysterious, benevolent, rewarding, and confusing as any of the major religions. One thing it is not, is dishonest. It's next to impossible to lie through the guitar. It always reveals truths. Truths about your effort, truths about accomplishment, truths about frustrations, truths about your ability, truths about sharing, and truths about ego. You just can't lie with a guitar in your hand.

Music, like any true omniscient being, waits for you to discover it. It puts you in an elevated state of awareness and a lifelong path of constant learning. You're never done learning your instrument and there are many instruments to play. It goes on forever. It never stops.

I graduated from the University of Illinois in 1985 with a BS in industrial psychology. While Illinois has a top five industrial psychology program, my degree could still be described as what my father would define "a worthless psychology degree." But I picked psychology as a major on purpose. I wasn't ready to join the workforce. Pete Townshend had my ear:

> They call me The Seeker
>
> I've been searching low and high
>
> I won't get to get what I'm after
>
> 'Til the day I die.

I became one of Pete's "Seekers." He was telling me to go out and see the world. So I did.

Seven months after I graduated, I found myself hovering over the tiny Luxembourg airport on a $390 Icelandic Air flight that had taken me out of North America for the first time. Sitting next to me were Michael Bathke, a high school swimming teammate and future guitar partner, and his wife Lori, who was five months pregnant with Emma, who would become an amazing mom herself. We had to rent a car and find the train station to pick up my brother Dan, who had been studying in London. Lori and I went to the baggage claim while Michael fumbled around the airport looking for the Hertz booth. Eventually, a pickle-faced Luxembourger, speaking what he thought was English, brought the car around to the baggage claim and gave us the key.

Suffering from our first doses of jetlag and completely disoriented, none of us were eager to take the keys. The Ford Escort looked like a Cessna to us. We loaded up the trunk, then Michael slowly pulled out of the airport. I navigated, while Lori was in the back trying to calm her fears about miscarriages.

I'd been to Montreal on a diving trip and Tijuana as a kid, but neither prepared me for the complete confusion of being immersed in a European city. On the North American trips, I sat in the passenger seat and looked out the window. This time I was responsible for finding my brother.

We trolled up and down the ravines of Luxembourg trying to navigate tiny streets that didn't go straight and kept changing names. The names weren't helping anyway, as I couldn't pronounce them, and Michael couldn't read the signs. Directional signals appeared to be telling us to make left turns, but every time we took the left, we got horribly lost.

When we weren't freaking out, we found ourselves in the most beautiful city any of us had ever laid eyes on. The ravines were supported by ancient stone walls rising high into the sky, forming castle turrets and church steeples. The cobblestone streets blended into the walls and tunnels. The oldest buildings in the Midwest are 19th-century churches, but this city was a 15th-century Gothic masterpiece. It felt heretical to be walking on the streets of this storybook town, let alone driving along them. Did people work in a city like this, or did they just ride single-gear black bicycles and hang out in boulangeries?

Once we figured out the tilted arrow signs weren't pointing left but were telling us to continue straight, things started to make sense. We were still panicked, but at least we could follow the map. Michael remembered that "gare" meant "train station," so after a few left turns and sprints down the opposite direction of one-way streets, we reached the Gare du Luxembourg.

I spotted Dan out of the corner of my eye and screamed at Michael to stop. Dan walked to the car, and we jumped on him as if he were Jehovah himself.

By this time Dan had been in Europe for four months and was an old hand at getting around. He'd been to England, Ireland, and had even done a Eurail trip on the continent, an unfathomable feat to us at this point. Dan hopped in the driver's seat, pulled out of the train station, and calmly drove us out of Luxembourg. With Dan at the wheel, my blood pressure dropped and I was able to navigate the brightly lit Belgian highway system.

Whereas Luxembourg City was a confusing maze, it was impossible to get lost on the perfectly marked Belgian highways. Space shuttle astronauts reported the only man-made thing they could identify from space was the Belgian freeway system.

As soon as we were on our way, Dan reached into his bag and pulled out a bottle of Bailey's Irish Cream. "Merry Christmas!" he said with a big laugh.

"Give me that!" Michael said. He took a long pull, closed his eyes and announced, "I'm all better now."

We skirted Brussels and sped through the countryside to the canal city of Bruges, not far from the English Channel. After checking into a hostel, Dan took us to a pub he'd visited a few months earlier. Nothing on site resembled any kind of bar I'd ever seen before. The strangely branded liquor bottles were corralled upside-down in single shot dispensers, and beer poured from long stemmed "pression" nozzles dealing out twice as much foam as beer.

Dan, Michael, and I were ready to toss a dozen of those tiny beers down our gullet, but Lori was getting sick from the saturation of unfiltered cigarette smoke in the bar. We drank well short of our quota and returned to the hostel to finish off the bottle of Bailey's.

The next morning, I woke at sunrise and walked to the city center to watch Europeans wake up. The buildings along the narrow twisting roads leaned on each other for support, especially in the town square where it seemed if I moved one small brick, the town would topple. The streets were lined with short brown poles serving as bicycle racks as well as traffic boundaries. The temperature hovered around freezing, but commuters went to work on single-speed black bicycles, with skirted women sitting side-saddle on luggage racks above the rear wheels. Their faces all seemed a little different too—kind of thin and crinkly compared to Americans.

I had some Belgian francs, but I was too afraid to walk into a boulangerie and order a baguette. Instead, I scampered back to the hostel and ate hard rolls and jelly with the crew.

After Dan walked us around the city, we got back into the Ford Escort and took off for Amsterdam. Dan named the car "Arthur Dent" after the main character in the Douglas Adams series, *The Hitchhiker's Guide to the Galaxy*. In Adams' books, Arthur Dent is one of two humans who escaped the end of the earth, which was leveled to make way for a celestial highway bypass. Dan thought it was appropriate to name the car after Arthur Dent because he was in constant search of adventure. Lori, Michael, and I thought it was appropriate because we felt like we'd never get back to our home planet.

It was New Year's Eve, and we headed to Amsterdam to party. There's not a better city in the world to spend New Year's Eve, but I was petrified with culture shock. Dan had spent a weekend in Amsterdam and scarcely needed the map as he drove us over a series of canal bridges, parking Arthur Dent up on a sidewalk in the city center.

The brownstone buildings made Amsterdam darker than the green ravines of Luxembourg. The lean of the buildings in the center of Bruges was nothing compared to this city's drunken architecture. We checked into the Hotel Kabul hostel in the middle of the red-light district and walked a few blocks to get our bearings. Dan seemed to know where we were, but every street looked the same to me. Exhausted from our first bouts with jetlag, we returned to the Kabul and crashed.

I woke up around 8:00 to see the Italian in the bunk next to me spiking his arm with a fresh dose of heroin. He nodded, drifted off, then offered me the needle. I'd seen my share of hallucinogens, but I'd never seen a drug needle before. I froze at the offer, so he shrugged his shoulders and put the needle back in his bag. I stayed iced the rest of the night. Michael and Lori were in the same condition. I'd heard of culture shock, but I thought it had something to do with migrant workers coming to America. I didn't think going to another western country could paralyze me.

Dan walked us through the Damplaatz and down Leidsestraat until we found ourselves looking at the world-famous Bull Dog Cafe. What is now commonplace in many US states was unthinkable in 1985. We were going to buy some legal weed.

All baggies cost 25 guilders (around $12 US at the time) so the produce was listed by weight, not money. The smaller the weight, the better the quality. We had our choice of Afghani and Kashmir hashish or five different grades of marijuana. Dan said the best buy was to go for the locally grown hydroponic Sinsemilla. Great pot at a reasonable quantity. We handed the dealer a 25-guilder note, and he gave us a small, sealed bag with the Bull Dog emblem printed on it. It smelled like a Christmas tree and stuck to Michael's fingers like fly paper. He rolled a doobie with papers from the dispensers sitting along the wall. We all smoked up except Lori, who was green with envy.

"Michael…" she said.

"I know," he replied, "I'm going to have to do a lot of babysitting for this one."

I thought the pot might take the edge off the culture shock, but instead it sent me into a paranoia-coma. Nothing seemed normal and I couldn't find a balance point to fall back on. I felt like I was living the very last night of my life. I began to miss Wisconsin. I had an insatiable urge to find a springboard. I REALLY wanted my guitar. Everything was so bizarre that I thought I would never be able to regain my normal brain. The language was incomprehensible, the canals looked like death pits, and all the buildings appeared to be not leaning on each other, but swaying.

We reached midnight and all hell broke loose. I remembered how crazy it was during Champaign's Halloween street parties when someone would blow off a single pack of firecrackers. But that would have gone unnoticed here. The Dutch strung gigantic ropes of firecrackers across major thoroughfares and danced in the streets, stopping traffic. The police didn't even flinch. At one point, there was an entire case of Roman candles burning in the middle of an intersection, shooting fireballs attacking the adjacent apartment buildings. A police car came up to it, circled around it and headed on its way. I thought I'd grown up in a free society, but Holland was kicking my ass.

The saving grace was Dan taking everything in stride. We tried to explain our culture shock, but he told us to chill out. "It happens to everybody," he said. "Give it a few days. It'll pass. Then you'll be kicking your ass for not chilling out." I didn't think I would ever get used to such a crazy place. And I could never imagine that in just 18 months, I'd be calling it home.

The next morning, we had breakfast at the Kabul, and I experienced a paranoia hangover. I was so stressed out from the night before I had a headache. I knocked down a few aspirin and began to relax for the first time since leaving the Midwest. When we walked out to the car, Amsterdam seemed much less frightening than the night before. We were off to England for a bit of normalcy, which seemed to take off the edge. That was a big mistake. I probably needed a little more edge than I'd anticipated.

Once again, Dan took the wheel of Arthur Dent and drove us out of town. I found a good blues radio station, and everything started to mellow out. As we meandered south into Belgium, Michael rolled a joint and we smoked out listening to some old Muddy Waters tunes. For the first time we could relax and laugh at our fears. The caged-in feeling of the night before was long gone as we hit the pastoral hills of southern Belgium. I even braved a stint at the wheel.

At this point, we'd crossed three borders and had yet to pull out our passports. As we neared the French border, Dan told us they'd stop us, so he took the weed from Michael and hid it. We slowed down for the border check, and a French douanier told us to pull over to a side lot.

"What's going on?" I asked.

"Don't know," Dan said. "On the trains they just match your ticket to your passport. I've never been through a road crossing before."

The guard asked for our passports and took them inside a small police hut on the French side of the border. A second guard came out, grabbed Dan and took him inside. We were baked, and all the paranoia we'd lost on the drive came flushing back three-fold.

"Where's the dope?" I asked.

"He's got it," Michael said.

Three minutes later Dan came out looking paler than his winter-white skin naturally looked. He gave us a strong glare and a very slight shake of the head, implying that none of us should say a thing. The guard pointed to me and motioned me inside. He brought me into a 10 by 10-foot room with a small table in the center. He pointed to my hip sack and ordered me to open it. He threw my bag on the table then pointed to my coat. I unzipped my parka and handed it over to him. He went through each pocket.

"Shoes!" he said.

I untied my Nikes and handed them over. He grabbed them, lifted the tongue and checked them with a tiny flashlight. Then he pointed to my feet with an impatient gesture implying I should take off my socks. I was still reeling from the joint, but I lost my buzz. There was a small, cracked mirror along one of the walls. I looked at my reflection and saw bleeding red eyes. They knew exactly what they were looking for.

The cop tugged on my turtleneck and motioned it had to come off. My face, which wasn't very tan coming from Wisconsin, had become sheet white.

The guard became impatient and raised his arms in a gesture of disbelief. He began shouting at me, but I didn't get what was going on. In French, he told me to take off my jeans, but I'd missed that vocabulary while failing French at Illinois. I caught his drift, dropped my jeans and put my hands on my hips as if I were on a diving board about to take an approach. "Oui, oui," he complained, as though I should have known the procedure all along.

I was standing in the dead of winter in a cold French guard shack sporting a bright orange Speedo I'd stolen before quitting the Diving Illini. "I'm already in prison colors," I thought to myself. He went through my pockets, then looked back at me in disgust. I was still slightly dressed and apparently I shouldn't have been. He motioned me to lose the Speedo and was not happy that I didn't understand him. The frontier guard was a chubby mustachioed man, and this had the makings of Midnight Express all over it. He made me turn around naked and bend over, but to my great relief, nothing went up the poop chute.

Disappointed that he didn't find what he was looking for, the guard pointed his nightstick at my stack of clothes and let me dress. Now it was my turn to walk out with a fear-stained visage and peer into Michael's eyes. Dan was standing alongside the car, but I didn't dare make eye contact. I had no idea how he could still be standing there. He was carrying the bud. Where the hell did he put it? How the hell did they not find it?

A third officer made us pull our bags out of Arthur Dent. He opened every zipper and poked through every single pocket. He kicked the side panels of Arthur Dent then looked in the ashtrays. There he found pay dirt. Sitting in one of the side ashtrays were the stems and seeds left over from the joint Michael had rolled in Belgium.

"What is this?" he asked.

"I don't know," I replied. "We were in Amsterdam last night. It was New Year's Eve. We were at a party and we took many people home. I didn't know any of them."

The cop clenched his fist around his booty and then tossed it in the brush. Michael came out from the shack tucking his Polo into his Levi's, Lori figured that whatever went down in the guard shack wasn't very good. When they asked her if she wanted a female cop to search her, she said, "I don't care, just get it over with. Search me so we can leave!" The guard stared at us disapprovingly then gave us our passports and sent us on our way.

Nobody said a word until we were over a hill two kilometers from the guard shack. Then Michael and I, in unison, screamed, "Where the hell did you put it?!"

"In my shoe," Dan said. "I just pinched the bag in my toe when I pulled off my shoe and used The Force. This is not the shoe you are looking for..."

The color had returned to my face, but it slipped right back to white. "They went through my shoes like there was fucking gold hidden in there!" I said.

"Mine too!" Michael said.

"Wow," was all Dan could muster. For the first time since we picked him up in Luxembourg, even he was freaked out.

"What did they do to you in there?" Lori asked.

"Strip search!" I said.

Now it was her turn to freak out. "That's not funny, you guys," Lori said. "I'm not going to have this baby in a French prison just so you guys can smoke out in Europe. No more pot on this trip! Michael, I don't need this kind of stress either, it's not good for the baby."

At that point we only had 20 miles to the ferry port in Dunkirk. Dan pulled out the bag, we split it into three equal piles and swallowed our contraband with an Orange Fanta chaser. High times on the road in Europe! The English Channel was choppy that night, and a lot of people got sick. The three of us were just fine.

After our Euro-baptism, we became road-hardened veterans and the trip went smoothly. We hit all the tourist spots in London and Paris then spent ten days eating with our eyes in the Alps.

Michael and Lori had to leave a week before Dan and I, so we dropped them at the airport in Luxembourg then traveled south in Arthur Dent to Italy. We drove ten hours and crossed six borders before sleeping in the car somewhere outside of Bergamo in northern Italy.

When we woke, we took inventory of our cash supply. We were desperately short. Neither of us had ever had a credit card, but I had one last paycheck coming to me from a restaurant job. I had told Michael to wire it to the American Express office in Verona as soon as he got home. It was a weekend, and we knew it wouldn't be there right away, so we had to make a decision. We could drive to Verona, get a hostel, and wait for the money, or we could gas up once more, drive to Yugoslavia, and sleep in Arthur Dent for a few nights.

With sober faces we found a gas station, filled the tank and headed for the Yugoslavian border crossing at Trieste. In a week we would be back in Wisconsin. What would a couple of warm nights in a hostel mean to us then? We had to keep going.

We had enough money to buy bread and apples for the next three days. We arrived in Trieste around noon and waited in a line of trucks for the border crossing to open. Neither of us had slept well in Arthur Dent during the freezing January night, so we left him in line and found cement slabs to suck up the warm Adriatic sun. When the truck line started to move, we boarded Arthur Dent, got tourist visas stamped in our passports, then took our first peek at a communist country.

As the sun went down, we drove the foothills of the Julian Alps to Rijeka on the Dalmatian coast. When we got to Rijeka, we locked up Arthur Dent and walked to the port. Shipyard workers were wandering the streets completely sloshed, but happy to come across a couple of Americans.

"Where you come from?" one of them asked me.

"Milwaukee." I replied.

He pulled up the lapels on his jacket, stuck his thumbs out and said, "Milwaukee! Happy Days! Ehhhh—Fonzie! Cool!"

Dan and I burst out laughing and returned the gesture. No matter what great feats anyone from our hometown will ever accomplish, the rest of the world would always remember Milwaukee as the home of the Fonz.

We returned to Arthur Dent and drove along the coast, looking for a secluded spot to crash. I'd brought a boombox from the States, and Dan had copies of the Grateful Dead *Red Rocks* bootlegs I'd recorded in September.

Just before turning off the lights, I pulled out a bottle of high octane Spittal rum I'd picked up at a train station in Innsbruck. A couple shots of old Spittal warmed us up and put us right out.

For two days we traveled the Istrian Peninsula of what is now Slovenia and Croatia. We stopped at the beachside resort of Pula and explored the remote citadel town of Pican. On the second night we caught a sunset from an Adriatic beach deep in the Limski Fjord. Not only was the peninsula beautiful, it was also cheap. Yugoslavia was much cheaper than Western Europe so we could afford cheese to go along with our bread—as well as a bottle of Yugo-Coke to mix with our rum. But it had been days since we had had a full meal. At one point we looked so emaciated that when we tried to spend our pennies at a bodega, an old shopkeeper took pity and loaded our sack with fresh produce for free.

January days along the Adriatic are sunny and glorious, but the winter nights are freezing. Arthur Dent offered little in the way of insulation, so we got no sleep. As our gas needle dropped, we were forced to return to Italy and wait for our cash. We made our way back to the expensive western world and parked our car outside of Mestre, the Italian city by the bridge leading to Venice. Arthur Dent had enough petrol inside him to get us back to Verona, but after that we were toast. We had three dollars and a long day in Venice in the morning. We were cutting it razor thin, but that was our bet.

Early the next morning, we left Arthur Dent in a secluded parking lot next to the three-mile-long bridge linking the Italian mainland to Venice. We crossed the span, then spent the last of our money on rolls and apples. We were broke in Europe and miles and days away from our flight home. We'd been sleeping in our clothes and hadn't had a shower in so long our skin flaked. Our only assets were fresh Grateful Dead *Red Rocks* tapes, a boombox, and the eighth of a tank left in Arthur Dent's belly—just enough to get us to Verona and the American Express office where we prayed Michael had sent my last paycheck. We ignored our plight, took the energy from the skimpy breakfast, and went for a walk in Venice.

Venice was spectacular, if not a tad smelly. We navigated the confusing spiral of streets and crossed the Rialto bridge, arriving at Piazza San Marco The pigeons in the square were an annoyance to most, but they looked like good food to us. We sat down on a bench and stared across the sea to the rich folks out on Lido. Most of them would drop enough cash on lunch to fill up Arthur Dent three times.

After a long rest, we turned around and made our way back to the bridge. Desperate, deprived, and with many miles already on our legs, we jealously watched scores of tourists hop on the train headed for Mestre on the Italian mainland. They were riding the Bridge to Venice by rail, taking in the scenery and drinking coffee. But we had to pound another three miles on the Bridge to Venice with no gas left in our tanks.

The sun began to sink as we took our first steps towards the mainland. With the golden silhouette of Venice for a backdrop we plodded onward towards Arthur Dent. And then, without any warning, the greatest and most powerful epiphany of our lives unfolded. We looked back at the paths we'd chosen to get to this starving moment on the Bridge to Venice, we concluded that not only had we made the right choice to stretch things to the limit, but we were also committed to stretch these limits the rest of our lives.

We were further from home than we'd ever been, literally and figuratively. We didn't have a penny to our names. Our older brother and sisters had taken the easy train to Venice, choosing challenging, albeit mainstream lifestyles. But Dan and I had set the stage for a totally new trip. This was a departure from the Baby Boomers and the starting-off point for Generation X. Even if we ended up tired, broke, and hungry we would experience the parts of Europe the tourists on the train don't know. And there was so much more of the world to discover.

We had to push the limit. The two gangly dudes on the Bridge to Venice didn't hold a candle to Kesey or Kerouac, but we felt like we were cut from the same cloth. Townshend said his father went off to France to fight in World War II, but Pete, "deprived of war," went to fight the Rock and Roll wars—to conquer the world. Now it was our turn. No longer was it acceptable to sit in Milwaukee and ponder the mysteries of the universe. It was time to go out into the universe and look for some answers—to conquer the world by getting to know it as best we could.

Europe was just the beginning. There was much more out there to discover. Gandhi went on fasts and hunger strikes not only for political causes but because he said it made him think more clearly. After the initial wave of hunger receded he could relax and let more important matters take over his thoughts. We didn't know it at the time, but the result of starving ourselves for four days in Yugoslavia was a clear look at the past and a sharp vision of the future. As we stepped off the Bridge to Venice we were no longer tired or hungry but driven. Our direction, however serpentine it would become, was set. We were dedicated to living extraordinary lives.

Unfortunately, while we were in Venice, someone had jammed a screwdriver into the lock on the driver-side door of Arthur Dent. The door was ajar and our possessions were strewn all about the back seat. We took inventory and discovered all they had gotten was the boombox—we still had the Red Rocks Grateful Dead tapes. The boombox had been our only source of entertainment, so having already exhausted every subject imaginable, we would have to crash with nothing to do but listen to each other's breath. We drove two hours through the night and pulled into a parking lot in Verona with Arthur Dent's fuel gauge flat on "E."

Six hours later, without getting any sleep, we followed directions in the Let's Go guide to the American Express office in Verona. The office was a small cubbyhole not far from Romeo and Juliet's castle. We walked into the office as if we'd fallen upon the Holy Grail. We asked the woman at the reception for our cash, but after taking in our query she replied in broken English, "No money here."

Dan and I looked at each other and started to shake. We didn't have a penny. We hadn't eaten a full meal in a week. Nor had we slept a full night. Our clothes were filthy; we smelled like ass; and now there would be no money coming. Next to Romeo, we were the two most desperate men in Verona. Before going to a US consulate and throwing in the towel, we had one last option. Dan went to a post office and convinced an operator to let us call Michael collect. He emerged from the post office, sat in Arthur Dent, turned to me and said, "Venice. The money is in Venice, not Verona."

We knew we had to go somehow. But first things first—with just a few drops left in the wounded Arthur Dent, we headed to the Hertz office and showed them the damaged door lock. The Hertz agent rolled his eyes and cursed his countrymen for making visitors feel so unwelcome. He looked at our paperwork and motioned for someone to bring us a new car. How unjust. Not only had Arthur Dent provided us transportation and shelter, he also just took a bullet for us. Now we were forced to abandon him in Verona for a Fiat Uno.

But that Fiat Uno had a full tank of gas in it. We signed the new papers then hightailed it back to Venice. Marco Polo started his great journey from Venice, but we had to get to Venice to end ours.

As we zoomed along the highway Dan looked over at me and asked, "What if Arthur Dent hadn't been broken into? We'd be screwed." The night before we were cursing our luck and saying things couldn't be worse, but if

Arthur Dent hadn't taken that bullet, one of us would have been hitch hiking back to Venice while the other would be looking for table scraps in Verona.

An hour later we arrived at the Bridge to Venice and drove onto the island, hoping there would be money at the American Express office to pay for the parking. I hopped on one of the canal boats that serve as city buses and prayed nobody would collect a fare. I found the American Express office just off Piazza San Marco, and sure enough, $185 was waiting for me.

I hopped back on the boat bus, this time with a ticket, and rode the canals one last time, not even noticing their exotic beauty. I leapt out of the boat and jumped into the Fiat, showering Dan with lira. He put the car in gear, and we cruised as fast as we could towards the Alps.

Our adventure ended with three phenomenal days in Salzburg, our favorite city of the trip. We looked on our map for the most whacked-out venue and settled on the small mountain village of Hallstatt in the Salzkammergut region. With clean clothes, clean bodies, lots of food, and fresh minds we set off deep into the mountain. We hiked along miles of half-frozen Alpine rivers leading to monster waterfalls just beginning to thaw. We came upon a 300-foot cascade where the ice cracked and fell, creating a crescendo echo that even the mountain goats stopped to take in.

At the far end of the trail, while sitting atop a three-stage waterfall with six pristine reflecting pools surrounding us, we declared our trip to Europe over. It was time to go home. The end of this trail was Milwaukee, Wisconsin. But the Bridge to Venice had been forever crossed. There was nothing but more trails ahead of us. The world was huge and we were young.

The Bridge to Venice Rule had been set: If you're not sure how deep the water is—jump in and find out.

• • • • • • • • • • • •

Bridge to Venice

Learning to Fly

I came back from Europe with a nifty new life philosophy, but I didn't know how I was going to apply it. Apparently, EVERYBODY comes back from these trips thinking they've found themselves, and within a year or two, they're back to where they started. But the stroll on the Bridge to Venice was pure and profound for me. I thought about it long and hard and then the answer came to me in the voice of an old friend: Diving.

The summer before I went to Europe, I drove to St. Louis with my Nicolet teammate, Pat, to watch the US Diving finals at Clayton Shaw Park, where Illinois held its summer training camp. Tom Scotty, my old teammate who would eventually coach UCLA, was talking to a coach at the side of the pool. I ran between them, jumped in the air, and yelled "Goehila!!!" before landing flat on my chest in the pool, making a massive splash.

"THAT'S THE GUY!!!" Tom screamed as he pointed at me. "He's the crazy one I was talking about!"

Tom was talking to Dave Lindsey, a diving show promoter who ran a high diving act in Lake of the Ozarks, Missouri. Lindsey gave me his card and asked me if I wanted to work a diving show. I asked him what I had to do. "Just toss a high dive and light your ass on fire," he said. I took his card, buried it in my wallet, and returned to Milwaukee, where I was in grad school going for a high school teaching certificate.

As much as I wanted to be a teacher, the walk along the Bridge to Venice stuck in my craw. I had to act on it. A few months after the St. Louis trip, I dug through my desk and found Dave Lindsey's card. My Illinois teammate Robin Duffy got involved with professional show diving after college and was flying all over the world doing shows. But Robin was really, really good—Olympic trials good. I never even made the finals of the Big Ten meet. I knew I wasn't good enough for the international stuff, but maybe if I worked a small gig in the States…

I called up Lindsay and he offered me the job on the spot. I told him I'd have to think it over, but I knew what I was going to do. I could stay in Milwaukee, tend bar, and take summer school, or go to Missouri and whip myself off a 70-foot ladder for five months. I was making about $250 a week

29

working part-time and going to school, but the job in Missouri paid $375 a week. The Bridge to Venice rule took over. I sent away for the contract and started training.

After a week on the diving boards the dives worked as easily as ever—even better. I was a year stronger, I'd had a lot of time to think about what I was doing wrong, and I was more patient with corrections. I put my 10-meter tower list back together, but it was still hard to imagine doubling the height. The big catch with the diving show was finishing each show with a 70-foot dive. I kept that out of my mind as I trained, but the thought of flatting from 70 feet was always there. One thing I had going for me was that, after talking to Dave Lindsey about his diving background, I discovered my diving experience was far superior to his. I dove in the Big Ten and he dove for a Division III school. But at one point he held the world high-dive record. If he could toss a 150-foot dive, I could manage 70 feet.

Lake Ozark and Osage Beach straddle a winding riverbed flooded by developers wanting to turn riverfront farm property into acres and acres of lakeside condos. Instead of farms that were barely breaking even, there were now miles of beautiful lakefront property. Bagnell Dam was built to create a complicated system of inlets and bays. What used to be pastoral farmland had turned into a haven for water-skiers. I was not privy to the local politics that have since been made legend by Netflix, but I was aware of the property value of the Lake of the Ozarks Water Show.

My dad took a couple of days off of work and drove me down to Missouri to make sure I wasn't involved in a scam. After ensuring I had a decent place to live, he returned to Wisconsin and I put my bike together. I became a bike commuter that summer and, as it turned out, for the rest of my life—until I couldn't anymore.

My first ride was a hilly four-mile run past strip malls and marine shops. The last hill was a steep drop almost to the lake level, followed by a quick incline up to a huge parking lot. I locked the bike to a tree, then walked into an office overlooking a 500-seat grandstand with a stage and a long blue ramp extending into the lake. I found the show office and introduced myself.

"I'm Tom," I said. "I'm here to do the diving show." I couldn't believe the words coming out of my mouth.

"Oh, you need to go see Dave Lindsey," the woman at the ticket counter said. "He's down there on the docks trying to get that diving board set up."

I looked down on the dock and recognized Dave from our talk in St. Louis nine months earlier. Had I known at the time what dire straits he was in and what a miracle find I was, I would have demanded he double my salary—and he would have gladly paid. But I was a rookie just learning the business. I walked down to the dock and called him, "Mr. Lindsey."

"Dave is fine," he said. "Glad you could make it. You ready to get dirty? We've got a lot of work. Grab that hammer and let's put this standard together."

I took off my shirt revealing a bit of a winter roll and a shiny white farmer tan. "We gotta work on that too," he said. "This is show business. People don't pay to see chubby people. And believe it or not, you're the star of this show. Get used to it."

I replied with a nervous laugh, sucked in my gut, and grabbed a hammer.

Setting up a diving show can be a business in itself. There are guys who work for companies that do nothing but set up stages, boards, and ladders, train a team, do the opener, and then go on to the next venue. It can be a complicated construction process and, even if you've got the procedure down (which is different for each location), you are still looking at a week of 12-hour days.

Being a rookie, I never thought about setup. All I thought about was the 70-foot dive. For three long, hard days Dave and I worked on building a three-meter diving board standard from scratch. The board was anchored to a floating dock. When the waves from the water skiers came in, the board would rock a foot from side to side. This definitely wasn't the Big Ten.

After the board went up, it was time to work on the ladder. Dave dove to the bottom of the lake with scuba gear and fastened the lower twenty feet of ladder to a base on a flat surface at the bottom of the lake. Eight feet of ladder stuck out of the water just next to the diving board. The ladder consisted of eight 10-foot sections of triangle radio tower. Each 10-foot section had to be fastened by guy wire to four anchoring stations. One station was attached to the show ramp, one was attached to a cement wall behind us, and two were attached to cement blocks sunk deep into the lake.

Dave did most of the ladder work and only asked me to hand him sections of ladder or tighten down the guy wires once he'd fastened them. Each section was hoisted on top of the previous section by a pulley welded to the top of a pole reaching high above the section that had just been secured. I worked on the dock while Dave locked his knee into the highest section on the ladder. I hoisted up sections and he did the rest. Any small mistake could prove costly—or potentially deadly. The ladder went up to 28, then 38, then 48 feet. It towered so high I got dizzy watching him work—and there were still three sections left on the ground.

"Let's call it a day," he said. "We'll set those three in the morning."

I was too shocked to even respond. The ladder was already 20 feet higher than I'd ever dived from. I nodded and cleaned up the tools.

Then Dave burst out with a fake sneeze. "Aaaaachoooo!"

That was the opening line of the comedy. I was beat and freaked out by the height of the ladder, but he wanted to rehearse. We were only three days from the opener, but we hadn't even gone through the lines of the comedy. I'd read the script a couple of times, but without the physical gags it didn't make any sense.

That night we drove three hours back to St. Louis to get some supplies. We rehearsed the entire way. Dave was upset I hadn't memorized it, but after 50 or 60 repetitions in the car, I'd gotten a handle on it. We crashed at his house, but I was too scared to sleep. Had the Diving Illini started their annual St. Louis, Clayton summer camp, I would have hopped a bus to their dorm and begged for a coaching job. Summer school at UWM was looking pretty good at this point.

In the morning we got back in his truck and rehearsed again. "OK, you've got the lines down," he said, "but your shit ain't funny. This isn't a college final. You don't get any points for getting it right. You gotta make all those people laugh."

I was just starting to feel good about having one part of the show down, and he was telling me I was going to embarrass the hell out of myself. At that point (thank God) I had a revelation. Tom Haig wasn't going to make 500 people laugh. I needed a character. I was in the Ozarks so why not be an Okie? I put on a country drawl and started talking as if I was stupid and pissed off (which wasn't too far from reality).

"That's it!" Dave shouted. "That's gonna work just great! Here we go. From the top…"

We went through the script and I stayed in my Okie voice. He was cracking up, I was cracking up, and for the first time I saw some light. Now I just had to light my ass on fire.

When we got back to the show site our announcer, Alex Jacobson, a Wisconsinite who had worked the famous Tommy Bartlett Water Show, was ready to rehearse. The standard dive show comedy is a 10-minute, three-person skit. The announcer asks the straight man if he wants to try a difficult dive he's been working on in practice. The straight man asks the crowd if they want to see the new dive. The crowd then screams their approval. Just as the diver is about to take off, the comedian, seated in the crowd, lets out an exaggerated sneeze, interrupting the diver. The rest is a series of goofy slapstick gags, interspersed with ridiculous banter.

Dave did the act first with me as the straight man, and then I took over as the comedian. After three or four rehearsals we had it down tight enough for Alex's approval.

"Dave," Alex said at the end of rehearsals, "You're doing the opener, right?" A day earlier that same comment and the lack of confidence in Alex's voice would have floored me. But I took it as a challenge.

Before we broke for lunch, Dave wanted to hoist up the last ladder sections. He climbed back up the ladder and we put on two more sections putting the tower at 68 feet. "That's enough for starters," he said. "Why don't you try this out, and we'll toss up another 10 feet in a couple of weeks."

"Yeah, that's a good idea," I lied. "I need to try out some dives first." What the hell was I saying? I didn't even want to climb the damn tower, let alone jump off. Doing a trick from 70 feet was inconceivable.

Dave went to lunch, and I decided I had to attack my fears. I was there for the summer, and I'd agreed to do this twice a day, every day, starting in two days. I'd signed a contract. He even pre-paid me for the first week. I put on a pair of cycling shorts, lifted one of the small diving perches sitting on the dock onto my shoulder, and started climbing the ladder.

When I got to 33 feet, I hung the perch on the ladder and stood on it to check out what the lake looked like from a three-story building. Ten meters always looked high. But on a 10-meter platform you can sneak up to the edge and peek over before standing up and tossing your trick. Here I barely had enough room for my feet while my back was flush against the ladder. If I let go, I was going to fall in.

I got my balance on the 30-foot perch, let go of the ladder and stood without moving. I raised my hands above my head, swung them in the air, and jumped as high as I could. I dropped into the lake and lifted my feet upon entry so as to not smash into the rocky 12-foot-deep bottom.

So far, so good. Back up the ladder. I dried off, climbed to the 30-foot perch and hoisted it on my shoulder. All the way to the top this time. I could have taken it ten feet at a time, but it was a pain moving the perch, and I was determined to greet Dave with good news when he came back from lunch.

I climbed up to the 60-foot mark and jammed the perch into place. I pulled myself over the lip of the perch and pressed my back against the crown. A 10-meter tower scared the hell out of me; 20 meters was just insane.

My legs began to wobble. I was high above the lake looking down on the roof covering the grandstand. I had a 360-degree view of the landscape, and although it was beautiful, I was ready to wet myself.

I stood on the perch for five minutes before the thought of letting go even entered my mind. I let go with one hand but re-clenched the crown. I kicked my legs out to release some of the tension, but when I tried to still them, they continued to shake.

When a diver is learning a new trick and is glued to the board, the coach will often count to three, and the diver has to go for the trick. I prided myself on never having to resort to counting. It wasn't my style. If I was going to go for a big trick, I got my ass ready and went for it. I hated people who needed to count, but this was a different deal altogether.

"One, two... three!" I let go of the ladder and started to jump. From out of nowhere, my hands stopped and grabbed the crown. I nearly lost my footing, but came back to a standstill on the perch. Now I was shaking harder than ever. My mind was ready to go, but my body said, "No." That's not a good sign. A diver relies on his body and muscle memory to take it places his mind doesn't understand. The body knows the difference between two and three twists—not the mind. When a diver lets his body take over, things work out for the best. Here, however, my body was taking over, and it wanted to climb down the ladder. There was only one thing to do. I had to force the issue.

I let go of the ladder with my left hand, lifted my right foot off the perch, then stepped off. The initial feeling of flight was familiar, but as I passed the wires at 40 feet, hyper acceleration took over. When we used to go to amusement parks as kids, we called all the big roller coasters that made us want to pee "dick ticklers." This was the king of the dick ticklers.

Before I could comprehend the acceleration, the water came fast upon me. I was squeezing my ass and legs like an innocent man on his first day in prison. My feet slapped the surface of the water, and I shot through like a bullet, except that I'd left my arms dangling off to the side. My arms slapped the water and felt like two pieces of seared meat trying to leave my shoulders.

My running backflip from 40 feet—the punchline of the Ozarks comedy routine.

I surfaced out of the water and climbed the ladder onto the dock. My triceps were blue and red, and my heart was thrashing. "Nice jump!" I heard from the girl in the ticket booth. She'd been watching me the whole time and it freaked me out. Then it hit me. In two days, I was going to flip off that thing—and lots of people were going to be watching.

Dave came back from lunch with smiles on his face as the ticket clerk had already told him the news. "Hey, I heard you stepped off that puppy!" he said. "Did you catch a little wind on the way down?"

"Nope," I said, "I caught a little water." I showed him my arms and he laughed.

"What the hell are you leaving your arms out on a high dive for? Tuck that shit away and cover your 'nads, you idiot."

Competition divers rarely go in the water feet-first because the sport is called "diving" not "jumping." When they do go feet-first, it's a practice lead-up dive before they put on the extra half flip and go in headfirst. In that case we let our arms fly above our heads to stop the momentum of the trick. High divers, however, grab their hands and tighten their arms, covering their cojones. Women do the same thing. Taking a nad-shot is rare, but it's a much tighter position.

Dave told me to go to lunch and take the rest of the day off to set up my room. He had business with the show owners and his girlfriend was coming in. I still hadn't done a fire dive, or a real high dive for that matter, but it felt great that he had enough confidence in me to think I could pull it off.

When I got to my apartment, a three-room bunkhouse off a dock on another section of the lake, my three water-skiing roommates were already moving in. Two of them were veterans, two of us were rookies, but we were all strangers. Being the diver in a water-skiing show was much like being the diver on a swim team. Twenty guys were doing one thing and I was doing something else. Just like being the left-handed guitar player.

I woke up on dress-rehearsal day a little fuzzy after dropping a couple beers the night before with my new teammates. The bike commute was a bit rough as I crossed the first bridge, but after the second hill I was sweating like a champ and going over the comedy lines in my head.

When I pulled into the Water Show the skiers were there, practicing their lifts, staging the equipment, and gassing up the boats. All I had to do was make sure my Okie costume was ready. Or so I thought.

"You ready to burn one?" Dave asked as he saw me walking towards the peer.

I hadn't put much thought into the "lighting my ass on fire" part of the deal. It didn't really scare me, but I was more than a little curious as to how it was done. Dave took me backstage and showed me a double-thick hooded sweat suit and three big fluffy beach towels hanging next to my Okie costume. Next to them on a small workbench was a spool of lamp cord, a dozen cable bugs (fasteners), a car battery, a tin of gunpowder, a box of baggies, a roll of masking tape, a case of flashbulbs (external mini light bulbs, one use each or four if a cube, that cameras used to light a dark scene before the days of built-in flash lighting), and 200 feet of electric wire.

Dave cut off a 50-foot section of lamp cord, split the ends and peeled off an inch of plastic on each side—just as if he were going to splice another wire into it. He sent me up the ladder and told me to tape the wire just below the perch at 28 feet. I climbed down the ladder to find him threading a loop of cable through one of the towels which had three inches folded over and was sewn at the top. "Here," he said, handing me the cable and some cutters, "you do that one."

I cut a section of cable, threaded it through the towel, then grabbed a couple of bugs and fastened the cable back onto itself. The result was a long cape with a cable loop that loosely fit over my head.

"Now we've gotta make some bombs," he said.

Bombs? I was still nervous over tossing a flip off the top and now he was talking about bombs? In order to ignite the fire dive, we had to make small pop-bombs out of gunpowder and the flash bulbs. Dave cut off a small section of wire and prepared both ends for a splice. He ripped open one of the flashcubes and pulled out a single bulb. He spliced the wire into the two small wires of the bulb then poured a little gunpowder into the corner of a baggie.

"Here's the trick," he said. "You gotta jam the bulb into the bag and tape it down tight. If it's loose, it won't pop, and you stand up there looking like a wet rat. If you crank on it, you blow up and you're a showstopper."

"Who lights it?" I asked.

"You gotta go over to the prop board at the ski show and sign up one of the skiers to come over here and touch the other end of the wire to the car battery. A half-hour before every show you go up and splice the new bomb into the main wire up on top."

I was nodding my head, but I was still a little confused. "And the fire comes from...?" I asked.

"Gasoline, Butthead! Go over to the gas tank next to the boats and fill this bucket with gas."

I returned with the bucket, and he set the two towels in to soak.

"All you have to do is put on the suit, jump in the water, and swim over to the ladder. I'll be waiting here with the cape. The cable goes over your head; you climb the ladder and wait for Alex to give you the cue. He'll say, 'Ladies and gentlemen, the Human Torch!' I'll be down here, and as soon as he says 'torch,' you cover up. Then I'll pop the bomb. Don't worry. You won't even feel the bomb. But make sure you look at the flags out in the parking lot. Always face into the wind. You don't want all that flame to come into your face. Burns the hell out of your nostrils."

I wasn't sure what was going to happen, but he was so nonchalant about it I assumed it was no big deal. I went back to thinking about what dive I was going to toss off the top of the ladder.

Walking off the ladder the day before was the scariest thing I'd ever done, but it also relieved me of a large portion of the fear. Aside from the bruises on my arm, nothing drastic happened. I'd tightened up my body just like I always did for tower diving. Even though the impact was much greater than a 10-meter dive, everything stayed in place. I didn't wrench my knee or torque my back. If I stayed vertical, I was going to survive.

After a dry rehearsal, everyone took off for lunch, but I stayed. As soon as the boats were gone and the parking lot was empty, I put my cycling shorts back on and climbed up the ladder. I was debating a couple of different dives but when I got to the top only one thing came to mind.

Throughout my diving career, gainers had always been my friends. Gainers, or reverse dives, are when a diver is standing forward but spins back towards the board or tower. They are the most difficult maneuvers to learn, but the easiest to control. I'd always scored highest on gainers, and I put them in a critical part of my list because I knew I could count on them. Now was not the time to buck the trend.

The view from the top of the ladder wasn't as shocking as the day before. The sensation of standing on the small platform wasn't as uncomfortable either. After catching my breath, I let go of the crown and stood on the perch with my arms on my hips. It still felt like I was up in the stratosphere, but I only had a small taste of the fear from the day before.

The most confident dive in my list was the reverse dive pike. It's a simple but elegant move that I always did well. I jump in the air, lift my legs above my head, touch my toes then look back for the water. In this case, however, I would look for the water, then tuck my legs over and land on my feet. High divers who do headfirst entries tend to have very short careers and brain damage. This dive was called a "three-position reverse somersault" because it uses all three positions used by divers: pike on the top of the dive, layout in the middle of the dive, and tuck just before straightening out to take the impact.

I raised my hands above my head and squeezed my body as tight as I could. For the second time in my life, I used a count. "One, two, three!" I swung my arms over my head, lifted my legs, touched my toes, looked back at the water and tucked the flip over, landing straight up and down. I shot to the bottom of the lake and stubbed my toe on a rock. But I was healthy, happy, and brimming with confidence. Just a couple days earlier I was ready to pack it in, but now I was a goddamn, bona fide high diver. Summer school my ass.

The dress rehearsal started at 5:00 but the skiers set up at 4:00. The Lake of the Ozarks Water Show was a 15-act, two-hour show. With all the music, lights, skis, boats, jet skis, costumes, make-up, and sundry props, it was easily as complicated as a Broadway musical. We even had "Magic the Water-Skiing Dog" to attend to.

My comedy was the third act. It went off without a hitch, but with an empty crowd there was no feedback. I was still wondering who the hell was going to laugh. Dave told me not to worry. "People will laugh at anything," he said, "especially during the night show when they've all been sitting at the bar. You did it just fine. Not as good as me, mind you, but just fine."

The fire dive wasn't until late in the second set, leaving more than an hour to kill. The delay made me jumpy, so when I saw a glitch, I stepped in with a suggestion. The rehearsal had stalled when one of the skiers couldn't change costumes fast enough between a ski act and a comedy act. The skit involved a spurned husband chasing his cheating wife around the grandstand.

"Hey Alex," I said, "I can do that part. I'll chase her up to the diving board then we'll do a backflip together." Alex and the skier looked at each other, we tried it out, and poof, I was a member of the ski team. I also had an excuse to mingle with the women skiers.

Before long it was time to do the fire dive. Dave told me to strap on the fire dive suit and jump in the lake. My cue to start climbing was the intro to the Pink Floyd tune, "Time." As soon as the bass thumps started, I climbed out of the lake and Dave put the gasoline-soaked cape over my head. I climbed the ladder, hoisted myself over the perch, checked the flags and stood facing the northerly wind. Alex gave the cue, "The Human Torch!" Dave touched the wires to the battery and I was engulfed in flames.

I thought my body would heat up like a bratwurst boiling in beer, but I couldn't feel a thing. My hands were covered in welding gloves, and my feet were in wetsuit booties. I slowly took my hands away from my face and looked around to see myself burning like a marshmallow that got too close to the campfire. I felt a little warmth on my shoulder and decided it was a good time to take off. I whipped off a front dive and squeezed tight as I hit the water. The biggest difference was the impact going into the water with the extra weight from the soaking clothes. The fire was no big thing.

"Amazing burn!" Dave shouted as I got out of the water. "I didn't think you were ever going to come down—I thought you said you've never done that before!"

I said thanks, but it wasn't a big deal. I just fell in the water from a seven-meter tower. I'd been doing that for years.

As I was taking off the fire dive suit, I saw Dave drop his shorts and get ready for the high dive. "Yo, Dave," I said, "my dive."

"You wanna fly this one?" he said. "You can't just jump off, you know."

"I got your frickin' high dive," I said.

"All yours, buddy," he said.

I pulled on my bike shorts and put the dive back in my head. Jump, reach, touch, look, tuck, squeeze. It was a lot to mull over, but I was more comfortable concentrating on mechanics than thinking of falling 60 feet.

After the ski jumpers did a series of long-distance flips and twists, the theme from Rocky came on, and I started my climb. I got to the fire dive perch, which was still a little hot, then paused to catch my breath and shake out my legs. As the music picked up, I turned back to the ladder and climbed to the 60-foot top.

Alex built the drama with a daredevil speech about an 80-foot high dive where I'd be traveling in excess of 70 mph and would have to stop in only 10 feet of water. When I got to the top, he announced, "The man who is going to attempt this death-defying feat for you is All-American diver, Mr. Tom Haig!"

The skiers sat in the stands playing mock crowd and gave me a fake ovation. My nerves were calm as I lifted my arms above my head. I thought through my mechanics, jumped into the air, did the trick, and ripped the snot (that's diver talk for entering the water splashless) out of my first public high dive.

When I came out of the water, there were real cheers from all the skiers. I took my bow then joined the skiers onstage for the big finale.

"Great job everyone!" Alex said. "Tomorrow's the real deal."

Dave came over and gave me a big bear hug. "Fuckin' A, Bubba!" he said. "You're gonna pull this thing off!"

I couldn't believe it myself. In one week, I'd gone from a bartender to a showman. I wasn't on Broadway or in the Olympics, but I wasn't serving martinis to alcoholics either. I cleaned up my props, hopped on my bike, and sprinted back to my room. The gamble was paying off. The Bridge to Venice rule had become more than just talk. I was beginning to live my extraordinary life.

After the first week of shows, all the fears I had about taking the job had disappeared. My body had toughened up to the 60-foot dive, the fire dive had become routine, and the two comedy skits were getting better each show. Daily show call was at 12:30 p.m., so I had no limits on how long I wanted to stay out or when I woke up. If we were at a party and everyone was too drunk to drive, I just crashed there. If I was into a book, I read until 5 a.m. If I wanted to learn a new song, I stayed up until it was locked into my fingers.

I woke up around 10:00 a.m., made a little breakfast, then hopped on my bike and rode the hills to the show. I timed every ride and tried to break my record each time out. My gut was rock; my body was tan; and as soon as the local schools were out, I was performing to two huge crowds every day.

Alex and I were having a blast with the comedy, often improvising and always getting the crowd involved. It was a rare day we didn't have people doubled up in laughter.

The one thing I wasn't happy with was the high dive being the finale. The skiers trained often and rehearsed for hours between shows. The more tricks they learned, the more money they made. I was making more money than anyone, but I never rehearsed a thing. Often, I'd ask somebody if they wanted to go for a bike ride or take a boat out, but they generally had to decline in order to practice. Most of them were younger, and when I was that age, I trained harder than the skiers. But I still felt guilty for being the big act. If my act was the finale it was going to have to be better than a simple gainer flip. I needed to up my game. And thus was born the Mifflin Street Dive.

Two weeks before leaving for Missouri, I had gone to Madison for the annual Mifflin Street Block Party. The Mifflin Street Block Party is in remembrance of a riot that took place in Madison during the Vietnam War. During the street festival, almost every house along the 500 block of West Mifflin Street has a live band on the porch, making a walk down the center of the festival a musical hodgepodge.

At one point during the festival, six of us climbed a tree and watched the goings-on from high above street level. When we ran out of beer, my brother Dan hopped out of the tree, went into a house, and filled our glasses. In the meantime, I'd gone to a lower branch and hung upside down from my knees. When the two of us tried the difficult task of drinking beer while hanging upside down, a photographer snapped a bunch of pictures. (Two weeks later our picture was spread across *Campus Voice*, a national college magazine.) After I polished off my beer, I lowered my hands above my head (if that makes sense) and put them in a handstand position. If I could hook my knees over a bar and lean back... nobody's ever done that before.

The next day I got to the show and figured out the logistics. The ladder was too thin to stick my legs through, so I found a sturdy two-foot section of pipe and duct-taped it five feet above a perch I'd mounted 10 feet over the lake. I climbed over the pipe, put my knees around it, then looked back until my hands reached the platform. I unhooked my legs from the pipe and straightened them, leaning against the ladder. I was upside down in a handstand looking at the water from a perspective that, in all my years of diving, I'd never seen before. Up until the late '90s, tower divers always did their arm stand dives facing the platform, never the water. I'd done tons of arm stand dives in my time, but always spinning forward, never backwards. As strange as the view was, there was no climbing back onto the ladder. I balanced myself into a tight handstand, then pushed off, and floated to the lake's surface on my feet. The Mifflin Street Dive was born.

I climbed back up the ladder and mounted the pipe above the fire dive perch at 30 feet. The ladder section above the fire dive perch was pitch black with soot, as was the platform. I climbed the ladder and draped my knees around the pipe. When I got to my handstand I was covered in black goo. The soot also made the platform slippery, so I didn't want to hang out very long. I got into position then pushed off, floating 1½ somersaults before hitting the lake. Although the visual was strange, the motion was natural. All I had to do was fall and look at my spot in the lake. Piece of cake. So now, up to the top.

When I climbed up to the top, I had to lower the platform five feet because the crown was too flimsy to support my weight. The other sections were anchored down, but the crown section was merely tied off. I taped the pipe to the last secure section of the ladder, then climbed down and waited for the show. Nobody had been there while I was practicing so I had a big surprise to throw at them.

The worst part about taking up a new trick is the high dive always comes at the end of the show. All I could think of was my new trick, but I still had to light myself on fire and do two skits. When it was time to climb the ladder, I was a nervous wreck. It had been more than three hours since my warm-up, and I felt as if I hadn't even done it. Alex was baffled as I climbed the crown and got into a handstand position.

"I don't believe I've ever seen this done," Alex announced to the crowd. It was the same opening line we used for the man-out-of-the-audience comedy, except this time it wasn't a gag.

The water looked surprisingly close, as my head was 10 feet nearer to the lake compared to standing on the perch. It took a long time to get into position, and the show music had long since run out by the time I got to my handstand.

"Here we go," I said to myself. The big, fat, 60-foot Mifflin Street Dive. No turning back. I started to fall, then gave myself a slight push to get the spinning going. One-and-a-half somersaults is not a lot of rotation for a 60-foot dive. In fact, you really don't need to push at all. I completed the 1½ somersaults looking right at the fire dive perch. That left 30 feet to fall and no more dive to complete. I flung my arms in the air to make my body longer and stall out the rotation, but all that did was create more bruised surface area when I landed flat on my out-stretched back.

I'd flatted a few times from 10 meters, but up there, you quickly learn your lessons. It's not the kind of thing you can grow old doing. This, however, was a new experience in the art of pain. The skin on my back was split and bleeding. My legs, butt, and arms were completely bruised. I had a splitting headache, most likely concussed, and I had to climb out of the lake and take a smiling bow.

The crowd was silent as the skiers rushed to the dock to pull me out. I managed to stand up and wave and the crowd gave me the kind of applause you hear when a football player is hauled off on a cart. I wanted to lie in bed for a week, but in just a few hours I was going to have to slap on my Okie costume and make people laugh. Welcome to show business.

The Mifflin Street flop would have dissuaded anyone else from trying any more tricks, but I knew I had a potential showstopper. There's an adage in diving that you must do three before you can quit. The first one is an experiment, the second one should be better, and the third time you go for confidence. Usually, all three take place in the same practice, but I wasn't about to climb back up that ladder and toss another one.

Two weeks later, after my skin healed and my bruises disappeared, I started over at 10 feet with a new idea—the Mifflin Street 2½. I would toss a fast arm stand 1½, split the dive, then do another somersault before hitting the water. The Mifflin Street 2½ would be more logical than the 1½ back splat. Sixty feet is just too much room for only 1½ flips.

It was a beautiful Saturday afternoon, and we had a packed house. Alex and I nailed the comedy, and I burned an extra-long fire dive just to build up confidence. When the high dive music started, I climbed to the perch and gave Alex a twisted smile. I was in the zone. This time I knew exactly what I was doing. I turned around and hoisted my knees over the pipe. When I got to my handstand, I looked at Alex on the stage, but he was staring at the ground. He didn't want to look. He'd seen my bruises and split skin from the last attempt and wondered why I hadn't just taken the damn pipe down. I checked out the lake then put the dive into my head one last time. Hard first 1½, split, then tuck it over, just like a split gainer double. Big time Mifflin Street Dive. One, two, three…

I shoved off the tower and spun as hard as possible. After 1½ flips, I opened up and looked at the landing area 50 feet below. I tucked back up, did another flip then kicked out high above the lake. I looked at my spot, clenched my body and slid through the water leaving only a few bubbles on the surface.

This time the crowd noticed. I could hear them from underwater. Alex was screaming into the mic, "Ladies and gentlemen, you've just witnessed history. This is the first time anyone has ever attempted an arm stand 2½ somersaults from 80 feet. [We were embellishing the height a little.] Let's give a tremendous round of applause for our Acapulco High Diver, Mr. Tom Haig!"

I had my showstopper, and I never felt bad about being the star ever again.

• • • • • • • • • • • • •

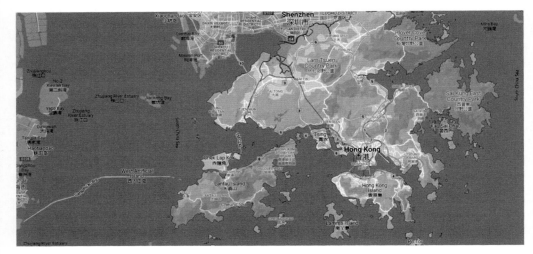

Hong Kong

Chinese Pancake

"Hello, may I speak to Tom Haig please?"

I didn't recognize the voice, but it sounded official. I assumed it was my student loan company wondering where my payments were. When I got back to Milwaukee after the summer of high diving, I continued working towards a teaching degree and was eligible for a loan deferral, but it never seemed to get processed.

"What's this concerning?" I asked.

"My name's Bruce Cant, and I'm with World Wide Productions out of Hong Kong. Tom sent us…"

"Yeah," I interrupted, "this is Tom. I was waiting to hear from you guys. My friend Robin (Duffy again—the University of Illinois All-American diver) said you guys were looking for show divers. I'm in the middle of a semester of school now. How do things look in January?"

"We need somebody today," Cant said. "Robin said you'd be perfect, but by January we'll be all full."

"I'd love to take the gig," I said, "but I can't just blow off a semester."

"Damn, we could really use you," he said. "Is there any chance of putting off classes for a couple of months?"

"I don't think so," I said. "But in January I'll be completely free."

"It doesn't look good," he said, "but we'll keep you on the list. Give me a call if you change your mind. We could use someone ASAP."

I took down his number and slammed my fist. I had just refused an all-expense-paid trip to Hong Kong. I pitched my Middle East History text into the hallway and went into the kitchen. I cracked a brew and thought about it again. If I was going to be a social studies teacher, what would be more valuable—a couple classes or a couple of months in the Far East? If I were a high school student, I know what kind of teacher I'd rather have. I'd take experience over book learning any day. I'd been in school for 18 years and even though I was studying what I was interested in, it couldn't be as rewarding as living those subjects.

It was time to act. I pulled out the course catalog to see if my classes would be offered the following semester. All four courses would be offered again in the spring. If I could convince my professors to give me an incomplete in my courses until I returned in March, I could pick up where I left off. It was out of the ordinary, but I had to give it a try. I hopped on my bike and pedaled six miles through a thunderstorm to the UW Milwaukee campus.

Surprisingly enough, three of the four professors (the history profs) were excited about the idea and let me take the extension. An educational psychology prof let me drop the class. I booked it home and as soon as I got in the door, the phone rang.

"Tom Haig please."

"Yeah," I replied. "Is this Mr. Cant?"

"Yes. I just wanted to ask you once more…"

"Yeah, yeah," I said, stumbling over my words. "I can do it! I'm good! I canceled my semester. You still got room?"

"Fantastic, Tom," he said. "Can you drive down to Chicago to pick up a plane ticket?"

"No problem," I said. "When do I leave?"

"How does this Thursday sound? We've got some big weekend shows, and we need an extra diver."

"Thursday's perfect!"

"We've got a 90-foot high dive here," he said. "Can you handle that?"

"No problem," I said.

"Great, now you need to go to…"

Cant gave me instructions to a travel agent in Chicago's Chinatown, but as I was writing, all I could think was "90 frickin' feet!" What the hell was I thinking? The ladder in Osage Beach was only 60 feet. This was almost a full 10 meters higher. It was three times higher than I'd ever dove only five months earlier. There was still time to bail, and most people would have. But most people hadn't walked The Bridge to Venice.

In those days you couldn't just show up at an airport with a phone and an ID. You needed an actual paper ticket. And you couldn't just print one out from a website. There were no websites. You had to go to a travel agent and pick up the physical ticket. And if you lost it you weren't going anywhere—those tickets were as valuable as the price on them. I drove down to Chicago and picked up what was only the third plane ticket of my life. The first one was to Oklahoma City for a college recruiting trip. The next one was the

Icelandic Air trip to Luxembourg. Now this one was to Hong Kong. Life had just gone into overdrive.

Three days later I was on my way to Hong Kong with a backpack and my guitar. I hadn't been on a diving board since leaving Osage Beach in August, three months earlier, and even there I didn't really do much diving. In Hong Kong, I was going to have to show up ready to toss my competition 10-meter list. I sent them a performance resume and listed my hardest dives. I never thought they would have a 10-meter tower at a diving show, but they did. It was a nervous, 24-hour flight.

One of the hairiest experiences in international travel was showing up in the Far East after a 24-hour flight and dropping into the old Kai Tak airport in Hong Kong. The pilot had to take a long arcing drop into an urban mountain valley lined by dozens of 40-story apartment buildings. As the pilot tried to stop on the shortest runway of any major airport in the world, you could look right into people's homes and see what they were having for dinner.

I got out of the plane not knowing what time it was, how much I'd slept, or even where the hell I was. I'd studied Europe for years before going there, but the Far East was new territory. I didn't even know where Hong Kong was before I got there. Apparently, I looked like a diver because Bruce had me pegged long before I picked up my bags.

"Tom," he said, "Bruce Cant—World Wide Productions. I can't tell you how glad we are that you could make it. The park's been rented out for a couple of extra shows tomorrow. You think you can handle it?"

"I don't really want to toss a high dive while I'm jet lagging…" I started to say.

"Oh no, don't even think about it," he said. "We just need you to do a couple of dillies and some three-meter dives. Can you handle that?"

"Sure," I said. I had no idea what a dilly was nor was I prepared to throw anything but the simplest three-meter dives. At least I wasn't going to have to toss my butt off a 90-foot ladder.

I dumped my gear into Bruce's car, and we drove on the left side of the road through a complex maze of tunnels and bridges to Happy Valley, the home of a massive horse-racing track and the offices of World Wide Productions. Bruce took me to a bar and handed me off to Dan Anthony (aka Dan-Bob), the show captain and a five-year veteran of Hong Kong show diving.

"Welcome aboard," he said. "Initiation time!"

A minute later five shots of tequila and a pint of beer arrived.

"Gombei!" he shouted.

I slammed my shot, and just like that I became a member of the American High Diving Eagles. From then on, every six months from 1986 to 1992, a new set of Eagles would step into my life, become great friends, then vanish into thin air, only to resurface on a different continent. As I sat around the table listening to their incredible stories of living abroad and doing shows in strange little storybook towns, I could never have imagined that in just a few months I would become an integral part of their history. Even though these Eagles were divers, they were nothing like my Illinois teammates. At Illinois we were just a bunch of college kids studying, diving, and having as much fun as we could. Some of my new teammates were in their 30s and married. I was 25, and never thought I would ever become a member of such a twisted family of circus performers. But seven years later, after it was all done, I would become one of their leaders; even marrying a high diver myself.

"The show's the easy part," Dan-Bob informed me. "Doing it with a tequila hangover is the rough part!"

He ordered another round and everyone joined in. They weren't as happy to see me as they were to have an excuse to knock back some tequila.

Six hours later I woke up feeling little effect. The divers were staying in the Hong Kong Jockey Club, a high-rise apartment above the Happy Valley racetrack. The Jockey Club owned both the racetrack and our show site, Ocean Park, an immense amusement park overlooking Aberdeen Harbor.

Just as I had done in Bruges 10 months earlier, I went outside before sunrise to watch the city wake up. It was 6:00 a.m. when I hit the street, but Hong Kong was bustling. Construction crews on bamboo scaffolding were busy at work and delivery trucks raced all over the neighborhood trying to drop their loads before traffic started. In Bruges I had noticed a small difference in people's facial structure, but in Hong Kong I was in a sea of Asian visages that, outside of a movie screen, I'd never experienced.

I was immersed in a flow of Chinese people and a never-ending sea of Chinese signs. I couldn't imagine people processing them as readily as I read English. The signs covered the urban landscape creating a multicolored forest with aluminum branches and cascading single-pane calligraphy. As swarming as the visuals were, the sounds were even busier. Businessmen and school children hurried onto buses; rickety food carts bustled into place; construction workers pounded on their projects and cab drivers honked at all of it. I looked up the valley to see steep tropical mountains scaled by daring switchback roads and skyscrapers clinging to every precipice. If there was any ledge to build on, it had long ago been exploited.

Our first show was at 11:00 a.m., but Bruce wanted us at Ocean Park by 9:00 to rehearse. I hopped a cab with two of the divers, and we dodged our way through traffic to the entrance of Ocean Park on the north end of the island. The divers introduced me to the security guard, who gave

Hong Kong 1986—a barrage to the senses.

me the Chinese name Fai-jaye. Properly pronounced with a rising accent on the first syllable it meant "flying boy." I found out a few days later, after another night of tequila, that when pronounced flatly it meant "fat boy."

Ocean Park is one of the nicest venues on the professional high diving circuit. The park, which houses an aquarium, several roller coasters, and the world's longest escalator, is situated on a series of cliffs looking across the South China Sea towards mainland China. The show site is an 8,000-seat auditorium built around a 20-foot-deep killer whale pool. Just beyond the stage, the boundary of the park drops off several hundred feet to the South China Sea. When you stand backwards on the high dive perch, you get the sensation you are doing a 400-foot high dive.

I wasn't going to be climbing that ladder anytime soon, but I needed to learn the show routine immediately. Doing a one-man performance and working with a team are two entirely different things. In the Ozarks, I got all the credit and took all the blame. Diving with a team required synchronization on the stage, the ladders, and even in the air. Everything from getting out of the pool to climbing the ladder had to be done simultaneously. I thought Bruce was kidding when he said he wanted us to climb the diving boards and adjust our fulcrums together. But after seeing it done properly, you cringe when you see it done sloppily. Bruce didn't care if we missed dives, but he was furious when you missed a stage bow. I thought I was in for a tough diving tryout, but they only cared where I was standing.

Fifteen minutes before the show, Dan-Bob made up the diving list.

"So, Haig," he said, "can you do a 1½ pike?"

"Too rough for me," I said.

A 1½ pike is just about the easiest dive in the book. The diving boards standards were even up on one-meter blocks, making the dive a four-meter dive instead of a three-meter dive.

"Fuck you," he said. "Hagar [my new nickname] is doing a tandem 1½ pike with Cathy [McPadden from Florida] to start out and a tandem 2½ pike with Bob [Torline from Minnesota] for the 6th dive. Can you remember that?"

My two partners sat next to me and told me that, even though Dan-Bob came off as a hard ass, he was really a softy. He just had a macho thing around new divers.

"Okay, for the mass dive," Dan-Bob said. "Dene and I are doing back doubles from the 10-meter. Hagar, can you toss a back double between us? Good, you're in."

The mass dive is the finale of the diving set. The more people you can put in the air at once, the more spectacular it is. I'd done plenty of back 2½s off 10-meter, but I'd never done a back double. It was a feet-first landing, and in competition it would never score well, so I'd never even thought about doing one. I just hoped it wouldn't be any different from the gainer doubles I'd done off the fire dive perch in the Ozarks.

The horn rang for show call, and everybody went to separate corners of the locker room where their suits were hanging up. "Red stripes!" Dan-Bob shouted.

Everybody stripped down naked, including Cathy, and got into their red-stripe Speedos. I looked over at Dan-Bob, and he was checking me out to see how I'd react to the co-ed locker room. I was trying not to drop my jaw, but my eyes did travel a bit. He whipped a red-striped Speedo at me and yelled, "Ladies and gentlemen, Mr. Tom Haig has just seen his first pair of professional tits!"

"Fuck you!" Cathy yelled. She turned to me completely naked and said, "He's just a pig."

Dumbstruck, I whipped on the Speedo and lined up to go onstage. The dive set went off without a hitch, including the back double, which I nailed right in time with the other divers. They told me to get ready for dillies, but I had no idea what they meant. Dan-Bob tossed me a clown suit and asked me what dillies I knew.

"I don't know what the hell you're talking about," I said.

"Dillies—clown dives!" he screamed. "Bruce, where the hell do you find these guys?"

Bob and Cathy came over and explained a few clown dives to me. I'd done clown shows with diving clubs, but I'd never heard the term before. I danced out onstage in a clown suit and immediately fell right on my elbow. The main function of the stage was to let Shamu the killer whale slide out of the pool to get fish. It was hyper slippery, but I didn't realize it until I started clowning around. I was in a ton of pain, but Dan-Bob lifted me up and made it all look like part of the show.

When the set was over, we ran backstage and another Floridian, Dene Whittaker, walked to center stage and started to climb the high dive ladder. I thought 60 feet was a monster height, but 90 feet was beyond absurd. They had a perch sitting at 50 feet they didn't even consider a high dive. I watched as Dene climbed up to the ladder, took a wave, then ripped the snot out of a perfect front double with a half-twist.

The crowd of 3,000 stood and cheered as Dene came out of the water and took his bow. I was as impressed as anyone. "Nice dive," I told him.

The 92-foot high dive at Hong Kong's Ocean Park.

"All in a day's work," he said. "It was a good dive, I gotta admit, though."

Cathy punched him in the arm and called him a conceited bastard. This was no love fest. No slack was cut at any time for any reason. My best bet was to remember my lowly position as a rookie and just try to take it all in.

"Okay, that sucked," Dan-Bob said at the end of the performance. "Let's practice before the next show."

When he said "practice" I thought he wanted us to work out and put some tough dives into the second show. Wrong. Dan-Bob tossed me a wet suit and told me to go outside and bounce the board. I put on the wetsuit and started bouncing the board.

"Not like that," he said. "Like this…"

He walked out to the end of the board and started bouncing, making a different clown pose every time he got in the air. When he jumped off the board, he struck a ridiculous position and held it until just before he hit the water. Dan-Bob didn't care whether I could do a 2½ or a 4½. He just wanted to know if I could make the crowd laugh.

The second show was better, and the third was even better than that. Normally we would only do three shows, but the Hong Kong Dairy Association had rented the park, so we had to do two more shows under the lights. There was a three-hour break before the night shows, so everyone got dressed and got something to eat. I was starting to feel the jet lag, so I asked Cathy to get me something to eat while I found a couch and took a nap. I went down hard, and it seemed like only seconds later when the show horn sounded. Dan-Bob tossed me a Speedo he'd been soaking in a bucket of Shamu's fish food. I didn't catch it at first, but once I had one leg in, the goo was all over me. He and Dene rolled with laughter, and I had to bust ass to rinse it out and whip on the team jacket.

The show music started, I stepped up onstage, and I hit my spot. It was night now, less than 40 hours since I'd left the comfort of the Midwest, and we were performing under the lights. I was in a complete jet-lagging daze but managed to get off the opening 1½ pike. I almost fell asleep onstage waiting for my second dive, but Bob nudged me out of my coma, and I climbed the springboard for our 2½ pikes.

We nodded to each other to start our approaches, but as I got to the end of the board, I couldn't remember what I was doing. I leaped in the air but didn't start rotating until it was too late. I was disoriented and didn't revive until I was stretched out horizontally above the water staring straight ahead at 5,000 Chinese dairy farmers. I should have been dropping vertically and looking at the pool, but all I saw were bright eyes and dropped jaws.

SPLAT!

Every square inch of skin on my front side hit at the same time. I didn't sink six inches below the surface of the pool. It was the mother of all belly flops. Being a killer whale tank, the water was cold, thick saltwater, making it every bit harder. I lost my breath and easily swallowed half the pool. I paddled to the edge of the tank coughing and gagging. The ladder was shaking, but I knew that couldn't be from my splash. I looked up to the first couple of perches and saw Dan-Bob and Dene laughing so hard they couldn't control themselves. I hoped their guffaws would lead to splats of their own, but the bastards nailed both dives in perfect synchronicity.

When we got backstage, the Eagles were crippled with laughter, and I was crippled with pain. "We can try something easier," Cathy said sarcastically.

I was hurting too much to respond. They were having a field day with me, while I was beet red and ready to throw up. I made it through the clown set and took the final bow before the acute pain subsided, leaving me with a dull, raw ache. After the show, Dan-Bob asked me if I wanted to take another nap. I was starting to get pissed, but if I let it show, I'd never hear the end of it. I felt like whining and saying, "You try to get off a plane on the other side of the world and learn a brand-new job in front of 5,000 people!" But I knew he'd done that a dozen times. Instead, a simple "Fuck you" came out. It was trial by fire, and I was burning up.

• • • • • • • • • • • • •

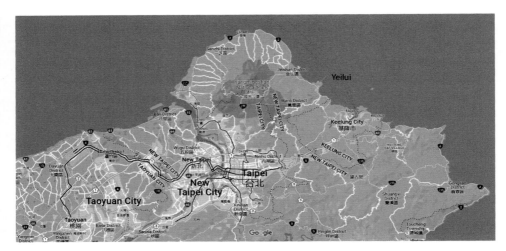

Taiwan

Frowning Clowns

The first day in Hong Kong may have been rough, but once I got over jetlag, I started having a ball. We were only doing three half-hour shows a day starting at 11:30 a.m. and ending at 4:00 p.m. A great audience in the Ozarks may have swelled to five or six hundred, but Ocean Park pulled in several thousand per show.

I'd taken my gainer double up to the 60-foot perch and told them I'd toss a high dive, but Bruce insisted I get used to the hard impact of salt-water before going up much higher. Everyone else could high dive, so they just wanted to make sure they had enough healthy bodies while the team rotated. With only three high dives a day and six high divers, there just wasn't enough show to go around.

My elbow was still sore from smacking it on the stage during the opening show, so I wasn't thinking of tossing the Mifflin Street Dive. I was just happy to be waking up every day in Hong Kong. At night I wandered the streets checking out hole-in-the-wall restaurants or surveying the markets of Kow-loon for bargain electronics.

During the long breaks between shows I resumed the reading habit I'd acquired in the Ozarks. For all the machismo and bullshitting that went on at diving shows, the one thing most divers did was read. There was just too much time to kill. There was no internet, no Gameboys, and only bad Kung Fu movies to watch on a VCR. Unless you had to sleep off a hangover, almost everyone had a book in their hands. While at Illinois, I was so busy with school, practice, and work I never read anything but required textbooks. I thought the summer in Missouri was a fluke, and once back in Milwaukee I'd go back to textbooks. But now I was developing a healthy reading habit.

Unfortunately, I wasn't in Hong Kong very long. I'd only been in there for 10 days when WWP pulled a fast one. I woke up one morning and walked into Happy Valley on a grocery run. It was a beautiful sunny day, and the city was bursting with energy. It was snowing in Wisconsin, but in Hong Kong I had to clear palm tree leaves from the entrance to my grocery store. I ran into Dene Whittaker at a chicken stand, and he asked me if I was packed and ready to go.

"Go where?" I asked.

"Taipei," he said. "Didn't Bruce tell you?"

"Tell me what?"

"Oh yeah, he should have talked to you about it," he said. "We're going to Taiwan to set up tomorrow."

I was thrilled. I assumed it was a weekend gig or a weeklong festival. I wasn't in the Far East just to see Hong Kong. "How long's the gig?" I asked.

"Contract's for four months—but they'll probably extend it…"

I was grooving on Hong Kong, and from out of the blue I found out I was going to spend my entire tenure in the Far East in Taiwan. Hong Kong was exotic. Taiwan sounded like a polluted hellhole. I envisioned rows of factories producing junk that ends up in America with "Made in Taiwan" tags. I'd never even heard of the capital, Taipei.

I'd been duped. WWP didn't need to rush someone out from the States to dive in Hong Kong. They needed someone in Taiwan. Ocean Park in Hong Kong is a major world-class tourist attraction in one of the most interesting cities in the world. Ocean World in Yehliu, however, is a small dolphinarium in a tiny fishing village along the north coast of Taiwan. They thought they had to trick me to get me to come. I was pissed off at being deceived, but they didn't need to pull the fast one on me. I would have come if they told me I was diving in the middle of the jungle in Vietnam. I was on the bus to see the world, not hang out in comfy cities. I wanted to meet interesting people, not play to big crowds. I could imagine one day seeing Hong Kong, but I never imagined I'd ever visit Taiwan.

When I got to Ocean Park, Bruce came over to me looking guilty. I thought about complaining loudly about pulling the fast one on me, but I didn't see what good it would do. Years later I would realize that a sudden change of plans meant I should ask for more money. But at the time, I just wanted to cooperate. He started to put a sell on me, but I interrupted him and told him I was excited to go. That way we both went into it with a great attitude. He also bumped me up to $65 bucks a day provided I was a daily high diver.

As opposed to the monster high dive in Hong Kong, the high dive in Yehliu is only 70 feet. But the pool was just 9½ feet deep. At Nicolet High School, the diving parents petitioned for a new pool because they thought nine feet was too shallow for our one-meter springboard. No parents were petitioning anything in Yehliu. I had to figure out how to do shallow water high diving or go home. Bruce said if I worked my way up the ladder, I wouldn't even notice it. I nodded, but I quickly learned nothing ever came as advertised in the high diving business.

The next day Dene Whittaker and I were on a plane to Chiang Kai-shek Airport outside of Taipei. Dene was a 35-year-old, 15-year show veteran. He'd been everywhere and seen everything. While I was as green as it comes, Whittaker knew every trick, every show venue, every comedy line, and every diver. I felt like the doting puppy dog following Spike the oversized boxer.

Our park contact, Vincent, picked us up at the airport and drove us to our temporary residence, the Angel Hotel in downtown Taipei. I thought the streets of Hong Kong were busy, but they were bush league compared to Taipei. Every sign in Hong Kong was in English and Chinese, but the streets of Taipei were lined with only Chinese characters. In Hong Kong, the streets were clean, and people obeyed traffic laws. In Taipei, everything was filthy, and a yellow light was the signal for 40 motorcycles to gun it through the intersection, the last dozen passing well into the red light.

None of the motorcycles were ridden by solo riders. Three people per bike was the norm, and it was common to see a family of five on a single bike. Just before we pulled into the hotel, I saw a family of eight riding a Yamaha 125 with a special bench adapted to the rear wheel. Dad was driving with a baby on the handlebars. Two children sat between Mom and Dad, and Grandma sat on the elevated bench with a kid on either side of her. You don't catch that act too often in Champaign, Illinois.

In the morning, we picked up a blue microbus that would be our transport for the next four months. Bill, an American who had lived in Taipei for 22 years, rented the van to us and warned us about the roads.

"They may appear safe at times," he said, "but believe me, they aren't."

Dene took over the wheel and started driving at a maniacal pace, darting in and out of traffic, cutting people off and jumping red lights. "If you want to survive here," he said, "you've got to play their game." I thought he was insane, but as I spent more and more time behind the wheel, I realized he was right. In a couple of weeks, I would be fighting it out with the best of them.

Dene blasted through town and hit the main highway north to the port city of Keelong. It was a clear day, but we could barely make out the mountain cliffs around the city. The pollution was so unbearable that people on the sidewalks wore face masks—long before COVID would make that a common sight. The freeway gave way to a tight coastal road cutting through small villages towards Yehliu and Ocean World Dolphinarium.

The drive along the South China Sea is spectacular, with plenty of switchbacks and high cliff roads draped in tropical flora. Taipei confirmed my impression of Taiwan being a hellhole, but the drive out to Yehliu was the opposite. I'd never imagined Taiwan as paradise, but most of the island is. On one side of the road were long stretches of beach and on the other terraced rice fields. Barefoot, cone-hatted farmers worked the rice fields that carved a mosaic high into a rain forest mountain range. Compared to Yehliu, the Midwest may as well have been Pluto.

Ocean World is in a national park along one of the most dramatic stretches of coast. After driving high above the ocean, we dropped down into the tiny fishing village of Yehliu. The Dolphinarium is a 3,000-seat amphitheater encasing a puddle of a dolphin pool. Just behind the Dolphinarium is a huge stone monolith jutting out into the South China Sea. Along the bottom of the monolith is a field of rock sculptures carved by eons of wind and salt erosion. Most of them look like giant shiitake mushrooms, but one of them appears to be a pompous woman with a beehive hairdo. The locals call it Queenshead, and it is the symbol of the park. The divers in Hong Kong warned me I would hate Taiwan, but so far I loved it.

The Dolphinarium featured a diving board and had it in place along with a permanently installed 30-foot ladder. All we had to do was set up four sections of ladder and learn comedy in Mandarin. Since my only setup experience had been watching Dave do everything in the Ozarks, I was still following Dene like a puppy dog. This time, however, he made sure I did my share. Instead of just working the pulley rope, he taught me how to tie off the wire, adjust the turnbuckles and lock my leg into the top of the ladder so my hands were free.

If I was going to do this for a living (grad school? what grad school?), I wanted to know every facet of the job. Not only would I be responsible for my own security, but they would have to give me full pay for setup duty. Until you've directed an operation the companies only give you half pay for setup days. Once you know how to do a complete setup you can make a lot of money just going around getting shows off the ground.

By sundown, the ladder was set. We had to bolt back into Taipei to pick up Alan Bell, a trampolinist from the University of Missouri who was taking a break from school to make enough cash to pay for a couple more semesters. It took two hours to get to the airport and another hour to get back to the city. By the time we got back to the Angel Hotel in downtown Taipei, I was wrecked. I took a shower and slid under my covers.

At midnight Dene shook me out of my slumber. "Wake up, Rookie," he said. "Time to go out."

I thought we were down for the night, but I did not know the ways of Taipei. Many young workers in Taipei keep their shops open until 10 or 11 p.m. before taking a shower and heading out on the town. Bars are empty at midnight, but by 2 a.m. they're packed. Thus, our social life for the next few months took place between midnight and 4 a.m.

After slugging a few beers and a shot of tequila we rotated bars to an English pub called "My Place." We ran into the English synchronized swimmers we were replacing at the Dolphinarium. They were going home after 18 months on the island. In the space of a half hour, I'd had three shots of tequila and was lit. It was 2 a.m., but in Taipei, the night was still young.

By 3 a.m. I was getting sloppy, but the girls, having weathered a year and a half of Taiwan social life, were energized and in great form. I went outside to catch a breather and was followed out by one of the swimmers. She grabbed me from behind, walked me over to the corner of a parking lot and put her tongue further down my throat than any foreign object had ever been. We groped each other, and only when we were whistled at from a passing car did we realize we were still in public. The Brit looked at her watch and panicked, thinking she'd missed her ride home. I told her we should just take a cab and she said, "Love to, dear, but I haven't packed yet and my plane's leaving in a few hours."

When I got back to My Place, Dene was gone and the swimmers were chasing each other in and out of every bar on the street trying to get organized. An hour later the swimmers had collected themselves but were also fending off a salivating tribe of Taipei locals looking for their last chance to make out with a pretty white girl. My new friend and I mauled each other goodbye, then I hailed a cab back to the Angel.

I got up to the room and slammed three glasses of water along with three Extra Strength Tylenol. In four hours I was going to be onstage in front of a couple hundred Chinese school kids trying to remember the lines to a comedy in Mandarin. I felt lousy, but if I made it through the first show, there was an hour-long nap awaiting me.

I unzipped my fly and took aim at the toilet when all of the sudden the ground started to shake. The drinking glasses fell off the sink and smashed on the floor. The light in the bathroom went off, and I thought I heard a locomotive pass by in the hall. For twenty seconds that felt like two minutes, the earth shook so hard it tossed me right on my butt.

I jumped out of the bathroom and looked over at Alan who had sprung out of his bed. "Was that an earthquake?" he asked.

Dene rushed into the room just as Alan uttered the words and laid into him, "No, idiot, that was the fucking elevator! They make 'em heavy here. OF COURSE IT WAS AN EARTHQUAKE!"

We looked out into the hallway and saw a hodgepodge of terror-stricken international travelers looking at each other and asking in 20 different languages, "Was that an earthquake?" I was freaked out, not wanting to die up on the seventh floor of a hotel in downtown Taipei. The Westerners had said if you die in Taipei you go straight to hell because it's not that far away. I grabbed the van keys off Dene's table and went outside to crash in the parking lot. I got a few hours of sleep before an aftershock woke me. By this time Dene had had enough. He woke up Alan and we took off for Yehliu.

When we got to the park, they told us the quake had registered a 6.9 and had killed 15 people just two miles north of the Angel. Alan hadn't even been in the country for eight hours and he'd already survived an earthquake. The show opener, with only three people onstage and less than 30 in the crowd, was a bit anticlimactic. My post-show nap, however, was heavenly.

Taiwan is an extreme place, and it seemed that not a week went by without something extreme happening. Whether it was the weather, the traffic, the pollution, the late nights, or the cultural confusion, we always seemed to be running into bizarre situations.

Although the show opened with three divers, we soon added two more. We did a four-man show three times a day, except for the weekends when we were a full contingent doing four shows on Saturday and five on Sunday. The weekdays were a breeze, but Saturday got rougher and Sunday was brutal. The first show on Sunday started at 9:30 a.m., which meant we had to take off from Taipei at 8:00 am. That doesn't sound too rough except Saturday night was the best night to go out, and it was pointless to show up at a bar before midnight. Since we worked in a small town where we didn't even live, pulling the late-night weekend shift in Taipei was the only way to meet people.

After a four-show day on Saturday we would drive back into Taipei and take long naps, waking up around 9 p.m. We took turns showering, ate dinner, then hit the pub district around 11. Depending on who was there, we'd stay out at least until 3 a.m. and more often until 4 a.m. Show call Sunday morning took place at 8 a.m. at a Taipei breakfast institution, Mary's Hamburgers. Whoever had made it back to the apartment the night before drove the van down to Mary's and scooped up the rest of the divers who for one reason or another hadn't quite made it home yet.

As winter arrived, Taiwan turned cold and rainy and things started to go bad. Air temperature at showtime could drop into the 40s. We wore wetsuits, which were heavy and restricted our dives, every day. My elbow hadn't healed well from the spill I took on opening day in Hong Kong. I did lots of ladder dives and high dives, and one day, on a simple front dive from 30 feet, it popped out. I thought I'd broken something, so I went to the Adventist Hospital in Taipei for X-rays. Thankfully nothing was broken, but I had to take two weeks off, and that meant divers were working without a day off.

Everyone was edgy and it resulted in one of the divers attacking Dene while he was driving the van home from the Ocean World Christmas party. The owners of the park were in cars right behind us and got a kick out of seeing a couple of gwailos (white devils) go at it. But it's scary to be in the van when the driver is pulled into the back seat while on a twisty mountain road.

Luckily January, which can be every bit as nasty as December, turned out sunny and warm. We put away the wet suits and laid out in the sun between shows. On days off I would venture into Taipei with my Chinese friend, Larry. He introduced me to his family and several friends, so I started feeling like a local. They taught me Mandarin words and phrases, then laughed like jackals as I screwed up the tones. These were the reasons I came to the Far East—not to sit in a musty dressing room or a smoky bar.

As my time in Taiwan started winding down, life on the island got crazier and crazier. February means Chinese New Year, and I'd never seen a festival like it anywhere. Ocean World closed for three days before Chinese New Year, as we would be working five shows a day for five days straight over the holidays. I took a train down the east coast of the island through the mind-wrecking Taroko Gorge. The Gorge is a tropical ravine with thousand-foot marble cliffs and Buddhist temples, often at the bottom of massive waterfalls. The island of Taiwan was proving to be 10 percent disgusting and 90 percent incredible. It truly is a hidden treasure.

When I got back, Chinese New Year was in full swing. For 48 hours we could hear firecrackers blowing off from our apartment and saw massive fireworks displays from our roof. When I was in Hong Kong, I'd bought a Walkman Pro 6 bootlegging deck so I could record Grateful Dead concerts. I turned the microphone out towards the city to record a half hour of fireworks. When I listened to it three days later, the popping noises were so dense it sounded like static.

All the stores closed except for restaurants and bars, which were filled with Chinese families. The streets of Taipei looked like a snowstorm had hit. But instead of snow it was mounds of firecracker paper. Everyone you saw greeted you with a warm smile and traditional Chinese sweets. The celebration went on for five days, subsided for a week, then, on the twelfth and final day, started all over again.

As February ended, it was time to pack my guitar and backpack and get ready to return to UW-Milwaukee and the second half of the semester. At the end of an epic four-month stay at Ocean World, we did our final show, then sat down with the dolphin trainers for one last round of Taiwan beer before leaving Yehliu. As we pulled out of the park, we saw two people trying to hitch a ride into Taipei. We hadn't seen any hitchhikers the entire time on the island, so we picked them up. They were a young Swiss couple cruising around Taiwan on their annual month-long holiday. Every year they pick another country to visit for a month…too bad the United States doesn't work like that!

Once back at the apartment Dene had a plan. "We're leaving Taiwan in style," he said. "It's time for a dilly party!" For dilly parties, we'd get dressed

Season finale dilly party in Taipei. The rage before the storm.

in our clown suits and put on even more extravagant makeup than we do for the shows. Then we'd head out on the town. A couple of replacement divers had come in, and we also collected our Chinese friend, Claire. We were an unruly gang of nine clowns when we burst into one of the local restaurants, owned by our black market currency changer. We ate like kings and put down beers like they were water. While we boozed like champs, Dene, the driver, hung out. The last thing we needed while all jacked up on booze and adrenaline was a drunk driver. "I'm chilling out now," he said, "but once we get downtown, I'm parking this damn van, we're all taking cabs. And each one of you bastards is going to buy me a shot!"

We gorged ourselves on plate after plate of Chinese food washed down by beers and Shaoshing rice wine. Our table was an absolute mess, but that was as big a compliment as you can give a restaurant in Taiwan. If you leave a neat table it means you didn't like the food. That obviously wasn't an issue.

We piled into the van and headed south on Chung Shan road to the President Hotel. The tunes were cranked, and we were loud and rowdy. Not only was this our going-away party, but it was also Dene's retirement party as well as his bachelor party. We had just passed Mary's Hamburgers when Dene put his hands in the air and shouted, "Look mom—no hands…"

He was holding the wheel with his knees, but Claire thought he'd gone crazy. She pulled the wheel and the van jumped across the boulevard, careening straight towards a pick-up truck. Dene grabbed the wheel and swerved back across the boulevard, putting the van up on two wheels. I was sitting in the middle seat against the right window. "We're goin' for a ride!" I screamed.

Our nice homey blue microbus teetered, turned, then smashed down on the right side, crushing the right front quarter panel and shattering every bit of glass in the vehicle.

Dene and Claire shot through the windshield and the rest of us remained trapped inside until we could get out through the hatchback. While we were trying to sort out the chaos, a huge crowd gathered to watch the eight gwai-los prance out of the wrecked van like a circus act. The people of Taipei aren't often treated to bleeding clowns—especially white ones.

By the time we were extracted, an ambulance was already there. It was a dark foggy dreamlike scene, with smoke coming out of the engine and glass spread out across both lanes. I tried to take a count of everyone and survey the damage. "Who needs the ambulance?" I yelled. "Who's hurt?"

What was left of our van, post-wreck.

Everyone was standing in a circle when two clowns said in tandem, "YOU ARE!"

In the midst of the chaos I hadn't noticed that my right side was a mess of glass, road, and blood. Nothing was broken, but my right knee was split wide open and bleeding all over my dilly. I took off the clown suit, leaving me in full facial makeup, no shirt, a pair of running shorts, and some green Nike waffle stompers. I hobbled over to the ambulance and sat with Dene, who had sliced his ankle going through the windshield. Claire wanted to come because she felt guilty. Unfortunately, the unlucky Swiss couple both received some good slashes and had to pile in as well.

"Adventist Hospital!" Dene was screaming. "No Chinese hospitals!"

"No," the driver responded in broken English, "Tien Mu hospital."

He took off with Dene pounding on the glass screaming "Adventist," but it was no use. We were in a public ambulance, and they go to public hospitals. When we arrived at the emergency room of Tien Mu hospital, they ushered us into a dark hazy room stuffed full of geriatric Chinese patients lying in beds and moaning in pain. We sat on some beds for a half hour then chased down a nurse and demanded treatment.

Only after squeaking our wheel did we get some attention. Dene went in one room, the Swiss couple into another, and I went in a third. Claire was feeling so guilty she wouldn't let a doctor look at her left arm, which had swollen to double its normal size. (Two days later she was diagnosed with a broken ulna bone.) Instead, she roamed from room to room, making sure we were all right.

A couple of nurses worked me over with tweezers and peroxide, trying to pull out the dozens of glass shards jammed into my right side. Finally, a doctor came in and looked at my knee. He stared at my knee then looked at my face. "You make whoopee wit big man?" I didn't understand what the hell he was saying until I caught my reflection in his forehead mirror. I was wearing no shirt, and I had lipstick as well as full eye makeup. He thought Dene and I had gotten into a lovers' spat and I had hit him while driving.

I grabbed a towel, wiped off my makeup and told the doctor to concentrate on my knee. The doctor pulled out a needle and told me it would "make pain smaller." I wasn't sure where the needle had been, but before I could do anything, he jabbed me with it. I shouted out in pain and Claire came running in. She was in tears, and she insisted I hold her hand while the doctor took another stab. I squeezed her hand until her fingers turned blue. "Keep holding," she insisted. I had to let go or I was going to rip her small fingers off.

Ten minutes later the doctor came back in with sutures. "I sew you now," he said. "You no feel a thing." Claire was still in the room, so I grabbed her hand just in case. The doctor stuck the needle in me; I screamed bloody murder.

"Medicine no work yet," the doctor said. "I come back in five minutes."

Five minutes later he came back and started again with the same result. Whatever they were using for Novocain in Taiwan, it didn't work. My only pain medication was Claire's hand. In the course of receiving 17 stitches, I nearly tore it off. They bandaged me up like a mummy and sent me to the waiting room. The Swiss couple was long gone, leaving only Dene, Claire, and me.

Dene leaned over to me and whispered, "Slip outside and grab a taxi."

"What?" I asked.

"Did you put your name on anything? Did you give them any info?"

"Nothing," I said.

"I gotta get on an airplane tomorrow night, and I don't want to be stuck here answering a lot of questions about who was driving what and how much did anyone have to drink."

I slid out the door as inconspicuously as any mummy can, flagged down a cab, and told the cabby to wait. Dene, still in his clown suit, came hobbling out seconds later. The cabbie didn't want anything to do with the fare, especially when an orderly flew out of the hospital chasing Dene. The orderly stopped my cabbie from taking off, but 20 yards ahead of us Claire had flagged down another cab. She dropped the guy a 100 NT tip ($4) and he took us without reservation.

Claire told the cabbie to hit it and we burned rubber away from the hospital with the orderly screaming and chasing us down. Dene looked at me in the rearview mirror and said, "You look lovely, buttercup."

The cab sped away from the hospital but took a wrong turn away from the apartment. I was about to correct him, but Claire put her fingers to my lip. She was born in Taipei, so I thought she knew a shortcut. The cabbie pulled over and let us out miles from the apartment. "We switch cabs," Claire said. She flagged down another cab that drove us just a few blocks from the apartment. We got out and walked in the wrong direction until the cabbie was out of sight. Then we turned around and power limped to the apartment. We'd made it! We hobbled up to our apartment guard, who didn't know what to think.

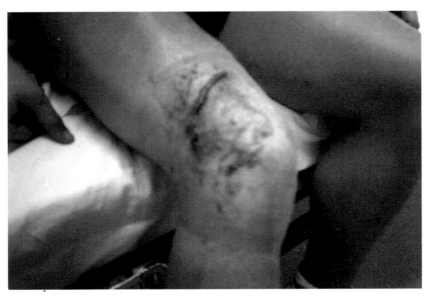

My knee just after it got stitched up at the Tien Mu municipal hospital.

Dene cashed him with 100 NT and said, "You know nothing. The divers were here all night, understand?"

The guard took the bill and let us in. We got upstairs and I sat on the couch while Claire prepared ice packs for us.

"Holy shit," I said, "I can't believe we ditched the hospital. That was genius."

"You think we're a real brain trust, do ya?" Dene said. "How many micro-buses full of white clowns do you think wrecked last night in Taipei?"

Just then the phone rang. I picked up the receiver and a voice speaking perfect English said: "Good evening. This is Tien Mu Hospital. May we speak with Mr. Whittaker?"

• • • • • • • • • • • • •

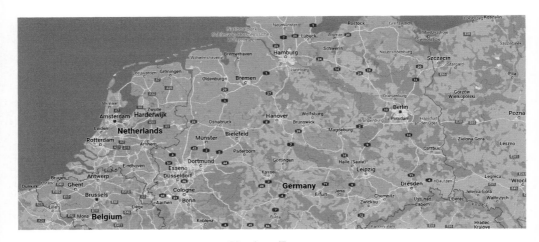

Northern Europe

Upside-down in Northern Europe

Two weeks after the wreck, I arrived back in Wisconsin with a crutch and a bag full of gauze bandages. My parents were ecstatic to see me in one piece and returning to school. After such a harrowing ordeal, I would surely come to my senses, finish my coursework, and look for a teaching job.

But that was the furthest thing from my mind. Where other people saw a fly-by-night circus operation, I saw screaming crowds, exotic tropical landscapes, and bustling international capitals. I had a meeting with my academic advisor to see if I could take some course work with me on the road, but he said I needed to get serious if I wanted to be a social studies teacher. But that ship had sailed. I wasn't a teacher, I was a performer.

Less than a month after I got home, Bruce Cant called me and I signed up for a six-week contract in Holland. It didn't start until after my semester ended, so I finished the schoolwork then packed some light summer clothes and my guitar. I appeased my parents saying I was just going to Europe to make some cash to pay for another semester. In the end, I wouldn't see America for nearly two years, and when I returned, I was a different human being.

My contract was in the idyllic former seaport town of Harderwijk, Holland. For nearly all its existence, Harderwijk had been a rugged coastal town. But when the giant Dutch polders (reclaimed land) were built, Harderwijk was no longer on the coast. It went from a town of rugged sailors to a haven for windsurfers. It also housed the Dolfinarium, which would be my office for the next two months. There was a massive indoor pool for their killer whale show, but the roof was too low for us. The Dolfinarium built us a pool by digging a deep pit on the beach and securing it with 40 horizontal steel girders. The water was pumped in from deep underground ensuring a numbing 55° F entry for five shows a day. It also turned out to be a viciously cold and wet summer, which meant we dove in wetsuits and spent the time between shows bundled up in towels instead of lying on the beach.

What on paper sounded like a hellacious contract proved to be yet another spectacular chapter in the impossible life I was cobbling together. What Holland lacks in the weather and topography department, it more than makes up for in its number one asset: stunningly beautiful and incredibly sweet women.

My new teammates were show veterans who had volunteered to come back to Harderwijk year after year. After we'd set up the show in driving rain and bitter cold, I had to ask them why in the world they opted for the north of Holland when they could take a contract in Spain or Hong Kong.

"Let's go to the pub," the captain told me. "I think you'll see why."

My first trip to Nikki's Inn, the centerpiece of the Harderwijk social scene, was spent slack jawed, fumbling awkwardly over a language (English) the locals seemed to have a better master of than I did. After the second night, I complemented myself for only getting busted staring on two occasions. But on the third night I was introduced to Linda, and I was smitten from the minute I laid eyes on her. My world was rocked, and it stayed rocked long past the date on my return ticket.

The one difference between professional diving and other sports is we rarely had to compete. We just had to stay healthy. We didn't even have to be particularly good. If you could stay in the high dive rotation and hit your cues, they really didn't care about your degree of difficulty. And for a cold-water, bad weather show like Harderwijk, the goal was to just stay healthy so everyone could take their one day off a week.

I fell into this groove just like all the vets. My knee had not completely recovered from the wreck in Taiwan and the ugly weather made it ache. For three weeks, I stuck to the script. I cranked out shows, then met Linda afterwards at Nikki's Inn. Aside from lighting myself on fire and jumping off the 80-foot tower, the job became a nine-to-fiver.

I might have kept doing this all summer long, but word of our next contract came up. One day my boss came in and announced we would be heading to Berlin to perform a one-off show in front of 40,000 people for the 750th anniversary of the city. If I was going to do a stadium gig, I wasn't going to just hop off the ladder. I was gonna blow 'em away with the Mifflin Street Dive.

The next day I started working my handstand up the ladder when the captain of our team came out from the show trailer to see who was making all the noise. "Don't be practicing," he said. "Pretty soon they're gonna make us all practice. And that's what the shows are for!"

I laughed then asked him to watch me as I climbed to the 40-foot perch and tossed my first Mifflin Street Dive in a year. It was the lowest one I'd ever done, but I spun it slowly and barely finished the trick before I hit the water.

"Looks like you need some more time on that one," he said.

"That's what the shows are for!" I said.

I was doing the last high dive of the day and I got pretty nervous when show time came. After four cold shows, all we ever thought of was getting warm and making it to Nikki's for happy hour. We had the habit of razzing Henk, our announcer, to get him to start the show early or cancel it altogether. Henk was a great sport, but his paycheck came from the Dolphinarium. He was a company boy and not a rule breaker. If show time was 3:30, the pre-show music went on at 3:25, whether anyone was there or not. I paced in the sand behind the trailer visualizing the Mifflin Street Dive. I'd done at least thirty in the Ozarks, but because of my injured elbow in the Far East, it had been almost a year since the last one. And this ladder was fifteen feet higher. I wasn't sure if I should float the top or spin it.

I did the fire dive to open the show, then came out onstage for a tandem reverse twister and the six-man mass dive. The team ran backstage and got dressed for the comedy, but I slipped out and got ready for the high dive. As soon as the team finished their dillies they ran backstage, hosed themselves down and toweled off. They were done for the day, but my day had just started.

Henk gave his dramatic high dive speech, and I walked out to the front of the stage. Before he said my name, I looked up into the bleachers and saw Linda and her friend, Babbs, sitting in the crowd. I gave them a wink and they sarcastically blew elaborate kisses with both hands, basically saying, "Get this over with so we can go to Nikki's and have a drink."

I climbed the ladder to the 40-foot perch and took a pause to catch my breath. I looked down at Linda, who pointed at her watch, telling me to hurry up. I climbed underneath the 80-foot perch, but instead of hopping up on top of it, I lowered the perch five feet so I would be putting my knees through a secure section of the ladder, not the crown that was only attached by a single wire. I got on top of the lowered perch then looked straight at Linda. She looked back and shrugged her shoulders as if to say, "What's the deal? Get off the damn ladder already."

I turned around, climbed the final five feet, and put my legs through the ladder, then looked back and placed my hands on the perch. I looked down at Linda, who now had her eyes covered with Babbs consoling her. I freed my legs from the ladder and stuck a solid handstand. I started the fall, then kicked my legs into the first 1½. When I split, I had a horrible visual. In the Ozarks, all I could see was the lake. Here, I was looking at the edge of the stage about sixty feet below me. The ladder was erected about three feet from the edge of the pool, and I wondered if I'd given myself enough room to clear the stage. Panicking at this point would do no good at all, so I tucked over the bottom somersault, spotted the water and zipped the thing into the pool just a few feet from the stage.

I came out of the water to the biggest ovation I'd gotten all year. I ran backstage to a team full of vets high-fiving (years before fist-bumps) me and slapping me on the arse. I wasn't the only trickster on the team, but I wasn't just a lazy staff diver either. I was somebody to come see.

I met Linda and Babbs on the way out and Linda was both amazed and pissed. She gave me a big hug and a kiss, then a sock in my arm.

"Why didn't you tell me you were going to do that!" she said. "You scared the crap out of me!"

"I guess that's kind of what my job is," I said. "I'm supposed to scare the crap out of people."

With that I received another sock in the arm—and then she grabbed it, pulled me close and we walked off to Nikki's.

Stage bows from the catwalk in Harderwijk, Holland. Great crowds—especially on bad weather days.

By the close of summer, I'd moved from the team hotel into Linda's one-room studio in the center of town. As the season ended, I felt an awesome sense of relief. I made it through the contract without any injuries and I'd even put away some money. Linda had scored me a job pulling boats out of the Harderwijk marina and prepping them for winter storage. The job wouldn't start until the weather got bad, so that gave me time to do the Berlin show and also take a four-week Euro-rail trip to all the spots in Southern Europe I'd missed traveling with Dan, Michael and Lori 18 months earlier.

Our train for Berlin left early in the morning, so when I woke up, I gave Linda a kiss and told her she should sleep in. She would have nothing to do with it. She got dressed and ran to the bakery to get some sandwiches for the train. When I tried to get on the train, Linda didn't want to let go. Only when the conductor yelled for last call did she tearfully release me. This trip was only going to last a week. What would she think when I took off for a month on the continent?

Five hours later we arrived at the East German frontier. In 1987 Germany was two separate countries and the thought of them reuniting was absurd. The train stopped at the border, and the East German policemen searched underneath the wagons with mirrors, lanterns, and dogs. Inside the train they went through every page of our passports and questioned us as to our purpose and length of stay. I was the only person on the team who had been an Eastern Bloc country before, but this shakedown was ten times more severe than the border check in Yugoslavia.

The train rolled through the drab East German countryside, a stark contrast from the colorful West. When the train slowed for a road crossing, every car I saw was the same: a smaller version of a 1969 Ford Rambler, a box on wheels driven only by men who all wore the same gray clothes.

When we passed into West Berlin, however, we pulled into one of the most vibrant cities in all of Europe. The contrast of this brilliant island to the sea of blandness surrounding it was shocking. The streets were lined with high fashion shops, and the buildings adorned with neon lights. A fleet of Mercedes, BMWs, Porsches, and Audis replaced the box-like cars of the East. Funky modern sculpture and loud posters took up any piece of open space. The posters advertised concerts, football games, track meets, and for the first time ever—The Acapulco Death Divers! The 750 Jahr Celebration was the biggest thing in town, and we were headliners. Not only were we on posters, but we were also on buses, billboards, and just about every kiosk in town.

We hailed a couple of taxis and headed to the Alt Mariendorf racetrack to meet Bruce Cant from Hong Kong and our booking agent, Jim Tieborg. Tieborg was an American promoter who had been living in Germany for more than thirty years. He used to work a trapeze act before getting into entertainment management. He smoked like a fiend and drank his share, but when it came down to hauling gear, Tieborg had no problems getting dirty with us.

Bruce met us at the racetrack and asked us how the season went. He'd heard about the Mifflin Street Dive and told me it would be a showstopper in front of the huge crowd. He was trying to pump each one of us up because he knew we were in for six days of butt-breaking work for one day of glory—followed by another day of torture to take it all down.

When he showed us the show site we thought he was joking. We were fifty yards into the infield of the track. One bank of seats was almost a quarter mile away from the ladder. One of the main reasons our show worked was because of crowd involvement. The closer they get to the pool, the more involved and active they get. How were people supposed to react to clown faces without seeing them? They couldn't even tell if we were happy or sad clowns. We were contracted to do two half-hour sets. One set would be straight diving and a tandem fire dive, and the other would be the carpenter-comedy act followed by dillies and the high dives.

"That carpenter act's gonna go over really well from 200 yards away," I said.

"It's in the contract, and that's what we're gonna do!" Bruce yelled.

We could tell negotiations with the Germans hadn't gone smoothly. Germans are horrible when it comes to diving shows. They have a rulebook for constructing radio towers, and technically that's what we were doing so we had to follow those regulations. An obese, red-faced inspector followed us everywhere making sure we were following the D.I.N. (Deutschland Industrial Norm). In Holland we could have set up a ladder with kite string in the middle of Amsterdam, and nobody would have even minded the traffic jam. In Germany they wanted to make sure we had regulation shoelaces on our clown shoes.

We were up early in the morning and waited for our equipment truck to arrive. The racetrack hired a construction crew to erect a stage, but it was up to World Wide Productions to provide a swimming pool. WWP bought a ten-meter wide, four-meter-deep oil holding tank with an enormous synthetic liner. The tank was composed of thirty-six heavy iron panels that would be bolted together in three concentric rings of twelve. Each panel weighed about fifty pounds, and there were more than 3,000 bolts holding it together. All we had to work with was an electric winch and a couple of power bolt fasteners. Before we could get started, a messenger from the racetrack came over and told us our freight container was held up in East German customs. We couldn't do anything without our gear, so Bruce reluctantly gave us the day off. We didn't waste it.

I suggested we go to Checkpoint Charlie and cross over to the east side. We'd be working all week in the West and this might be our only chance to check out the Berlin Wall and East Berlin. Everybody thought it was a great idea, so we went back to the hotel, packed our cameras and took the U-Bahn to Checkpoint Charlie.

The Berlin Wall was a horrific symbol of communist oppression. It wasn't one wall but two walls, one on each side of "No-Man's Land." The wall on the west was covered with colorful yet inflammatory graffiti against the Soviet regime that held half of Europe captive. The eastern wall was covered in soot.

Checkpoint Charlie was a small white building in the middle of the street with fortified gates on either side. The museum next to Checkpoint Charlie was a testament to the brave Germans who tried to escape, many of whom died in the attempt. The most ingenious solution was to cut open the spare gas tank of a semi-truck. The escapee would climb in the empty gas tank with a scuba tank and a welder would seal them in and cover his weld. The driver would wait in the long line at the border for the truck to pass customs. Once on the other side, the semi would pull into a garage and the driver would smash the loose weld open. It worked for a few months until an East German tattletale informed on the driver. The driver was never seen again.

We crossed through the checkpoint and strolled along the drab streets of the East until we came upon the central district with dozens of government buildings. We found a restaurant and ordered up a couple of plates of the nastiest schnitzel I'd ever tasted. We stopped eating when someone found a dead worm in their chicken broth.

The centerpiece of East Berlin was a 300-meter-high radio tower open to the public. We bought tickets and rode the elevator high above the city to the observation deck. From there we could see all of Berlin, including the racetrack, Brandenburg gate, Olympic stadium, and the bombed-out Kaiser Wilhelm Memorial Church in the center of West Berlin. We shared the observation deck with a class of school children who were looking at West Berlin for the first time. They were excited to see sites they'd read about in their textbooks. These were world-famous monuments of their birth city. But they would never visit them as long as the wall stood.

We walked around the center looking for something to do or buy, but there was nothing. We were getting tired and bored until we stumbled upon a pub not far from the radio tower. We ordered a round of beers and couldn't believe they were only one East German mark apiece. In the West, most beer cost four West German marks a pint. We told the waiter what a great deal we thought we were getting, and his eyes lifted.

"How much did you pay for your East Marks?" he asked. At the border we were required to change 25 West marks (1.6 Deutsch marks = 1 US dollar) for 25 East marks. We thought the normal exchange was a one-to-one ratio.

Putting a "Fat Man Rocks" sticker on the Berlin Wall. Jerry Garcia would have been proud.

"Don't leave," he said. "I have a friend you might want to talk to."

His friend, a spitting image of Colin Hay from the band Men at Work, came over and asked us if we wanted to change money.

"I'll give you five to one," he said.

I thought it was a scam, but when he opened a wad of East German marks from his pocket and started counting out money, I knew it was real. Not only were the beers we were drinking one-fifth the price they were in the West, but the currency was devalued one-fifth. After doing the math, I figured we were paying about fifteen US cents for a huge mug of beer. And it was damn good German beer, too.

We loaded up on East marks and went back into town looking to buy trinkets for birthday presents or any kind of souvenir. There was a big market near the train station not far from the pub. We strolled over, ready to throw wads of cash around but there was absolutely nothing to buy. I was looking for a T-shirt or a postcard or some funky hat or scarf for Linda, but everything was complete junk: broken toys, old appliances, ragged work clothes.

We regrouped at the train station and decided the only good use for our huge stash of East marks was booze. We took a table in the middle of the bar at the train station and ordered a round of beers. "This one's on me," I said. "I can afford half a buck for you guys."

We pounded the beers and took turns buying rounds. All around us were East German rail workers sipping their beers at the end of a hard day's work. They were depressed and looked a little peeved at us as we started to get louder. Then I had a tremendous idea. I called the waiter and ordered a round of beers for the table next to us. It cost me all of 60 cents. Everyone caught on and started buying rounds of beers for every table in the bar. Before we knew it, the whole place got loud. After an hour, we were spread all over the bar trying to learn card games and taking pictures with our new friends. We got the place rockin' and it didn't even begin to dent our supply of East marks.

It was getting late, and Checkpoint Charlie closed at 11 p.m. We only had one-day tourist visas so getting caught in East Berlin after the gate closed was not an option. The four of us started our way back to the gate, but now we were lit and in a rowdy mood. At one point my teammate Jeremy climbed on the hood of a car and yelled, "I am the richest man in East Berlin!"

We all laughed until a bunch of cops ran up to us and took Jeremy away in cuffs. We only had a half hour to make the time check, but now one of us was in a lockup. Our team captain Darren, fueled by a half dozen pints, took matters into his own hands. He told our teammate Jennifer and me to head to the gate, while he was going to get Jeremy out. It would be best if at least some of us were at work in the morning.

Jennifer and I made our way to the gate and prayed we would see Darren and Jeremy before they shut it for the night. Then, with only five minutes to spare, we saw our teammates sprinting for the gate.

"Don't ask!" Darren yelled as the four of us passed through security and made our way to the subway stop in the West. Once we were all settled, Darren gave us the scoop.

"I told them I was Ronald Reagan's nephew," he said. "And unless they wanted a whole bunch of trouble, they had better let this American go immediately!"

"You're kidding me!" I said. "They bought that?"

"I doubt it," he said. "But I think we just looked like more trouble than we were worth…"

After a week of delays, setup, and rehearsal, it was time for the show. We were headliners, but there were also six harness races, a sway pole act, and hovercraft races. The crowd trickled in when the gates opened at noon, but by 1:30, 40,000 Germans were in their seats pounding beer. After the first harness race, people turned their attention to the sway pole, a 60-foot flagpole anchored to the ground by a five-foot cubed water tank. The performers climb to the top and get the poles rocking back and forth as hard as they can. They do handstands and even switch poles in midair, but they were getting little crowd reaction. They got one roar, but that's when one of the guys slipped and almost fell. When he did it again, we realized it was a rehearsed move. We'd introduced ourselves to the sway pole team earlier in the week, but being a band of Swiss circus gypsies, they kept to themselves.

After a few more harness races, we were up. Our show music came on. We ran out to our stage positions and waved to the crowd, but there was no reaction. We could barely hear the stage announcements, as all the speakers were pointed into the crowd. We had no stage monitor, so Tieborg sat under the stage and cued us when to go. We could tell the crowd was politely applauding the dives, but it was hard to hear. Finally, when we did a mass dive with six of us flying through the air at once, they responded with the ooohs and ahhhs you normally hear at the 4th of July fireworks.

We closed the first act with a tandem fire dive that got the crowd going. We set up two perches at 25 and 35 feet. Darren, the bottom diver, lit himself on fire and Bruce Cant, the top diver, quickly caught on fire. After about ten seconds of burning, Bruce screamed he was going, and they both flew off their perches into the tank. The thrill of diving in front of the huge crowd got the most of Bruce. He spun into a flying front somersault, then ate it hard when he hit the water.

We were the only ones who even noticed Bruce had done the front flip. Unfortunately his cape came up on his face and burned his forehead and cheek. He took his bow gracefully, and then came running backstage looking for a hose to freeze his face. He wasn't seriously hurt, so we circled around him and laughed. Bruce tried to spray us, but he couldn't keep the hose off his blistered face long enough to take good aim. "So, this is the guy who signs the checks," I said.

A couple more races went off, and then it was time for the big finale. The reason we came to Berlin was at hand. High dives are almost more impressive from far off than close up. We were finally able to appease even the people a quarter mile away at the paddocks. The first two high dives went off well and the crowd responded with collective gasps followed by huge applause. I was up next. I climbed up to the perch and lowered it again so that my knees would be hanging over a secure section of ladder. I waved to the crowd, then turned around, climbed up the ladder and put my legs through the rung. I stayed tucked up in a ball for a couple seconds because I wanted to prepare myself to take the mental snapshot I would never forget. I could hear the crowd's murmur rise as they were trying to figure out what I was doing. Then, as slowly as I could, I laid my head back and took a look at 40,000 upside-down Germans.

To this day I can still clearly see that crowd and hear their voices rise. I took it all in, then remembered I still had to do a pretty tough trick. With the tank being 10 feet off the ground and me being upside down, the visuals were disorienting. Although I was 85 feet in the air, I only had 73 feet to make the dive. If I spotted the ground, I was going to eat it. I had to make sure I saw the surface of the pool and nothing else.

I released my legs from the ladder and got myself to a perfectly straight handstand. I held it longer than I usually do just to take in the crowd one last time. I burst off the ladder, spun the first 1½, split, caught my spot, and then dropped the second flip into the tank. I missed my rip, but when I came to the surface the crowd was going crazy. I felt like Gorman Thomas hitting a homer at County Stadium. Getting the Dolphinarium crowd to react was one thing, but a huge ovation from 40,000 Germans was the most amazing thing I'd ever heard.

The Berlin Mifflin Street Dive: 80 feet up in front of 40,000 upside-down spectators.

I collected high fives from the team and took one last bow for the crowd. At Illinois we were lucky to get fifty or sixty people to come to our meets—and we trained hard for those meets. This was the payoff for all those morning workouts and heavy 10-meter tower crashes. Reluctantly, I stopped my wave and dropped back in line.

Jeremy, one of the great high-dive tricksters of the '80s, was last to go. He knocked the snot out of his mid-turn triple to the same ovation I'd gotten. We took one last bow as a team, and the crowd went nuts a final time. It was an incredible end to yet another unbelievable experience as a high diver. I felt sorry for the good divers who never got to experience anything like that. Then again, they didn't feel sorry for me in college when they were kicking my ass.

That night a few of us decided to go back to East Berlin to see what kind of celebration the communists were putting on. We'd already seen enough people in the West having a blast, and we figured we could see the fireworks from anywhere. We took the subway to Checkpoint Charlie and crossed over hoping to find a bunch of people celebrating the 750th anniversary of their beloved Berlin. An hour later we crossed back. After a military parade early in the day all the stores were ordered closed, and the streets were empty. West Berliners were having the biggest party in the history of the city while East Berliners were told to go to bed.

• • • • • • • • • • • • •

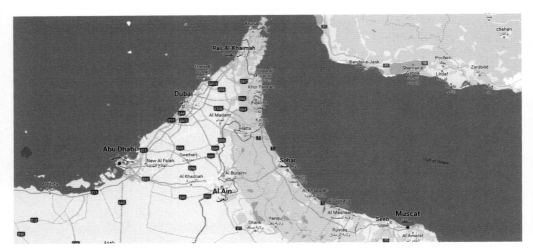

The United Arab Emirates

Instant Karma

The thrill of Berlin was just the beginning of what would prove to be the most intense six months of my life. I returned to Harderwijk, but only had a few days before taking on a month-long Interrail trip. While my life was whipping around at 100 miles per hour, Linda's life consisted of getting up and going to work. She asked me again to cancel my trip, but that was out of the question. In the back of my mind, I was still in grad school to be a social studies teacher and this was an opportunity I couldn't miss. I'd only be gone a month and then I'd be in dark rainy Holland through winter.

Life on the rails in Europe sounds like one big party, but that's not how I took it. For me it was a matter of seeing as much as I could before my pass ran out. People say you shouldn't rush through Europe. But I was living in Europe and I knew the difference between being a local and being a traveler. For one intense month, I was going to be a road-hardened traveler.

In 30 days I got all the way to Istanbul, saw all the capitals of southern Europe I'd missed on my first trip, and even made it to Africa. Along the way I climbed Mt. Olympus (Bursa, Turkey), ran the course of the ancient Olympians, threw coins into the Trevi fountain in Rome, and saw a bullfight in Madrid. I stayed in super cheap bunk rooms or slept on overnight trains and boats to save money. Like most travelers in the era, I didn't have a credit card. I used travelers' cheques and found money changers in each new city. My cheques were in Dutch guilders and by the end of the trip I'd traded them in for more than a dozen currencies. I had visions of riding the rails all the way to Casablanca, but got held up by a pair of drug dealers in Tangiers. Robbed of my travel funds, I had money in my bank in Holland, but no way to access it. I headed back to Harderwijk penniless, hoping the conductors didn't notice my train pass had expired. I found myself broke and traveling around Europe— just like I'd been on the Bridge to Venice.

When I got back to Holland, it was time to start my new job. Linda had gotten me work at Eerland Marina, a small winter boat storage business in the port of Harderwijk. I worked without a work visa, but that was to the benefit of both me and my boss. If he put me on the books, he had to pay a 100 percent employment tax. Five guilders to me, five guilders to the government. This way he paid me 7.5 guilders an hour ($4) and no one was the wiser. It was full-time work and believe me, I wasn't taking a job from anybody. Nobody wanted that job besides me.

I was out the door by 7 a.m. and spent my entire day scraping fiberglass, lifting engines out of boats, and preparing small yachts for winter storage. It rained constantly and by the time December came around, we had less than six hours of daylight. I rode my bike to work in the dark and rode home after work in the dark. Holland is a very tough place to winter, but then again, I was living with a beautiful, caring woman. It was rough, but I still wore a smile most of the time.

I was ready to stick it out, but instead World Wide Productions came calling with an interesting proposition. They asked me if I wanted to do a show in Abu Dhabi.

In 1988, just a few years before the first Gulf War directed everyone's attention towards the Persian Gulf, few people in America had ever heard of places like Abu Dhabi and Dubai. I imagine many high school geography teachers would have been hard pressed to find countries like Qatar or Bahrain on a map. The only Westerners who had ever heard of Muscat, Oman were wealthy retired Brits or oil executives. When I was told we had a gig lined up in Abu Dhabi, not only could I not name the country it was in, I took a stab at the continent and even got that wrong. I'd heard of diving shows in Egypt and South Africa, so I thought I was headed to Africa.

Instead, I was off to The United Arab Emirates, deep in the heart of the war-torn, socially repressive Arab Middle East. Linda was less than pleased. She thought I was going to be in Harderwijk at least until summer, but now I was leaving before Christmas. But high diving money is much better than dock-worker money, so I had no choice.

Linda and her sister drove me to Schiphol Airport in Amsterdam and sat with me while I waited for the plane to arrive. I assumed I'd be getting advance pay on arrival, so I only took a 100 guilder ($50) note with me for the trip. While we were waiting, Linda asked me for some cash so we could get some fries. I gave her the bill and forgot about it. I didn't notice until I ordered a beer on the flight to Dubai that she had forgotten to give me the change. When I dug into my wallet, I found moths. Not only was I going to the strangest place I'd ever been, but I was also going with 50 cents in my pocket. The Bridge to Venice rules were one thing but being broke BEFORE the trip even started was pushing the limits.

At the time I wasn't worried, because WWP was always good about advances at the beginning of a show. After a week of setup pay, I could pay them back and start saving money. But that was assuming this was a normal diving show. Nothing in fact would be normal until I landed back in Holland four months later.

Just after the sun set on Israel and Jordan, the KLM flight touched down at Dubai International Airport in the United Arab Emirates (UAE). This was long before the tragedy of September 11, 2001, and thus most airport security was lax. Today armed guards are not unusual at an airport. Back then it was shocking to see. Luckily, I could see my contact, Dan-Bob Anthony from Hong Kong, sitting on the far side of customs. Had he not been there, I'd have been screwed. I didn't have enough money for a Coke, let alone a hotel room.

Getting a work visa in an Arab country was quite difficult. I had to submit a letter of invitation from my UAE employer and present customs with two copies of every page in my passport (more than 50 stamped pages at this point) and four passport pictures. When I passed through customs, they took my passport and gave me a receipt number.

"Where do I pick up my passport?" I asked.

"Your passport will be kept at the Ministry of Work," the clerk told me. "When you are ready to leave the United Arab Emirates, you will be issued an exit visa, and you may pick up your passport then. Your sponsor will have all the necessary information."

I had only been in the country for ten minutes and I already broke the first rule of international travel: Don't lose your damn passport. I was as far away from Wisconsin as I'd ever been, and I didn't have any money or travel papers. If I wanted to get any farther from Milwaukee, they'd have to put me on a spaceship. When my dad heard I was going to the Arabian Peninsula, he sent me a book by Sandra McKenna called *The Saudis*. McKenna tells stories of expatriate workers getting tossed in jail and abandoned for months on end because nobody could find their passports. In one scenario, a clerk from the Ministry of Work let a man rot in prison for three months because the clerk used his passport to prop up an uneven desk. The worst part was the man was in prison because he went to report someone else's traffic accident and was mistakenly locked up. The only law in the Arabian Peninsula is power, and I surely had none.

But from what I'd read, the UAE was a different kind of place than Saudi Arabia. Whereas Saudi was an ancient kingdom and the motherland of Islam's most sacred sites, Mecca and Medina, the UAE had only been a country since 1971. The seven Emirates of Dubai (Abu Dhabi, Ajman, Sharja, Fujairah, Ras al Khaimah and Al Qurayya) had been separate sheik-doms loosely controlled by the British Crown, which called them the Trucial States. In 1971, just after oil was discovered, Sheik Zayad, the leader of Abu Dhabi, united the sheikdoms into the United Arab Emirates.

For all practical purposes each emirate was its own country with its own laws. They were Sharia Islamic states, but if one sheik wanted to loosen up the laws for Westerners, that was his business. The unification meant citizens could get a recognizable passport, and Zayad had a seat in the UN. More importantly, he had a powerful say in the petroleum cartel OPEC as well as the Gulf Cooperative Counsel, the regional coalition that included Iran and Iraq (who were at war at the time), Saudi, Kuwait, Bahrain, Qatar, Oman, and Yemen (at that time both North and South Yemen).

After more than an hour of processing papers and obtaining a work visa, I picked up my bags, passed through one more security check, and was released into the country. Dan-Bob gave me a big hug and told me not to say a thing until we got in the taxi. The air of paranoia that was to last the next four months had been established. Years later I met Ricky Poole, a grizzled old show veteran, who cringed when he talked about working in the Middle East. "It's a nervous place to work," is all he could say.

Once in the taxi, Dan-Bob reported things weren't going quite as well as they'd expected. We were working for a Moroccan woman named Jamilla, whom Chip Humphrey (WWP co-owner and my boss in Harderwijk and Berlin) had met in Taiwan. She had seen the show and was sure it would be a big hit in the Emirates. She had come up with enough money to ship a freight container of show equipment to Abu Dhabi, but since that time, they'd run up against a nightmare of red tape and didn't even have permission to unload the container.

"There's some ground rules here," Dan-Bob said. "Absolutely no drink-ing. Legally drunk here is anything greater than .00 percent. Cab drivers can take you into the police for a bounty. It's going to be a long, dry haul but in the end, we'll save a lot of money."

Was this the same Dan-Bob who had forced tequila down my throat in Hong Kong? And how the hell was a team of high divers going to exist without knocking back beers after work? It's what we did to maintain sanity.

Before we took off, five lanky camels wandered in from the middle of the desert and drank out of a trough next to the airport exit. Just across the street was a yellow triangle caution sign with a camel silhouette and the words "Camel Crossing" written below it. I thought I'd drifted into a movie set: Dan-Bob and Tom on *The Road to Abu Dhabi*.

Ten minutes out of town, the driver turned to Dan-Bob and said, "Okay, I think it's safe, now."

Dan-Bob cracked a Coke and pulled a fifth of Johnny Walker Black out of his bag.

"Just kidding about the booze," he said. "But not about the cabbies; if they think you've been drinking, they can take you in."

"This is true!" the cabbie said. "Last month I have many professional wrestlers. Two of them went to jail. It is not a good way to enjoy the country."

"Tom, this is Adul Josuf," Dan-Bob said, introducing the cabbie. "He's our manager. If you've got problems, talk to Adul."

"Yes," Adul said, "I can get you anything—except the things you want." Adul laughed hard from his belly. He was a diminutive man of thirty with a warm, trusting soul—something we would soon find was a rarity in the Emirates.

"I am not Arab man," Adul said, "I am from Sudan. I am Christian man. Christian man like to drink sometime. Arab man say he no drink, but he drink more than Christian man."

Again, he laughed hard. By the end of the two-hour drive to Abu Dhabi, we'd become fast friends. Before he left us, he put his arm around me and whispered, "Remember, I am not an Arab man. We laugh and have good jokes. If Arab man laugh with you, be scared."

Then he looked me straight in the eye. "Serious this time, man."

I told Dan-Bob about my cash snafu and asked him if he could spot me during set-up. He gave me the equivalent of $20 in UAE dirhams and told me to talk to Chip in the morning. I went up to my room in the Corniche Residence, a business hotel that would be home for much of the next three months. I was sharing a room with Ricky Tennant, one of the best divers in the world and the only high diver I knew from my amateur days. Ricky greeted me with a big hug, then plopped down on his bed and said, "This place is fucked up, man."

In the morning I met Chip for breakfast and asked him for an advance. "Things aren't working out that well so far," he said. "Mae [Chip's wife] is coming in a week or two, and she'll have some cash for us. In the meantime, you get one free meal a day at the hotel."

I couldn't believe what he was saying. I only had $20 in my pocket, and he couldn't spot me a dime. Bruce had given me a hundred bucks coming off the plane in Hong Kong. Something was way out of whack. I asked him what time we were going to set up, and he told me we didn't quite have the location nailed down yet. He should have told me there wasn't a show at all. I walked back to my room, stunned, and sat next to Ricky.

He took one look at my face and said, "I told you man, it's all fucked up. We don't have dick going on here except six divers and five swimmers."

"Swimmers?" I asked. "What swimmers?"

"We got five British chicks working with us. Really green too. I think they're all pretty freaked out about it."

"So, what's the deal?" I asked. "Why aren't we working?"

"Contract's all fucked up, dude," he said. "We're not working in any park. This Moroccan woman Jamilla is selling us as a separate 50-minute show. She thinks people are going to pay $10 just to see us."

"What? Like we're the freaking Rolling Stones?"

"Exactamundo," he said. "They're still trying to get a license to set up at some tourist club on the other side of town."

"So why the hell did they send for us?" I asked. "I could still be working in Holland!"

"I bet you're pretty pissed you stepped on that plane," he said.

I wasn't just pissed. I was outraged. And scared. Unemployment was not in my grandiose scheme to make a Dutch-American relationship work out.

Ricky and I went up to the hotel pool where I met Jerry Grimes, one of the smartest high divers in the business. Jerry was pulled out of the Colorado high school coaching ranks at the age of thirty-three to work in Hong Kong. He dug it so much he hadn't been home in three years. He could do great tricks off the springboard, but he was along for the ride because he was as funny a dive-show comedian as there was. Ricky introduced me and the first words out of Jerry's mouth were, "Pretty fucked up, eh?"

The three of us sat down to a bitch session, but Jerry told us to chill. The synchronized swimmers were walking up to the pool deck, and being rookies, they had no idea how screwed up things were. No sense in everyone panicking.

Tracy Golding, the captain of the swimmers, was a Taiwan veteran and a sweet spunky Brit from London. She always had a great attitude and tried to maintain it even though she was aware of the problems. She told her girls delays were normal, and soon enough they would be performing for thousands and taking home paychecks. The team consisted of four more Brits: Rachel, Mandy, Janet, and Lesley. Tracy introduced Jerry and me to the swimmers. I greeted them all with a quick hello and a handshake until I came to Lesley.

Lesley was hyper-cute and had a smart-ass air about her. We shook hands but something else was in the air. The girls went back to the pool, and Jerry and I went back to our books. But as Lesley slid into the pool, we busted each other looking back for a peek. I shook it off and reminded myself I was with Linda.

We sat at the Corniche Residence for more than two weeks with no sign of work. I finished *The Saudis* and passed it around the team. That left me with nothing to do, and also sent a wave of paranoia through the troupe. The swimmers were excited when they arrived, but after reading a few chapters of *The Saudis* and waiting without work they realized they were in trouble. They stopped working out their routines and sat around watching CNN and US Armed Forces Television in their rooms.

I did my best to explore Abu Dhabi, but I didn't have any money and there wasn't much to see. In 1987, the city was an offshore island sitting on one of the biggest oil reserves in the world. Just twenty years earlier there had been nothing there. Since the discovery of oil, skyscrapers were springing up like dandelions. On the surface, little was left of the nomadic Arab culture that had existed since the beginning of time. But underneath the big new skyscrapers, it was all still there.

It was interesting to watch the parade of bizarre characters walking up and down the Corniche (sea strand) but without any money it wasn't even fun to check out the souk (market). I played guitar hours a day. If it weren't for David Letterman and live NFL and NBA games (usually at 2:00 a.m.) on US Armed Forces Television, I would have jumped off a cliff.

To fill out our squad, Nancy Clarke, one of the rare female high divers, flew in from Hong Kong with Chip's wife, Mae. Nancy was always bubbling over with energy which, considering our situation, annoyed the hell out of me. How could anyone be so happy when we were in such a crappy situation? As soon as she caught wind of what was going down, even Nancy started to get pissed—and I began to like her a lot more. Nancy always went to whichever one of us she thought was feeling the worst and tried to pick us up. She ended up being one of my favorite people in all of pro diving.

Jamilla, the show broker, stayed at the Abu Dhabi Intercontinental, which provided us with our best source of entertainment. The Intercontinental was located on a private beach, and Jamilla arranged for us to use it as her guest. Had it been just the divers, they never would have let us in, but because we were traveling with six young single white women, the most valuable thing on the Arabian Peninsula, we were all invited.

It was a cab ride away, so I had to rely on anyone with money to spot me the fare until we got paid. A couple times a week we would make it to the beach to play volleyball or go for a swim. As long as the girls were with us, the volleyball games were stocked full of oil-rich Arabs trying to hit on them. Local protocol required the Arabs to ask us if they could talk to "our" women. Somehow by entering the country the swimmers had lost their independent status and become our possessions. Even though most of the Arabs at the Intercontinental were educated in the West, in their eyes, the swimmers were our harem.

We thought it was funny, but the girls thought it was great, as it kept slimy guys from hitting on them. When they found a cute one, though, they let us know he could play in our volleyball game. One of those cute ones turned out to be Said, the son of Sheik Zayad, the president of the country and one of the richest men in the world. Mandy took a liking to Said and vice-versa. He wasn't a bad friend to have in our camp.

None of the girls were adept at volleyball except Lesley. Lesley wasn't just a pretty face. She was an aggressive, competitive athlete. She was all over the sand, diving after balls and spiking at the net. If her side was down, she had no problem reaching under the net and holding down someone's shorts so they couldn't spike. The two of us hit it off immediately and started hanging out.

One night we were watching TV, and she leaned over and kissed me. I kissed her back, then pulled away. She was one of the most attractive women I'd ever met, and at any other time in my life, I wouldn't have thought twice, but this just wasn't that time. I sat her down and told her I was with Linda. I told Lesley that she was a magical bright spot in an otherwise fucked-up trip. She tossed away the Linda story and held on to the "magical" part.

Finally, after three weeks, we got the go-ahead to set up. Our location was on a V-shaped cement pier owned by the Abu Dhabi Tourist Club. We were diving into the Persian Gulf, which has a severe and irregular tide. In the morning, the water at the edge of the pier was six feet deep, and fifteen feet deep where we would land our dives. But by mid-afternoon when the tide went out, there was five feet of beach directly underneath the springboards. At low tide, the height of the diving boards went from four meters to six meters. We had to push dives out—and even then the water was only 10 feet deep. Before any of us dove, Dan-Bob went into the landing area with scuba gear and pulled out enough metal rebar to create a small prison.

We were working, but still had no pay. I was borrowing from Nancy just to eat more than one meal a day. We got the show set up, rehearsed, and were scheduled to start on December 21st—my birthday. But on the morning of the opener, Jamilla met us at the Corniche Residence and told us we were back on hold. I went to my room depressed as hell and ready to take a plane flight out of there. Then I heard a blast from Ricky's radio that was one of the nicest birthday presents I've ever gotten.

Before 1988, the Grateful Dead got absolutely zero airplay outside of the occasional "Truckin'" on a retro show. Ricky was listening to the US Top Twenty on Armed Forces Radio when I heard ol' Jer belting out "Touch of Grey." The Dead had been playing the tune for years but hadn't put out a studio album. Sometime over the previous six months the Dead had released *In the Dark.* The single, "Touch of Grey," had become a US hit. Some called

Getting ready with Dan-Bob Anthony to do a cold night show for seven spectators in Abu Dhabi.

it the demise of the band, but from where I was sitting it was the best tune I'd ever heard.

When Garcia busted out with the refrain, "WE WILL SURVIVE!" I put the first genuine smile on my face in months. I pulled out my guitar and jammed along. A few minutes later Nancy and the swimmers came down with a birthday cake. We were all broke and the hotel beers were unbelievably expensive, but we gave in and threw ourselves a party. We needed it.

I'd only called Linda once since arriving, but I'd been writing a couple of times a week. She seemed in good spirits, getting ready for Christmas, but we missed each other a ton. I called her on Christmas Eve and told her the continuing bad news about the show. She told me I should give it up and just come home. She was right. Reading news clips of Iranian gunboats being knocked out of the water fourteen kilometers from Abu Dhabi wasn't exactly putting her in the Christmas spirit. I told her I'd be coming home soon.

The next day Chip announced we were tearing down our setup and moving to a sports park in Dubai. I told him I'd had enough and was ready to go home. He insisted that Dubai was a sure thing, the contracts were signed. We were going to work and we were going to get paid. I threatened that if there was just one more delay, I was out. But who was I kidding? I was still broke, and I had neither my plane ticket nor my passport. He said he was going to make it work out. I had no choice; I had to stay.

I called Linda back and said I was going to try to make it work in Dubai. She was not happy. For the first time I could hear the sound of resignation and doubt in her voice. Keeping us together was going to be more difficult than she thought. Me living in a war zone with no money was not helping our progress.

Two days later, it was Christmas, and we had a brief reprise as Sheik Said and his friends invited us to a huge barbecue. His people had stuffed a boat full of enough meat, salad, bread, and Heineken to feed an army. We traveled on a 30-foot powerboat to a deserted island just off the Abu Dhabi coastline. The day before, they'd mounted a makeshift hut out of scrap wood. It felt like we were at a catered lunch on Gilligan's Island. We made up a baseball game with some of the equipment they'd brought out on the boat and took turns playing with their snorkeling gear. I brought out my guitar, and we made up songs and drank like fish. As the sun dropped into the Gulf, Said and his buddies broke down the hut and used the wood for a huge bonfire.

We were good and sauced, singing like Brits in a pub, when Lesley asked me to go for a walk. We took off under the moonlight for the far side of the island. When we got to the far shores she asked me if she could kiss me. I couldn't say no. We started making out and nature just took its course. We'd had a sexual tension and an incredible chemistry between us ever since we met. I'd held off for four weeks, but the exotic scene lubricated by booze and a beautiful woman was too much. We took off our clothes, slipped onto the beach, and made love in the surf.

I woke up the next morning with a splitting headache and the worst guilty conscience I'd ever had. I'd never been one to cheat on a girlfriend, and this was big time cheating. I tried to rationalize it, which even scared me more. I told myself that if Linda were around there's no way I would have been in that situation. It was kind of like a soldier-at-war cheating—except I wasn't about to die in a bunker anytime soon.

Nope, I figured this was heinous businessman cheating. I envisioned myself a fat loser in Thailand buying factory widgets, then taking up with hookers. But that wasn't fair to Lesley. Where did she fit in all of this? I wasn't looking for anything and all of a sudden a beautiful woman I really respect darts into my life. I'd already told her that I was with Linda! It was her fault! Then my rationalizations stopped. The reason it happened was because I wanted it to. No sleazy slut was going to make me cheat on Linda. It happened for one reason. I really liked Lesley. Nice way to complicate an already completely screwed up situation. I hid in my room and didn't talk to Lesley for the next three days.

Instead of getting the go-ahead to rehearse, we got the go-ahead to tear down our equipment and move to Dubai. Everyone came to the show site ready to work, including Lesley—who stared me down and gave me a long extended middle finger. After taking down the first couple sections of ladder, Chip sent the two of us out to pick up lunch for everyone. Lesley looked at me with daggers in her eyes and said that it was a smashing idea. Silence wasn't the way to deal with this woman. She was way too strong for that.

She grabbed my arm, nearly putting her thumb through my elbow and escorted me to the cabstand. "Feeling a nip guilty, are we?" she said.

"Lesley," I said, "you gotta understand—I'm not over here to fuck around. I'm broke and I need the cash. That's what I'm doing. What would you do if your boyfriend was off in the Middle East fucking around on you?"

"Look," she said, "we're all stressed, we got pissed on Christmas, and I'm sorry but I really like you. Is that such a sin?"

"No, but…"

"And I didn't notice you complaining either. You seemed to bloody well like it, too. You're Catholic, are you? Got a wee case of guilts, have you?"

"I'm not a fucking Catholic!" I protested. She'd hit one of my buttons and she got a big kick out of it.

"Have we got some issues?" she asked, with a big smile.

She nailed me and there wasn't much I could do about it. Again, there probably wasn't much I wanted to do about it. "Oh, piss-off then!" I said in my best John Cleese accent.

"Was that supposed to be an English accent?" she said.

I could have killed her. Instead, I playfully socked her in the shoulder, resulting in a wrestling match in the back of the cab. The driver, a good-natured Pakistani, smiled at us through his rearview mirror and said, "Whatwillwebehavingforlunchthen? Weshouldbethinkingofsandwiches—notwrestling?"

The team met the move to Dubai with skepticism but also a certain degree of fatal optimism. We were broke, and Jamilla had lied to us so many times that if the show didn't take off, even Chip was going to pull out. On New Year's Day we packed our bags into a pair of Datsun minivans and took off for Dubai.

A few of the swimmers and I had already been to Dubai for an afternoon, and we liked it much more than Abu Dhabi. Dubai, a former pirate haven, is a cosmopolitan port city with a rich teeming market and an active nightlife. Foreigners were allowed to drink, and all the major hotels had bars and discos.

We were more than ready to set up and start working, but the venue and the schedule were ridiculous. The swimmers were happy because the club had a clean, competitive eight-lane swimming pool that leveled off at one end into a fake beach with a wave pool. We weren't so lucky. We were diving into the receiving tank of a giant waterslide. It was a small peanut pool, half of which was only four feet deep. The half we would be diving into was only 30 feet wide and 8.5 feet deep. We were going to have to do a 67-foot high dive into a puddle. The Nicolet diving parents would have had a field day with this one.

The setup was incredibly difficult because the sand on the desert floor wouldn't hold any of our mooring stakes. We ended up nailing guy wire to palm trees and weighing down the springboards with oil drums filled with water. The oil drums worked great for the springboards, but the trees were problematic. When the wind blew, the trees swayed, taking our ladder with it. It wasn't very comforting to be on top of a 67-foot ladder knowing that if you timed your jump wrong you would plant into four feet of water. And even if you timed it correctly you had the "luxury" of eight and a half feet.

On an average day we drew a total of 100 people over five shows. One hundred people spread out among five shows is ridiculous. At best, a diving show is a headline attraction for an amusement park, but not the kind of show people pay specifically to see. We put on a great show, and kids loved us, but it was asking an awful lot for people to leave their homes and drive in just to see a 50-minute water show.

Waiting for the fifth show of the day was torture. Temperatures during the day would rise to 90 degrees, but nighttime in the desert could drop below 50. We had a sunny patio to hang out during the day, but at night we huddled together in a hallway underneath the giant waterslide. We bundled up in towels and prayed that nobody would walk through the door. Our contract stipulated that we wait five minutes after show time before canceling a show. One day we were seconds away from canceling when Tracy walked backstage and announced there were five coaches (tourist buses) coming into the parking lot. It was a freezing night and we were furious. As we started to strip down and get ready, she poked her head around the corner and said, "Psych!" We chased her around the pool and tossed her in fully clothed. From that day on "five coaches" was our magical term for "canceled show!"

During the day we would occasionally get a decent crowd, but even then they were the strangest crowds I'd ever performed for. One time we performed for a sheik, his five wives, and his thirty children. Another time we had a family of four from Scotland and a group of forty Saudis. As soon as the Saudi men saw the girls come out in their pink suits they ordered their families to get up and leave. We did the rest of the 50-minute show for the family from Scotland. They got very wet.

Tuesday was Women's Day at the club. The crowd consisted of a few hundred young women covered head to toe in burkas. They were bussed in from their harems for a few hours while older women looked after their children. Islamic law prohibits women from talking to men outside of their immediate family, so getting crowd reaction was tough. Jamilla took over the microphone so the women could applaud and laugh, but it was a muffled laugh as they held up their veils and covered their mouths. Before the last clown dive, we would run into the crowd and ask them if they wanted to see one more. A normal crowd responds by screaming, "YES!" These women smiled silently (but enthusiastically!) and nodded their heads. They were going crazy and we were hearing crickets.

As nice as the afternoon weather was, running around in tight Speedos wasn't going to cut it in the UAE. Instead of doing shows in competition suits, the entire troupe wore head to toe Lycra body suits. The divers looked like 1920s circus strong men and the swimmers looked like they were wearing bright pink full-bodied pajamas. The pink suits were nearly see-through when they got wet and even more see-through, it turns out, when reprinted on newsprint. Jamilla put a full-page ad in the local Arab newspaper showing the whole troupe waving to the camera. In black and white, the pink suits came out the same tone as skin. It looked like an ad for a strip club and the paper had to pull it after the first day.

The show was one bizarre happening after another, but at the end of the day, we were working and getting paid for it. Nobody promises routine work when you're performing in foreign countries, so all the anomalies ended up being just a bunch of exotic stories. Once the paychecks started coming in, life in Dubai was agreeable. Nancy and the swimmers grew to love Dubai because every night one of the hotel bars had a ladies' night, and they drank for free. Tracy was their ringleader, and she had the town mapped out after the first week. Intercontinental on Monday, Hilton on Tuesday, Hyatt on Wednesday. They had no reason to stay home.

While the girls could party for free, drinking was incredibly expensive for us. Beers were going for six dollars a pint, which was triple what any of us had ever paid. After missing a month of work, boozing wasn't in any of our budgets, so the only time any of us went out was to chaperone the women. Adul told us we should never let the women go out alone because Bedouin slave traders were known to kidnap foreign women.

The clubs made Dubai a fun place to go out at night, but Dubai was also a great place to spend a day off. From our apartment we could walk to the Dubai Creek, the main waterway splitting the town, and take a boat taxi across to the main bazaar. There were camel races, museums, the famous gold souk and plenty of great restaurants and shish houses. Abu Dhabi was brand new and stale, but Dubai was an ancient pirate city with plenty of cultural outlets

Lesley and I cooled it for the first two weeks in Dubai until the Sikh maintenance workers at the park threw a big party for the team. They

Waiting with Jerry Grimes to take a bus to watch a race on the three-mile Dubai camel racing circuit.

had foreign resident liquor permits and said if they could use our apartment, they would cook some Sikh cuisine and get us sloppy on Indian rum drinks. We got the apartment ready, and after our final show of the day, the Sikhs showed up with cases of beer, bottles of rum, and some of the tastiest kabobs and rice dishes I'd ever eaten. We started a loud game of Mexican dice, and in no time we were all polluted.

Lesley and I sat next to the table, and as the drinks went down, we got closer and closer until she was sitting in my lap. Not long after that we were out on a porch making out. We both had the next day off, so we slid down to her room and didn't leave for the next thirty hours. I've never been one for the "if you can't be with the one you love" argument, but I'd never been in the same situation that Steven Stills was in when he wrote it either. I just dropped the guilts and lived for the moment. All rules were off in the UAE. I couldn't control what was happening around me, and I obviously hadn't demonstrated the ability to control what was going on inside me. After that night, Lesley and I were together.

Just as soon as the team got in a groove in Dubai, Chip told us we were packing up and moving back to Abu Dhabi. All the permits had been signed, and we were promised bigger, higher-paying crowds. That same day Adul came running in telling us he convinced a school district to

The Abu Dhabi show poster. I have absolutely no idea what it says.

bring in school groups. The last week in Dubai was incredible as we were performing to over a thousand school kids a day. There was only a small grandstand, so packing 500 people into the tourist club felt like playing to 5,000. They arrived in droves and sat on the pool deck, leaving us almost no room to perform. They went crazy over Jerry's comedy, and every time I did a high dive, I heard blood-curdling screams all the way to the water.

When I took my bow they mobbed me, and I would end up signing autographs for an hour after the show. I had no idea what they wanted with a high diver's autograph, but they were happy as hell to get it. And after weeks of not having any crowds, I was happy as hell to sign them.

After the horrible month in Abu Dhabi, I remember Dubai as a great triumph. We were the first diving troupe to play the Arabian Peninsula, and even though the financials were all red, we did our job. The crowds loved the shows too. Everyone from the big school groups to the dozen people who would squash our buzz by showing up just before the last show of the day, cheered wildly. The company was taking a hit, but all we could do was take the stage five times a day with a big smile and give it our best shot. If you can perform under those conditions you can perform anywhere. And we were "anywhere."

Once back in Abu Dhabi, Jamilla's promise of big well-paying crowds proved to be a crock. We returned to playing for a couple dozen people and praying for "five coaches" at the end of the day. The show site wasn't the greatest place to perform either. The diving conditions were safer than in Dubai (even though the escaping tide made the comedy pretty dangerous), but the swimmers had horrible conditions. The Persian Gulf is one of the saltiest bodies of water on Earth and their bodies were too buoyant to sink. And even with goggles, it was very difficult to see each other through the murky water. Any number of creatures would float into the show site, including big sea crabs that disrupted their routines and made a mockery of their figures. The introduction to their routine was a dance sequence on the deck followed by a line of sideways dives into a pool. Instead of diving in, they had to climb down a ladder, wade through some muck and dive from there. On top of that, there was a loud prayer siren right behind us that tended to go off—appropriately enough—in the middle of their Madonna number.

I wasn't so happy about diving into hard salt water, but I was pretty psyched about the deep landing area. Although the water depth was dangerously shallow at the end of the diving boards, it dropped off sharply leaving a bottomless pit for the high dive. We put up eighty feet of ladder, which left a 90-foot high dive during low tide. I was standing up my entries and drilling every dive. My tailbone had been getting sore from diving into eight-and-a-half feet in Dubai, but after a couple of days on the big ladder with lots of water, I was puffing every high dive I did.

Back at the Corniche, I played a ton of guitar, plowed through books, and cooked my own meals. Lesley and I were now a constant thing, though she would still scoot back up to her room in the middle of the night. She roomed with Rachel, and she felt like she was abandoning her friend by shacking up with me. Time with Lesley was fantastic, but time away from her was driving a nail in my head. I wasn't supposed to be feeling guilty about this, but the longer it went on, the more I knew I had to bring it to an end.

A week before the contract was up in Abu Dhabi, it was time to call the Lesley adventure to a close. There were rumors that the team was either going to Oman for a couple of weeks or (we were praying) a one-month gig in Sydney. Whatever the scenario, it wouldn't be long before I was going home, and I wanted to put this little affair I was having to bed (or out of bed). I'd gone through all the rationalizations a hundred times, and the only way I was going to half-reconcile myself was to talk to her face to face and end it.

The swimmers were going to ladies' night at the Abu Dhabi Meridian, and I decided it was the night to break it off. Six of us took cabs over to the bar after work and settled into a couple of pints. Lesley was looking fabulous (as she always did), and we sat together in a booth with her knee draped over mine. We started with the usual bitch session over the salt water, the small crowds, and the freezing last show. Nancy, always the optimist, told us we should be happy we're all still together and making some money. As much as The Middle East Tour had been a painful and trying experience, long after we quit show business, we would remember it as our craziest adventure. She ordered a round of tequilas, and we toasted the first high diving tour of the United Arab Emirates. After we slammed them, we all got a little somber. Lesley leaned back against me, squeezed my hand, and told me she was really going to miss me. I told her we needed to go for a walk.

The Meridian was only a couple of blocks from the Corniche Residence, and it wasn't long before we were just across the street from our hotel. She assumed we were going upstairs to bed, but I told her we had to talk outside. We went behind a wall across from the Corniche where there was a new hotel under construction. It was a beautiful starry night, and her face was glowing in the moonlight. I was beginning to fall under her spell again. I couldn't believe I was going to break off a relationship with one of the most energetic, beautiful women I'd ever been with. What the hell was I thinking, dumping someone like this? It would have been much easier to just start kissing and take her up to my room. But I was in love with Linda and I had to stake that claim in my mind. This was a fling and the only way I could rationalize it was to break it off.

Lesley put her arms around me and stared into my eyes, but I pulled them back over my neck and put them at her side. "Listen," I said...

"Oh fuck," she said, "is this the 'I'd-love-to-but-I-can't-anymore chat?'"

I laughed and said, "I'd love to, but I can't anymore."

"I reckoned this was coming," she said. "She must be something special, this Linda, then?"

"She's special, and I made a big promise," I said. "I don't like breaking promises and the only way I can reconcile this to myself is to start making another promise to her right now."

"Suppose it won't wait, will it?" she said. "I won't tell, I swear!"

We laughed, and then she started to cry. I had my arm around her shoulder squeezing her tight when, from out of nowhere, a flashlight beam blared in our eyes and we found ourselves at the end of an automatic rifle.

"What the hell is that?" she screamed.

Two UAE policemen had their guns pointed at us, yelling in Arabic. I pointed to the Corniche Residence and slowly reached in my pocket for my room key.

"Corniche Residence," I said. "Room 715. We go home now."

Nothing doing; the rifle didn't go down and the cops were even more agitated. They called for backup, and finally an English-speaking officer came to the scene. "There's some misunderstanding, officer," I said. "We were just on our way home and we sat down to talk."

"This building off limits," he said. "What you do here?"

"Nothing, officer," I said. "Just talking."

"You have drinking?" he said.

"No sir." I lied.

"You make sex?"

"Absolutely not, sir," I said. "We live right across the street. We're on our way home."

The cop didn't buy my rap. He cuffed me and tossed me in one car, then tossed Lesley in his. "Where are we going?" I demanded. "Where are you taking her? Hey, we didn't do anything—we're just walking home!"

I was talking into a Plexiglas divider and the cop on the other side wouldn't have understood a thing I said anyway. The lights started flashing, and the two cars raced through empty streets to the Abu Dhabi police station. Talk about people having a little time on their hands. I could see Lesley trying to explain the situation to the English-speaking cop, but he obviously wasn't deterred. We were going to jail in the UAE.

The cops hauled us into the station and I asked if I could call the Corniche so they could verify who we were. "This Abu Dhabi," the cop said. "No sex, no drink. This not filthy England."

I wasn't holding any cards (or a passport for that matter) so I had to listen and keep Lesley from freaking out. The three cops were rifling off their plan in rapid-fire Arabic when I asked them if they could remove the cuffs. "This one to jail," the cop said pointing to me. "Woman go to women's jail."

"Where's the women's jail?" I asked.

"Twenty kilometers."

"Twenty kilometers!" I said. "She's not going anywhere—I want to call my embassy."

The cops thought it over for a couple of minutes and decided I might know somebody in the US Embassy who might know their boss. There are no laws per se in Abu Dhabi. It's all a series of complicated precedents, any of which can be broken if you know someone's boss. In this case they weren't sure, so they let Lesley stay.

"The girl stays in the office," the cop said. "You go to jail."

He walked me to an isolated corner of the station and tossed me through a small door into a room that resembled a one-story racquetball court. He took the cuffs off and told me to wait until morning.

"Please let me call the Corniche Residence," I said. "They can straighten this all out."

"We call in morning," he said.

He shut the door and locked me in. There was a small barred window in the door, and I tried to look out to see what was happening to Lesley. Behind me were my two new roommates, a Filipino and a Sri Lankan. I slammed my fist on the door and the Sri Lankan told me to take it easy.

"Nobody goes home tonight," he said. "Get some sleep, big day tomorrow."

Ten minutes later, Lesley slid her head through the bars.

"What's the deal?" I said. "Did they release you?"

"'Fraid not," she said. "They don't seem to mind if I wander, though. If they've got one of us, they've got us both."

All the spunk and energy of her voice was gone, and her beautifully tanned face was white with fear. "Maybe it's best if you go back to the office and try to catch some sleep. You don't think those cops will try anything with you?" I asked.

She started to cry, and I put my hand out for her to hold. Just then the cop came around the corner and walked toward the door with the key in his hand. I was hoping that he'd called the Corniche and they verified who we were. Lesley stepped away from the door and he opened the cell.

"All clear?" I asked.

"Now we go to hospital," he said. "Take blood sample."

"What blood sample?"

"Alcohol sample," he said. "You are much drink."

"I'm not letting you put any needles in me," I said.

"Let's go," he said. "Girl, too."

He cuffed me and tossed me into a police car, this time with Lesley in the back seat with me. The cuffs were tight and I couldn't sit in any position without them digging into my wrists. I was in pain, and Lesley was helpless to do anything about it. I was supposed to be the strong one here, and I was starting to crack. We got to the hospital, and the cop removed the cuffs. He took us to the emergency room and spoke to an Indian nurse in Arabic. The nurse pulled out a needle, and I adamantly refused. "You can toss me in jail," I said, "but you can't put that crusty needle in either one of our arms."

The nurse looked at the cop and shook her head. She knew I was refusing and she wasn't going to have any part of doing a procedure without a patient's consent. "You refuse test?" the cop asked.

"Absolutely," I said. "No needles are going in either one of our bodies."

He looked over at Lesley. "You refuse…"

He didn't have to finish as Lesley was already shaking her head. I'd never known her to be without words, but this was as good a time as ever to bite one's tongue. The cop scribbled some Arabic on a piece of paper and told us to sign it. I signed in as Jerome Garcia and Lesley penned in as Madonna.

Once again I was cuffed, tossed in the back seat of the car with Lesley, and taken back to the police station. Lesley was sent upstairs and locked inside the Chief of Police's office while I was tossed back in the cell, the population of which had grown to about six inhabitants.

By morning the cell was packed with more than twenty people. All of them were heavy smokers, and I could barely make out the door through the haze. I made my way up to the window and peeked out. The hall was now full of lawyers, wives, and children, all trying to get some answers. I sat down ready for a long day. Show call was at 10:00. Lesley and I would be docked a day's pay, but that was the least of our problems.

Before anyone else was called, a cop yelled my name through the window. I raised my hand and hastily made my way to the door. He let me (and an enormous cloud of smoke) out of the cell and escorted me to a room where Chip was talking to an American. Chip had steam blowing out of his ears as he introduced me to Robert Barry Murphy, the US Consul in Abu Dhabi. The cop escorted Mr. Murphy and me into a waiting area where we could talk. Before we got started, Lesley was let into the room. I went over to give her a hug, but Mr. Murphy coughed loudly and looked me in the eye. "That's what got you into this in the first place," he whispered.

"So," he started, "Let's take it from the top…"

I told him the story from top to bottom including how much I'd had to drink and what the two of us were not doing on the bench.

"Looks pretty good for you," he said. "We should be able to get you deported out of here without doing much time. Where's the last place you were before here?"

"Holland," I said. "But what's all this about being deported? Don't they put some nasty marks in your passport if you get deported? And what kind of 'time' are you talking about? I mean, I didn't do anything."

"The cop's report says you were drunk, trespassing, and having sex in public."

"That's ridiculous!" I exclaimed.

"I never!" Lesley said.

"Now, you're British, are you, miss?" he asked.

"Yes," she said, "do you reckon they'll be sending anyone over?"

"Nooo, I don't think so," he said. "The Brits have enough trouble over here. They have lots of teenagers coming to meet divorced fathers and getting drunk. This is a dime a dozen for them. They'd rather just stay out of these small matters. As a matter of fact, there's not a lot I can do for the two of you either except monitor your location and let your families know you're O.K."

"You can't do anything?" I asked. "I'm a freaking American citizen, and the US Embassy can't call bullshit on this thing?"

"If you were the CEO of an oil company you'd be in much better shape, but a circus performer doesn't have much clout—unless you know someone in the government."

Lesley and I both had the same thought. Mandy was still seeing Sheik Zayad's son, Said. If that didn't do it, what would? "We're good friends with Sheik Said," I said. "One of the girls on our team is dating him." I was sure I was holding the trump card.

"Zayad's son?" he asked.

"Yeah!" we responded.

"No good," he said. "If Zayad finds out Said is fooling around with some white circus worker, he's not going to be very happy. You might just be getting your coworker in a lot more trouble than she bargained for."

We were hosed. Chip had to go do the morning shows, but he told us he'd be back after lunch. They let me sit up in the office with Lesley, but I was convinced I was going to jail for god knows how long before getting deported to Holland. I could just hear Linda, "The charges were drunkenness, trespassing, and what?"

Four hours later Chip returned, this time with our Palestinian promoter, Mr. Fouad. Mr. Fouad told us he would have us out in no time. We sat down in the office of the Chief of Police, who warmly embraced Mr. Fouad. As it turns out the Chief and Mr. Fouad went to college together. In a matter of minutes, we signed confessions written completely in Arabic and were released.

"Get your ass home," Chip said. "This thing is far from over."

The two of us grabbed a cab and went directly to the Corniche, which was looking like a palace in the clouds compared to my jail cell. Lesley and I were completely fried from the experience, so we went to my room and held each other until we fell asleep.

It would have been nice if we could have taken the rest of the day off, but we still had the evening shows to do. We slept hard and barely made it to the tourist club for show call. When the two of us made it backstage, the team jumped all over us, wanting the story. We were both exhausted and asked everyone to let us just get dressed and do the shows.

"No problem," Jerry said. "Oh, by the way, jailbird, these two fire dives—these two high dives—they're all yours."

I figured something like that was going to happen. We did the first show for about thirty people, and I was feeling wrecked. We waited silently after the first show, dying for Tracy to come running through the curtain yelling, "Five coaches!" Instead, she said, "Ten people."

We geared up for the last show, but by this time I was feeling extra hazy. I got through the fire dive but went short on a 2½ pike from a five-meter springboard (2½ pike has been in my ONE-meter springboard list since my junior year in high school). I did a couple clown dives but bailed on the last one to get ready to jump off the ladder. When the clown set was over, the announcer said my name, and I waved to the crowd but had trouble focusing on them. I climbed the ladder up to the midway point and almost slipped when turning around to look at the landing area. It was a poorly lit night dive, but I'd never had problems with it before. Now, I couldn't tell the surface of the water from the cement pier. I climbed to the top but, before stepping up to the perch, I had to repress vomit. I got on top of the perch and started hallucinating. Arab holding cells hold more than prisoners. They also do a great job holding contagious viruses.

I turned around to an 85-foot-high panorama of the Persian Gulf, which was swirling like water in a toilet bowl. My legs felt wobbly, and I considered walking down, but the thought of navigating 85 feet of ladder with several malfunctioning senses was too much to fathom. I had to go with the old diver's adage: Let your body do the trick. I jumped in the air and did the first flip of my double gainer but had no idea if I'd done a fast one or a slow one. I split the dive and tried to focus on the landing area but all I saw was an olive-green void. I tucked over the last flip, stretched for the water but instead of landing feet first, I took three quarters of the Persian Gulf up my ass.

I made it out of the water to take my bow, but Jerry and Dan-Bob had to help me backstage. "You look like shit." Jerry said.

I was sick as a dog, and my ass felt like I'd jumped out of an airplane onto the left field foul pole at County Stadium. I shared a cab with Nancy back to the Corniche, and she helped me balance as I walked through the lobby to the elevator. Just before we got on, a bellman handed me my mail.

Sitting on top of the stack was a letter from Linda. Nancy got me into my room and tucked me in, and I opened the letter.

> Dear Tom,
> I've been thinking it over and I don't see how we can ever make this work...

Linda dumped me. Instant karma.

* * * * * * * * * * * *

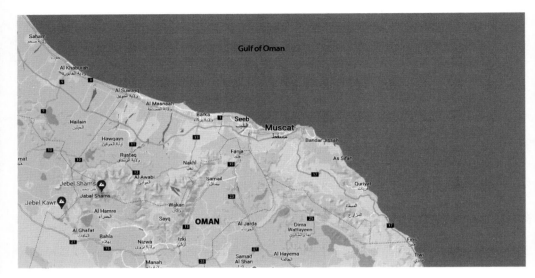

Oman

Middle East Mifflin Street

Lesley and I were given a state-ordered curfew to return to our hotel room after the final show each night. It was house arrest. But come on, who wouldn't want to be locked in a room with her for a week?

With a couple of days left in the Abu Dhabi contract, Chip announced we would be packing up and going to the Sultanate of Oman instead of Australia. We were pissed, but Chip had his reasons. The Middle East Tour was his baby, and we were losing our shirts on it. A few weeks earlier, an Omani businessman had approached Chip about bringing the show to the capital, Muscat. By this time Chip was a savvy Middle Eastern businessman and he agreed, provided all the money was up front. He had the show bought and paid for before we took off from Abu Dhabi.

The biggest drawback of the deal was that we had to trim one person on each team. Lesley had been talking to an agent in England who had a full season lined up for her in Geneva if she could get out of this contract. All the swimmers were more than ready to go home, but since Lesley had a gig lined up, they agreed she was the one to go. She came down to my room after their meeting and told me we only had a week left.

Whatever bad news I had coming to me about women I figured I deserved; in fact, I'd expected it. But instead of going into a litany of promises to write and visit, I asked Lesley if we could just not think about it until it was time to go to the airport. She thought it was best, too. We just went about business for the next few days, as if the show were to never end.

Several days later we got taxis and headed off to the airport. Lesley was on her way to Geneva; Nancy was on her way to Hawaii; and the rest of us were on our way across the desert to Oman. Lesley and I had learned our lesson about public displays of affection. We had our goodbye at the hotel and promised to write and visit over the summer. After her plane pulled out of the gate in Abu Dhabi, I never saw her again. We only re-established contact via Facebook in 2019. She's become an amazing and spirited mom and runs her own photography business. And she hasn't aged a day.

The rest of us thought we were stepping out of the frying pan into the fire, but as it turns out we took a right turn at hell and ended up in heaven.

The Sultanate of Oman on the southern edge of the Arabian Peninsula is about the size of California south of San Francisco. Its terrain is mostly high desert, but when the mountains hit the never-ending palm tree beaches along the Arabian Sea the result is an unspoiled paradise inhabited by some of the friendliest people in the Arab world. When an Arab from the UAE offered us hospitality, we were suspicious. But the oil windfalls hadn't yet affected the Omanis, and their offers were genuine.

Passing through customs was an interesting experience, as no Western tourists were allowed in the country at the time. Aside from a few oil company-sponsored lounge singers, we were the first Western entertainers to ever cross the border. The customs agents went through our bags and confiscated videos we'd made of the show in Abu Dhabi. They claimed images of the girls in their pink full-body performing suits were pornographic.

An official of the Ziadfleet Company, our sponsors and hosts, picked us up at the airport for our 17-day stay. They took us to the newly constructed Holiday Inn in Muscat and told us we could see the show site as soon as we rested from our travels. (Muscat is only a 45-minute flight from Abu Dhabi.) They told us they had a springboard set up so all we had to bring was the ladder. I assumed we were going to be diving off cement buck boards into a Holiday Inn pool.

They drove us to the site and I couldn't believe what was laid out before us. The Sultan Qaboos Sports Complex in Muscat, Oman, was a brand-new multi-sport facility with a 40,000-seat football stadium, an indoor gymnasium, fifteen racquetball courts, six regulation basketball courts, a fencing salon, a weight room, and the most comprehensive aquatic facility this side of Miami.

Sultan Qaboos was the supreme leader of Oman and held power until his death in 2020. In 1970, with the help of the Brits, he effected a palace coup over his father, who managed to shoot one invader before accidentally shooting himself in the foot. He was exiled to England where he lived out his final two years in a luxury hotel.

The swimmers were performing in a 10-lane, 50-meter competition swimming pool. We had a 25 by 25-meter diving well with virgin one- and three-meter springboards and a full tower complex. The water was clean and warm, and the stands around the pool could seat 3,000. On the opposite side of the pool from the public stands was the Sultan's royal box with a 20-foot-high royal Omani gold emblem mounted behind 100 plush reclining seats.

Nobody wants to be uncomfortable at a swim meet, do they? I could just picture my mom and dad sitting on the hard, wooden bleachers enduring three-day-long swim meets at Nicolet.

As we gazed over the facility with our jaws dragging, a Filipino dressed head to toe in Speedo gear came out to talk to us. He had been the assistant Olympic coach for the Filipino national team, but after the Seoul Olympics, he took this job at five times the salary. He gave us a tour of the facility but told me he wasn't going to finish the last year on his contract. As well as he was paid, he only had 15 swimmers on his team, and the most dedicated came to practice just three times a week. Aside from his team, no one was allowed to use the pool—and we would be the first divers to ever go off the towers.

We went into the locker rooms, which were as luxurious as any health club in America. In Abu Dhabi we went home itching from cold salt water and sticky from the occasional oil spill. In Oman we had warm showers and could soak in a whirlpool or bake off the night's chill in a sauna. The Sultan Qaboos Sports Complex was also equipped with a sports medicine clinic and three German physical therapists. After three months of setting up, tearing down, and running around jerry-rigged stages, we were full of dings, scrapes, and bruises. The therapists were so psyched to see real athletes they booked us for full workovers. Before the day was over I was having ultrasound done on my knee and an electronic nerve stimulator unit jolting electricity into my kinked neck. The ladder setup was a little tricky because we didn't want to break any of the pool tiles. We were used to throwing things around during setup, but the Sultan Qaboos pool tiles had been imported from Italy and cost 25 bucks apiece. We could lose a day's pay just by dropping a section of ladder.

Since the show was already rehearsed, we were ready to go with a day to spare. We took a rare team holiday and went to discover Muscat. Muscat had been a Portuguese trading colony in the 15th century, and its most famous resident was Sinbad the Sailor. Sinbad was a pirate, but he had been a hero to the Omanis, especially when he pulled into port with a haul of loot. The old Portuguese forts are still in place with their cannons pointed out to the sea. We climbed above a hill behind the city and looked over the luxurious diplomatic quarters next to the Sultan's palace. Even though the Iranians were shooting at US gunboats in the Gulf a few hundred miles across the desert, the American and Iranian embassies were right next door to each other.

The Muscat souk was full of Arab clothing, pottery, tapestries, and antiques. The food, like almost all the Arab cuisine we'd tried, was as good as any food on the planet. We couldn't find a cab to take us back to the hotel so we thought we would be daring and try hitchhiking. We split into groups of three and I wasn't on the road more than a minute before my group was picked up. As the car pulled over to pick up more and more passengers, we realized the Omani transit system is a fleet of rideshare minivans. There are no bus stops or taxi stands. You stick your finger out on the main highway, and you get scooped up and dropped off somewhere in your town.

We were given one meal a day at the Holiday Inn, but this wasn't your average roadside Holiday Inn. This was a luxury resort with an enormous buffet prepared hot at any time of the day. The swimmers smiled at the waiters our first day, and after that the staff never cared when or how often we came. There was a hotel bar with shockingly expensive beers and drinks, but I don't think we paid for one the entire time we were there. One patron was so happy to see young white women that he went up to the bartender and announced, "I don't want them to ever see the bottom of their glasses!" It must have cost him a fortune.

Working in Oman was rewarded with nothing short of rock star treatment, including an opening press conference. We were seated at a long table in a makeshift pressroom at the Holiday Inn. We each had a name placard in front of us and journalists went down the line asking us who we were, where we were from, and what our specialty was. The Acapulco High Diving Show was a big deal in Oman, so the press conference was covered live on national TV—as was the show opener.

We worked without days off, but none of us wanted to miss these shows anyway. We had big appreciative crowds and occasionally the royal box hosted dignitaries. One day then-Egyptian President Hosni Mubarak's family stopped in on their annual vacation to Oman. We asked if the Sultan would be making an appearance but our sponsor, Mr. Ziad, didn't think the girls' pink suits would go over well next to the Sultan.

Ziad, a Clemson University grad, loved the pink suits, and one Sunday invited us to his mansion for a catered lunch. Ziad's lair was a multi-level labyrinth of Italian marble and intricately carved wood. It was so opulent we were nervous just walking in the door. But Ziad made us feel welcome. On one level he had a home theater with an NBA game playing, and a full wet-bar and billiard parlor on another. Instead of putting a mirror behind the bar he had an underwater window into his swimming pool. He watched the swimmers do routines in his pool while we shot snooker at the bar.

World Wide Productions had a strict company policy against drinking before shows, but Ziad informed us that he was waving that formality. He had a couple cases of Heineken ready for us, and he wanted to see them finished. We looked at Chip and he told us to do whatever we wanted. "Ziad's signing the checks," he said. "And these checks aren't bouncing!"

The tradition in determining who does which high dive is to play a game of seven-card no-peek poker before the first show. Whoever wins gets to pick a dive or even sit the day out if there are more high divers than shows. We had four high divers but only three shows. Whoever won the game could get liquored and waltz through the shows not having to think of jumping off an 80-foot tower. Whoever took second could sober up for the last dive. The third-place finisher would have to pace themselves for the second dive, and the loser couldn't drink much at all as he would have to do the first dive. Jerry won the card game and was a mess the rest of the day. Chip took second, and not being a big drinker, took the first dive. I ended up with the second dive, and Dan-Bob got the last one.

By the time we showed up at the pool the girls were loud and sloppy, and we were trying to focus on what dives we could still do. Ziad, who had also been drinking, came in as we were figuring out the dive list. "The other stipulation of drinking at my house," he said, "is that you have to let me call the dives."

We laughed at first, but he was serious. It ended up being one of the funniest nights of shows I've ever done. Ziad took the microphone and made us do some of our hardest tricks with our heads still floating somewhere around his billiard parlor. I've never seen more splats and ugly diving in my life, but the guy signing the paychecks was laughing the loudest.

Normally once a show routine gets going nobody practices, but with these facilities we stayed after the morning shows and worked out. There was a one-meter springboard to do practice dives, and I had a great coach in Jerry. As we came down to the last few days of shows, I was putting together my old college list and getting in great shape. These four months were without question the strangest time in my life, and I wanted to do a big finale to commemorate it.

I hadn't pulled out the Mifflin Street Dive the entire tour because the conditions had been far too dangerous. In Dubai the water was too shallow and the ladder too shaky to do handstands. When the tide was out in Abu Dhabi the landing spot for the Mifflin Street Dive was a sandbox. But the pool in Oman had 17 feet of warm fresh water and ideal lighting. It was a perfect place to high dive. The Mifflin Street Dive was going back into rotation, but I wasn't going to stop there. I didn't want to leave the historic Middle East tour without putting a big exclamation point on it.

One of my best 10-meter tower dives had been a reverse 2½. The Sultan Qaboos pool had a competition five-meter tower so I started working the dive back into shape. I did a bunch of gainer doubles from the five-meter platform, jumping as high as I could and spinning them as fast as I could lift my legs. The doubles were dropping better than they ever had before, but instead of thinking of the reverse 2½ from the 10-meter, I began thinking of a split gainer triple from the 80-foot ladder. I knew I could do the trick, and once the thought was in my mind, I had to take it up to the top of the ladder.

That night I climbed the ladder for my dive, took a little extra time to visualize the trick, then swung my hands over my head and tossed my first reverse triple. A gainer double is a controlled trick. You spin, check out the landing spot, and tuck over the last flip. You have lots of time for adjustments and several places along the way to slow down or speed up the spin. The triple was different. It was one big hot blast of energy. I jumped as high as I could and spun like a yo-yo. I kicked out at the double and spotted the surface of the water. I'd spun the double at just about the same height as I did my single, so the last flip seemed natural. I stood up the bottom and ripped the bejesus out of it.

The team loved it, but that wasn't the trick I wanted to end the tour on. The second-to-last night of the show I went up to the top, brought the perch down five rungs, and went upside down for the first Mifflin Street Dive I'd done since Berlin. I spun the top much faster than normal then kicked out for a long split before tucking over the finish. I stood the thing up on the bottom and stretched as hard as I could. It disappeared in the water. The stage was set for the biggest, baddest dive of my life.

I was going to toss the first-ever Mifflin Street 3½. It was the pinnacle of everything I was all about. It was going to be the most exotic dive in the most exotic place at the end of the most exotic trip. The last show didn't just mean a lot to me, it meant a lot to all of us. The people of Oman showed us the best three weeks of our lives after we'd spent the worst three months with their neighbors.

When we got to the Sultan Qaboos Sports Complex that night, there was more than the usual energy in the air. This was our last hurrah as a team and we knew we'd never be together again. The first couple shows went off with everyone in a good mood, but we were all thinking of the final. Ziad had become a partner in crime and wanted to announce the last show. He wanted to be part of the team, and we were cool with that as long as he was ready to be initiated with a full bucket of water. When it came to the bucket gag, Jerry and Dan-Bob came at him from both sides and nailed him in his full Arab dish dash. He looked like a wet rat, but in good spirits, he tackled Dan-Bob into the pool. Ziad came out drenched, picked up the mic, and continued to announce the show.

Finally, it was time to put the tour to bed. It's customary for all the high divers to do one last high dive at the final show of a contract. Normally we would have done it in Dubai and Abu Dhabi, but none of us wanted to celebrate anything there except the packing of our bags. Oman was a special place as well as being the end of the fabled Middle East tour.

Jerry went first and zipped a beautiful flying gainer right through the water. Chip went next and power ripped the same trick. Dan-Bob was into the spirit of the night and tossed a back double, his first in over a year. Now it was my turn. I took off my jacket and handed it to Tracy at the bottom of the ladder. I climbed to the 40-foot perch and focused on the landing area. This dive was going to be such a madhouse I'd be lucky to even catch a glimpse of that landing area while I was spinning.

I climbed to the top of the ladder and waited for the music to fade. From 80 feet in the air the girls looked like Barbie dolls and the guys looked like G.I. Joes. I looked over the horizon and saw the tips of the Omani mountains on a clear starlit night. I was nervous and my legs began to shake, but this wasn't their trick. It was time for my arms to do the heavy lifting. I turned around, climbed the ladder, and put my knees through the top rung. When I leaned back, I took time to picture the elm tree on Mifflin Street where my brother Dan and I had hung upside-down drinking our beers. It was late March, and by now Madison had come out of hibernation and that elm tree was sprouting its first buds. The tree had no idea that on the other side of the world, its finest moment was about to take place.

I placed my hands on the perch and took a deep breath before releasing my knees. I hadn't told anyone what I was going to do so I could have punted the trick and done the regular 2½. This was my last chance to bail. It was

The warmup for the Mifflin Street 3½ in Oman.
The real dive came during a night show.

tempting, but if I gave up on this trick, I would be giving up on me as a person. Giving up now would be turning away from the highlight of my diving career and the potential highlight of my life. This dive was way beyond the dreams of the 12-year-old kid watching Keith Potter dive in Wisconsin. I'd gone for big tricks on a 10-meter before, but this was different. Nobody had ever done this trick before. I didn't have a coach telling me how it was done because nobody had ever done it. This dive was mine and mine alone.

I unhooked my legs, placed my hands on the perch and leaned my thighs against the ladder for a few seconds. Enough thinking about what it meant; I needed to concentrate on what I had to do. I had to toss this thing just like I had the triple: super-fast on top; try to get a peek at the landing during the split, then squeeze for all I was worth on the bottom. The dive was ready. It was time to go.

I tightened my wrists and pulled my legs away from the ladder. I was balanced on my hands on a one-foot square platform, 80 feet above an anxious crowd on the edge of the Arabian Peninsula. I was tight as a nail and my body didn't budge even in the slight breeze. I took a long deep breath and looked at the landing area one last time.

I kicked as hard as I could and spun the top with every ounce of force in my body. Down below Dan-Bob, Jerry, and Chip were the only ones in the pool who had any idea what was going down. The top 2½ took much longer than I'd expected; much, much longer than the top two somersaults of the gainer triple. I split the dive and tried to focus on the landing area but all I saw was a big blur. I tucked back up and I had the awful feeling of disorientation divers get when learning their first scary dives off the one-meter board. My mind no longer knew where it was or what it was doing. I was falling faster and faster into an abyss of potential pain. I had no choice but to trust my body. I hadn't done anything wrong so I should have been in the right place. I just had no freaking idea. I was in no man's land—and this was real no man's land. No man had ever been there before.

My body jerked out of the tuck and tightened up like a metal rod. I felt water on my feet and, just like that, it was over. In fact, I actually hit the damn trick.

I was told when I was winning meets in high school it was bad manners to come out of the water screaming after you hit a dive. You should take it in stride like a big leaguer hitting a home run. But I couldn't control myself. Life wasn't going to get any sweeter. This was my game seven, bottom of the ninth homer. I sprung out of the water with a loud scream and pumped my fist in the air.

Dan-Bob grabbed the mic out of a stunned Ziad's hands and screamed, "Ladies and gentlemen, this is the first time in history anyone has done an arm stand 3½! You've just witnessed a world record!" The Omani crowd went crazy and Jerry pulled me out of the water with a big bear hug. The swimmers, ever the professionals, stayed at attention and did their final bows.

The Middle East Tour was officially in the books. There would be some drastic highs and lows over the next few years, but life never got better than that day.

• • • • • • • • • • • •

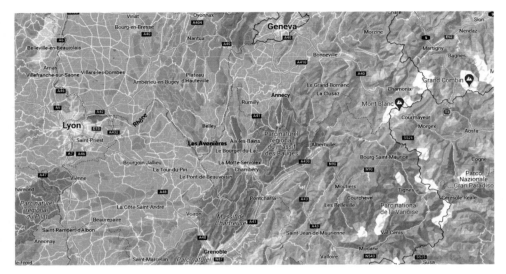

Les Avenieres

Chez Moi

There was a moment of clarity during the insanity of the Middle East tour and that came in the form of a rare World Wide Productions business meeting. While we were in Oman, Chip showed us the business plan for the new and improved World Wide Productions. Before 1988, WWP had at most worked in four cities at the same time. But during the summer of 1988 we would expand to nine shows throughout Europe and the Far East. At the time of the meeting, I'd been on the road for a year and had just been booted from my girlfriend's apartment. Nothing would ever get crazier than the Middle East tour and no dive would ever be bigger than the Mifflin Street 3½. I was thinking of calling an end to my high diving career and finishing school.

WWP said they needed me and would give me a raise and my own show to run. But I didn't want to work in a gigantic corporate amusement park on the outskirts of a big metropolis. Then they showed me where they were planning on sending me—the French Alps. The park was called "Avenir Land" located in Les Avenières, a town so small I couldn't find it on my map. I was told it was somewhere between Lyon and Geneva. The only thing I saw on my map between Lyon and Geneva were mountains. Big, huge, Alpine mountains—the same mountains that drew me in on my first trip to Europe. I didn't think about it very long. I wasn't going to pass up living in a small town in the French Alps. I signed the new contract.

Ten months after leaving America on a six-week contract, I landed in Les Avenières in the French department of Isère. In that span of time, I'd worked in five cities, visited twenty-two countries on three continents, set a world record, lived with a woman, had an affair, and been thrown in jail. It was time to pull up the reins and take stock.

When I arrived at my new home, a 100-year-old farmhouse in Buvin, a hamlet three kilometers north of Les Avenières, I knew I'd picked the right place to detox. I was more than ready to settle in, but I had no idea I was putting down roots that would last the rest of my life.

The Ranch Marin (that was painted on the barn door—and just happened to be where the Grateful Dead offices were north of San Francisco)

121

sat on the corner of a rural farm road a few kilometers from the Rhone River. I used the captain's prerogative to claim a large room on the second floor with a dramatic view of the first Alpine cliffs carved out by the Rhone. Directly in front of me lay a fallow field with two grazing horses. Across the street was a small farmhouse and off the back window was another field leading up a steep ridge to the richer houses in Buvin. I'd never lived in a rural setting before, but this place was nothing like small town America. This was darkest France where the cheese stinks, old women ride their bicycles with baguettes in their panniers, and no one would ever consider sitting down to a meal without a bottle of table wine. Americans like to claim we're the greatest country on the face of the Earth, but there's not much to complain about when you live in rural France.

I had a week to put up a ladder, install two springboards, and rehearse a show with four rookie divers. I wanted to get the equipment up as fast as possible so we could spend at least three days rehearsing. This was the ninth ladder I'd set up in the past two years, so I had the drill down. I had three bilingual Québécois on my team, making the hardware store runs much easier than if I had to explain stuff myself. Two weeks into my stay in Les Avenières I'd found only two people who were fluent in English. (After four years in town, that number rose to three.) But at this point my French was barely good enough to order a beer.

The equipment went up without any major hassles, leaving us two days to rehearse for the opener, which was a picnic show for park employees and friends. Because the Canadians spoke French, I had assumed one of them would do the comedy and I would do the fire and high dives. I showed them the script for the comedy, and all three of them disapprovingly shook their heads. Richard, one of the Québécois, was adamant against doing it.

"This thing won't make French people laugh," he said. "The French people know bullshit and this thing is pure bullshit."

"The comedy works in every language," I said. "The jokes are physical. Just translate the script and we'll get the announcer to rehearse it."

Begrudgingly they translated the script, but I was going to have to learn some French because the Canadians weren't going to do it. I'd had crowds howling in Osage Beach and in Taiwan, and I knew I could get people to laugh at the lines. It was all in making yourself appear to be a complete idiot doing silly gags the audience would never think of doing.

In the end, they realize you're not an idiot, you're actually fooling them, and that makes it even funnier. The Canadians were afraid of making fools of themselves in front of people they were going to be seeing in town. I had no problem with that.

While the Canadians practiced diving off the ladder, I sat in a room with our show announcer, Jean-Pierre Wallemacq, a gregarious Belgian thespian. Jean-Pierre had serious theater credentials but needed the day job to support his wife and daughter. He read through the script and had the same problems as the Canadians. After reading the translation he looked at me with the raised eyes of a French skeptic and said, "Tommy, I think we have problems…"

The problems were with word gags that are killers in English but make no sense in French. We tossed them out, then rehearsed the lines. He still didn't think it was going to be funny, but I assured him it would fly as soon as he saw the physical gags. We took it to the pool where I picked Richard, a chiseled gymnast, as my straight man. Richard was a great diver with a six-pack for a gut, but he didn't like being made fun of. His job in the role of straight man was to be mocked. When he got naturally embarrassed, he fell right into character.

After a few rehearsals, Jean-Pierre suggested we go into town, get something to eat, and continue rehearsing at a bar he knew. We'd been working hard for days, so a little relaxing sounded like a great idea. Avenir Land bought the team a brand-new Polish Fiat wagon (named "The Polski") that would not survive our four-year tenure in Les Avenières. We piled in and followed Jean-Pierre to the Café des Platanes, which shared a parking lot with the church in the main square.

The Canadians had already discovered the Platanes and had made some friends. Robert, another Canadian on the team, introduced me to the bar owner, Gerard, and Gerard's girlfriend and bar matron, Monique. Gerard had worked for a medieval equestrian show that had been the main entertainment at Avenir Land for three seasons. Their team put on a great show, but they also had a penchant for drinking while working. The previous year they got sauced and set off an explosion on their set, blinding one rider and blowing the thumb off their emcee, Pascal Chanal.

I thought Gerard might hold a grudge against us, because we had taken their contract. But he bore us no hard feelings and realized we would not only be his best patrons, but we would also bring in every worker from the park for happy hours. He bought us a round of drinks and asked if he could help with the script. (The Canadians had already told him it wouldn't work.) Monique served our first round of beers, and just like that we had a new home in Les Avenières. Eventually we spent so much time at the Platanes that we used their address and phone number as our official contact numbers.

The five of us rehearsed our lines in Gerard's back room as Monique kept bringing us beers. After we were comfortable with the rehearsal, we returned to the main room and came upon a raging bar scene with two Avenir Land workers, Marc and Stephan, holding court. I didn't understand a word they said, but I couldn't stop laughing either. If either of them could dive, I would have hired them on the spot.

The day of the grand opening arrived, and Bruce Cant came down from Holland to check out the equipment and watch a wet rehearsal. He wasn't happy with the bows, so he worked the Canadians through the routine while Jean-Pierre and I went through the comedy a few more times. Bruce declared us ready, but the Canadians were still not convinced with the comedy. Bruce told them I would work magic with it, and it would be a hit. Working for Bruce was a kick. He always let me know he had faith in me. There's no better way to get a stronger performance out of employees than to instill confidence in them. Any employee worth his scratch will repay the compliment a hundredfold.

Bruce had to have confidence in me because this was going to be my show. I was doing the fire dive, the high dive, and the comedy. It was just like I'd done every day in the Ozarks, except this was in French and I had to whip off the acts one after the other. There were no barefoot water ski acts between the comedy and the fire dive, so I had to move fast.

I peeked out from backstage to see a hundred people bundled up in leather jackets and jeans. We started the pre-show music, and the crowd rushed to be seated. When it was time to take the stage, Jean-Pierre looked at us and said, "Merde!" ("shit!"), which is what French performers say in place of "Break a leg!"

Jean-Pierre pounced onstage, whipping out the opening monologue while the Canadians ran to their stage positions. I was backstage soaking in a warm bathtub, wearing a brand-new fire dive suit. One by one he introduced the Canadians, then went into the fire dive speech. I walked onstage and took a bow, being careful to keep the hood over my head so the crowd wouldn't see my face. I climbed the ladder, lit myself ablaze, and tried to stay as long as I could. There was a nice steady breeze from the rear, so I covered my face and turned to the crowd, leaving my entire body engulfed in flames. I plunged in the water, climbed out, then took my bow—again keeping the hood on so the crowd wouldn't recognize me when I sat down to do the man-out-of-the-audience comedy.

I ran backstage, ripped off the suit, dried my hair, and got dressed in obnoxious day-glow French vacation wear. I found my seat in the crowd before the Canadians finished their dive set. The bows and stage presence were far from what they would become, but they hit the water together on the mass dive, and the crowd was into it. Jean-Pierre called Richard back out for the start of the comedy. Because this was the season opener, everyone believed he was going to do a spectacular trick.

Richard went into his hurdle, and I sneezed as loud as I could. Nobody at Avenir Land knew our act, and a couple of security guards surveyed the crowd when Richard fell onto the board. The next time I sneezed, I said my first few lines and my accent gave the gag away. But that never mattered. Only the most obtuse spectators ever fell for the act. The sight gags were always good enough to carry it.

The Canadians watched from the sidelines as Jean-Pierre and I went through our shtick. The last gag of the comedy involved me betting Jean-Pierre I could do a back somersault, a twist, and then a front somersault all in the same dive. Jean-Pierre told the audience that it was an impossible trick, but he'd really like to see it done.

"Moi aussi!" I shouted.

It's the kind of line that looks horrible on paper, but always works if delivered properly. The crowd roared with laughter as I walked to the back of the board and started my big trick. I walked out to the tip of the board; tossed a reverse flip; landed on the board; did a twist on one leg then did a clown flip into the water. The Frenchies roared, but more importantly, the Canadians saw the stuffy French crowd laughing at what, on paper, they thought would never work.

When I climbed out of the pool, Jean-Pierre put the mic in my face and asked, "Who taught you how to dive like that?"

"My coaches," I said.

"Your coaches?"

"The aquamaniacs!!"

The Canadians, now dressed in their clown suits, hopped onstage and did dillies while I snuck backstage and got ready for the high dive. I was winded, but it was a great crowd, and I was jacked up on adrenaline. It was a Mifflin Street kind of night. I climbed the ladder, lowered the perch and waited for the show music to stop. I stuck my knees through the ladder and leaned back to see my new home crowd. I balanced into my arm stand and right before taking off yelled, "Vivre Avenir Land!"

Rocking out in front of the Avenir Land fire dive billboard in Grenoble, France.

The park workers screamed as I pushed off the ladder and ripped the Mifflin Street Dive right to the bottom of the tank. I shot out of the water to a standing ovation. When I got backstage, Bruce was all smiles. "You're an 'A' level performer," he said. "You're on anyone's starting lineup."

I should have asked for a raise right on the spot, but I was just happy to be on the map in my new hometown. The park held a banquet after the opener, so we got dressed and made our way over to the party.

As we sipped champagne, a beautiful blonde 40-year-old French woman came up and asked me if I spoke French. I understood her question but needed Robert to translate my answer. He told her I didn't speak French now, but I was going to make a big effort to learn it over the summer. Then she asked me if I liked French food. This time I didn't understand a word but again Robert translated.

"Oui, oui!" I responded. "J'aime la cuisine Français."

The woman struck a flirty pose and said, "Si vous aimez la nourriture Française, attendez, vous n'avez pas encore goûté une fille Française."

I was stumped on that one, but Robert and the woman were dying.

"What did she say?" I asked Robert with a nervous look on my face.

"She said, 'If you like French food, wait until you taste French girls!'"

The woman, Jeanine Couty, would one day save my life. But for the instant, she scared the shit out of me. I had to get busy and learn French as fast as I could or I was going to be a laughing stock.

I'd been traveling nearly constantly since I'd left Harderwijk, so it took me a couple of days to realize I wasn't going anywhere. For the first time since December, I stored my travel bags and started using a chest of drawers for my clothes. It also occurred to me I was in horrible shape. Aside from the diving shows, I hadn't done any exercise in over a year. The last time I was in tip-top shape had been almost two years earlier when I rode my bike every day in the Ozarks. It was time to get back in the groove.

I cashed my first paycheck and went right over to Chez Petit, the local bike shop in Les Avenières. Mr. Petit, a jolly old bike mechanic, took one look at me and told me he had the bike for me. I dropped him a couple thousand francs and picked up a 12-speed Peugeot road bike.

Our first show wasn't until 11:00 a.m., so I had plenty of time to get up, eat breakfast and sprint the seven kilometers from Buvin to the park. There was a decent hill between Les Avenières and Buvin where I could see the entire Epine Ridge that separates Les Avenières from the Savoyard capital of Chambery. The first morning I rode, I felt the weight of every French fry I'd consumed since leaving Osage Beach.

The first week of shows ran a bit like a boot camp, as I made it clear I didn't plan on doing every act all summer long. Anyone could learn the fire dive, and it shouldn't be very hard for a bunch of native speakers to whip off the comedy. The big trick, of course, was getting them up the ladder. I wasn't getting a day off until at least two of them could high dive.

Richard and Robert were quick studies and motivated by the extra pay they would get as high divers. They took their dives up the ladder 10 feet at a time until they were ready to snap one off the top. In the meantime, Chip had been talking to my college friend, Robin Duffy, who suggested that the younger sister of an old teammate of ours from Illinois would be a great fit for the small French park. Jen Kelly was a sophomore at Illinois, but she'd had enough of competitive diving in the Big Ten. It was clear she wasn't going to do the big tricks the top divers in the Big Ten needed to compete, but she had enough difficulty in her list for us, and a beautiful set of required dives. That and her good attitude were all we needed. She'd been taking French and wanted to live in the country to learn the language. As soon as Jen finished finals in Champaign, she hopped on a plane and showed up in Les Avenières. The original Avenir Land High Diving team was set.

It had been an unseasonably cool spring in Les Avenières, but the day Jen arrived, the sun started to shine and summer pulled into full swing. With morning dew covering the Rhone Valley and Alpine foothills stretching toward the sky, the high dive at Avenir Land was one of the most dramatic on the circuit. The only dive more picturesque was the incredible seascape of Yehliu. But at Avenir Land we didn't have to worry about gale force winds coming off the South China Sea.

With the show running smoothly, it was time to relax and melt into the lifestyle of a small Alpine town. My mother sent me my college French book, which ironically was the only college textbook I didn't sell back at the end of the semester. I went everywhere with my French book, an English-French dictionary and a notepad to write down vocabulary words. When it wasn't busy at the Platanes, Monique sat down with me and went through chapter after chapter of my textbook. I changed my internal dialogue from English to French and wrote down every word that didn't jump into my head. Before long I had pages and pages of vocabulary words. After testing myself a few times and using them in everyday conversation, I could throw out the early lists. Those words had become part of me. When I first arrived, everyone at the park communicated with me in broken English. After a month my French was at least as good as their English, so I made a point to communicate to them in French. They could see I was making the effort, so they dropped their English and spoke to me in French.

With my limited vocabulary I could carry on a discussion about the show but that was pretty much it. At night I would go to the Platanes and try to catch what was going on, but I couldn't understand much. Sentences would fly by lightning fast, and I would be stuck on the first few words. I tried to express myself but after just 15 or 20 minutes I would get a headache. For a while I tried practicing with Robert. He was always patient, but after two months he told me, "You think you are speaking French, and there are French words coming out of your mouth, but that's not French!" Learning this language was not going to happen in a few months. It ended up being a life-long process.

The Canadians didn't have any of these problems and were doing well for themselves in town. It wasn't long before each of them hooked up with a French girl, and the Ranch Marin was the place to be in Les Avenières. Closing time in rural France is midnight, but that just meant it was time to come to our house to party. As soon as the Platanes closed, there was a line of cars stretching from Les Avenières to Buvin. On Fridays and Saturdays, it was common for us to be up until 3 a.m.

Eventually I understood some of what was going on and I started to make friends. Hypolite and Vincent were two musicians who belonged to the Maison des Jeunes, the French YMCA. They had a small building for meetings, and it came equipped with a drum kit. We tried to make music, but it was difficult, as we had very few common musical references. The Dead never made it in France, and I'd never heard one note of French rock. We played lots of "Blues in A" with drunk Frenchies singing over the top. It wasn't pretty but it was fun just to be playing with people.

As we rolled into full summer, I got into fantastic shape. The seven-kilometer ride to and from the park had turned into time-trial sprints. The first time I'd taken the hill between Buvin and Les Avenières I had to stand up and put the Peugeot in its lightest gear. Now I was topping the hill in a low gear and not even lifting my butt off the saddle. My gut was gone, and on my days off I went on longer 30- to 40-kilometer rides. The diving show was gliding on all cylinders as the Canadians had learned to fire dive, high dive, and do the comedy. Avenir Land was getting 4,000–5,000 people a day, so the mid-summer crowds were huge. On days with overflow crowds, all of us wanted to do the comedy. But if I wanted to do it, I simply reminded them, "the French people would never laugh at such a stupid skit," and I'd take it. Nothing felt better than making a crowd laugh before ripping a Mifflin Street Dive.

One day in late August I rode my bike to the park, walked around and greeted everyone I knew before changing out of my bike shorts and slipping into show clothes. It was a seemingly pedestrian morning until it hit me: I didn't speak a word of English. I was able to tell everyone what I did the night before, what I was going to do that day, and what I was thinking of doing on my day off. I understood their responses and was even able to understand their polite jokes. Four months earlier it would have been impossible. That day I realized I was home. I no longer felt like a Wisconsonite. I was an Avenièran. 35 ans plus tard, j'en suis toujours un! (35 years later, I still am one!)

Performing the world-record 11-man mass-dive in my home pool in Les Avenières,
France. From top to bottom, left to right: Jerry Grimes, Roger Graham, Randall Dickeson,
Rachel, me, Robert DesChampes, Ann Marie Beavis, Vince Fabbris, Jean Marie Senna,
Minnow Wadsworth, and Jacques, le maître-nageur.

•   •   •   •   •   •   •   •   •   •   •

Acapulco, Mexico

Living and Dying in Acapulco

Just like that, I became a Euro. For four years I lived in a small French farming community and only returned to Wisconsin a few weeks a year. My days consisted of riding my bike to Walibi (Avenir Land was bought out by a giant entertainment conglomerate and changed its name), knocking off a few shows, grabbing a beer at the Café des Platanes, then riding home to read or play guitar. Although it got routine, it was still show business, so there was never any shortage of insane people and events. As we were big celebrities in a tiny town, there was plenty of drama. Divers were always hooking up with townies and our Polski Fiat seemed to always break down far away from Les Avenières, leading to grandiose efforts to make it to the shows on time.

I became addicted not only to riding my bike, but to the sport of cycling as well. Greg Lemond was the king of cycling during this time and our Tour de France victory parties were the stuff of legend. My friends still talk about those parties and refer to our four years there as "The Belle Epoch" or the "Golden Age" of Les Avenières.

One event during that time stands above the rest, but it didn't even happen in France. It took place in Mexico. I was sitting in my office at Walibi when Bruce Cant stopped in to give me some great news. World Wide Productions had secured the rights to the Acapulco Cliff Diving Championships and I had been put on Team USA. When he told me I was speechless. I'd never even qualified for US Nationals and now I was going to compete as part of our national team. It was the culmination of everything I'd ever worked for as a diver. My best high dive was the interrupted double gainer, but Cant told me it was impossible off the cliff because you have to clear 10 horizontal meters of rocks just to hit the water. While he brushed it off, I took it as a challenge. If I got in the best shape of my life, I could clear those 10 meters and win the contest on heavy difficulty.

For the rest of that summer, I rode my bike longer and harder than I ever had in my life. I was doing 20–30 miles a day and up to 100 miles on my day off. And I wasn't just pedaling—I was jamming, grinding the gears as hard as I could on nearly every stroke. I watched and read cycling, so I had the play-by-play voice of Patrick Chêne, the Tour de France announcer, pushing me every step of the way.

The season ended two months before I had to be in Acapulco. I went back to Wisconsin, but instead of hanging out in Milwaukee, I bought a Cannondale touring bike and embarked on a 17-day cycling odyssey to Houston. I packed a tent, a sleeping bag, and an air mattress, and slept in state parks along the way. I thought it would take a month, but once I got going, I was knocking off more than 100 miles a day.

The Acapulco Cliff Diving Contest was not only a great promotional vehicle for WWP: it also served as our first company Christmas party. The three principals, Mickey, Chip, and Bruce, were there, as were all the show captains. We'd seen each other a few times over the years, but we'd never all been in the same place before. Dene Whittaker, Dan-Bob Anthony, and Bob Torline were there from my Far-Eastern Tour. Darren Duffy, Jeremy Willens, and

The photo from the *Milwaukee Journal* article covering my cross-country bike trip to train for the Acapulco cliff-diving contest.

Johnny McPadden were there from Harderwijk. The current World High Diving record holder, Randy Dickeson (who had just worked with us in France), was there, as was Roland McDonald, a tremendous high diver whom I'd met in Italy. Filling out the team were two retired WWP vets, Mike Murphy and Craig Lesser. There was no women's contest, but they flew in Nancy Clark from the Middle East Tour, Cathy McPadden from Hong Kong, and Bruce's wife, Maaike (also a show diver) for moral support.

After spending three weeks with my old teammate John McGhee in Houston, I packed up my bike box and boarded a flight to Acapulco. I deplaned to find all my teammates at the airport waiting for transport to our hotel. A van took us along the Acapulco strand before climbing the northwest cliffs leading us to La Quebrada, the most famous venue in all of diving. The moment I set eyes on the cliff, a streak of terror ran up my spine. The height was nothing to fear, but when Bruce told me I had to jump 33 feet out to clear the rocks, he wasn't exaggerating an inch. The cliff drops straight off the top, but as it reaches the bottom it slides out into the channel. Every time I looked at the cliff it seemed to slide further into the channel. I had my mind set on the double gainer, but I had to start thinking of a plan B. There's no way I could have prepared for what I was about to try.

Everyone was talking about what dives they were going to do, but Bruce told us we'd change our mind once we stood in front of the Clavidista's altar on top of the cliff and looked at the landing area. We weren't diving off a ladder, and we weren't landing in a show tank. The only thing that was normal was the height. And that used to be the scariest part.

The first practice session was scheduled for 11 a.m. Bruce took us to the spectator's platform on the opposite side of the channel.

"Before you jump off this thing," he said, "you've got to know what you're landing in. We've cleared away most of the coral and sea urchins but there's still plenty of jagged rocks down there. Who wants to check it out?"

He held up a mask and snorkel, and I volunteered to hop in and scout out the bottom. I dove into the channel and was tossed 20 feet beyond the landing area by an incoming wave.

"Don't underestimate the waves," Chip said. "The water can be as deep as 15 feet or as shallow as eight. It's easy to time the waves, but you don't want to miss one."

I swam back to the landing area and saw a thick stalagmite shooting out from the cliff right at the base of the takeoff rock.

"Damn!" I shouted up, "there's a spike right at the bottom of the cliff."

"Sure is," Chip said. "sometimes it's out of the water, and sometimes you can't see it. It's always there, though."

I snorkeled along the edge of the cliff and saw hundreds of sea urchins with foot-long needles. I came up to report it when a huge wave crashed into me, taking my breath and scraping me along the underwater cliff. My hip grinded against the jagged rock, then suddenly my foot felt like it was on fire. I came up and could barely get the message out:

"Stay away from that frickin' wall," I gasped, "It's armed!"

I swam to the viewing cliff and climbed back up to the divers. I looked down at my foot to see 50 black sea urchin needles sticking out of it. Juan Obregon, the head of the Clavadistas Diving Club, took one look at me and his eyes opened wide in horror.

"Quick," he shouted in Spanish, "Get me the first aid kit."

"Don't panic," he said. "If we get them out quickly, they won't do any damage."

He started pulling out the needles as the rest of the team stared on in disbelief. Not only did they have to jump past the cliff and avoid smashing their feet on the bottom, but they also had to worry about being poisoned.

In the meantime, the rest of the divers had taken their turns checking out the wall, albeit from a safer distance. The Mexican divers went along the cliff and removed as many sea urchins as they could. I was hoping they could plant some dynamite under that big stalagmite and blow it out of the water, too.

The next order of business was getting up to the diving platforms. In order to participate in the contest, each diver had to climb the cliff at least once. The Mexican divers, who grew up on the cliff, could scale the wall like giant spiders. But I was having trouble just getting out of the water. I had to wait for a big wave to lift me high enough to grab a rock, then hold on as tightly as I could while the water receded, leaving me dry-docked. If I didn't get a good grasp and cling to the cliff, the next wave would come by and knock me back into the channel, hopefully far away from any sea urchins.

After three tries, I pulled myself onto the cliff and scurried above the level of the waves. Watching the Mexicans scamper up the cliff made it look like there was a nice easy route to the summit, but I struggled the entire way. The first 20 feet were manageable, but from there the cliff shot up 30 feet before bending back towards the top. A wiser man would be using climbing shoes, rope, and a harness, but I was barefoot and wearing a Speedo.

I inched my way up the cliff, supporting my full weight on a few fingertips and toes. As much as I loved mountains, my body type is more like a rugby player than a free climber. I'll go all day on a steep incline with a full pack, but this vertical wall just wasn't my gig. A couple of times I was caught dead in my tracks, and one of the Mexican divers had to scale down from the summit and direct me. At one point a diver pointed out the finger holes he used, but when I tried them it was obvious my fingers weren't going to support my weight. I had to traverse the cliff back and forth to find cracks big enough for my whole hand. After an hour of struggling, I made it to the top. My foot was bleeding, as were both my knees. I left a trail of red all along the cliff.

I peeked over the summit perch and put an image of the double gainer in my head. I wasn't ready for it yet, but at least I had a visual image of what I was up against. Before going off the top, I wanted to toss a dive off the lower level. The contest consisted of two dives, one from a 50-foot perch and the second from the top, 20 feet higher. I wanted to make sure I hit my first trick to build confidence for the double gainer. I scaled down to the 50-foot perch and sized up a flying reverse somersault layout. It was an easy trick that I could rip even after the most festive nights at the Platanes. The channel didn't look as imposing a leap from the 50-foot level, so I called out to everyone that I was going and leapt off the cliff.

One factor I hadn't considered was that the ladder perches, although seemingly solid, had a slight spring to them. The cliff was as solid as solid gets. I felt deadness in my knees where there usually had been a slight pop. Normally I didn't bend my knees at all when doing a flying gainer, but I had to tuck this one on the top. I barely had enough flip to get it around. Nothing would come easy in Acapulco.

I climbed out of the channel, and this time took only 45 minutes to reach the top. My toes were bleeding so much I was slipping off the cliff. There was a quarter-mile path around the hotel to the take-off perch, so after that dive, I always took the hike instead of climbing the cliff.

My next attempt from 50 feet went much smoother. I used the strength that 1,400 miles of cycling gave me to fling off the cliff and stick a nice tight pose. It wasn't completely laid out, but I put the trick in the water with just a slight tuck at the finish. I had a week to work on it, so I was confident I'd hit it in the contest.

Meanwhile, the other divers were flinging their bodies all over the channel. Only four of them had ever been off the cliffs before, and I wasn't the only

Standing atop of La Quebrada in Acapulco—the most famous site in all of high diving.

rookie to make mincemeat out of my body. Johnny McPadden was the first to try anything more than a front flip off the top. He went for a double somersault with a half twist, a rudimentary high dive. He pushed out over the cliff but didn't have nearly enough momentum to get the spin going. He tried to bail out halfway through the trick and ended up plummeting uncontrollably into the channel. He hit with a nasty thwack that none of us wanted to hear. That was his last attempt at the double half.

Jeremy Willens was next to toss a big trick. He stood backwards on the top and launched the first-ever back triple off the cliffs. Unfortunately, he got so much going on the trick that he ended up doing close to a back 3¼. He wrenched his back so hard he could barely walk. Jeremy was as good a high diver as there was in the business, and La Quebrada took him to the cleaners on a trick he could do with his eyes shut.

With those two unsettling dives in the back of my head, it was time for me to start working up the gainer double. I found a perch on the viewing cliff that was about 20 feet above the water but a good 15 feet away from the water. The first time off I leapt like a long jumper to see if I could clear it. I made it into the channel, so I climbed up again and went for a gainer flip. This time I was going to have to leap like a broad jumper, then tuck over a flip, spinning back into the cliff. I was pretty sure I could make the trick, but any errors would lead to a concussion or a broken leg.

I took a couple deep breaths to collect myself, then cranked off the flip. Again, the cliff wasn't as springy as the high dive perches, leaving me with much less rotation than I'd expected. Nonetheless, I put the trick safely in the channel. I did one more lead-up and was ready to take my bloody body up to the top of La Quebrada.

I hiked around to the top and sat next to the Clavidista's altar to the Virgin Mary. I watched as some of the most experienced high divers in the world sized up their nemesis. Everyone except Jeremy, Roland, and I had given up on the big dives they were talking about while high on tequila. Almost the entire field of trash-talking high divers had caved in and decided to hurl the easiest trick in the book, a flying front somersault.

I stood on top of the cliff and looked down at the spike tucked in the landing area. All I had to do was clear that spike, and I would have a trick that could win the whole thing. Then again, if I didn't clear it, they were going to carry me away in a body bag. It was that simple: succeed or die. I envisioned diving beyond the edge of the pool in Les Avenières, and I was positive I could do that. The challenge was being able to toss two flips back towards the cliff from a non-springy take-off.

If I put every pedal stroke from Milwaukee to Houston into the jump, I could clear the cliff. I was rested, light, and feeling as strong as I'd ever been in my life. It was time. I knew I had the trick. I toed the edge of the cliff and raised my arms above my head. Then my legs started shaking like an alcoholic with the DTs. I was ready to go, but my body was doing a double-take.

The last time this had happened was the very first time I'd been off a ladder in Osage Beach. I stepped back from the takeoff platform and tried to collect myself. Stepping back from the cliff was not where I wanted my head to be. I wanted to be strong and aggressive, not timid and scared. Nobody had ever attempted this trick before, and the rules committee would have to give it the highest degree of difficulty in the contest. If I put it in the water, I was going to win the contest. That's where I wanted my head to be. I just had to convince my legs to stop shaking.

I re-addressed the cliff and thought of the dive the same way I had the Mifflin Street 3½ in Oman. Nobody had ever done this trick, so nobody could tell me how they did it. I trained harder for this trick than anything I'd ever worked for. I'd prepared it in my head and done the successful lead-ups. This was my trick and I was going to get it. I raised my arms above my head and again my legs started to shake. They really didn't want me to toss the trick. But this wasn't their choice. It was mine.

I shook them out and then tightened them like a taut rubber band ready to explode. I took one last look in the channel for a wave but realized that wave-watching was futile. I couldn't stare at the incoming water to do this trick. I had to keep my head in line, looking straightforward. Looking down and sideways was counterproductive to the spin. I couldn't worry about waves. There would have to be enough water when I got there.

I swung my arms up in the air and exploded off the cliff with 50 million pedals of force. Just as I was sure I'd reached the full potential of my jump, I snapped my ankles above my head. The jump felt good, but I wasn't spinning anywhere as fast as I was used to. But I was spinning enough, and 70 feet is a long way to fall. I opened the flip after the first somersault and checked out how I was doing. I expected to see water at the end of my toes, but all I saw below me was a pile of sharp jagged rocks.

I'd blown it. I was going to eat it. I'd gone one step too far. Thirty-three feet was, in fact, too far to toss a gainer double. The Bridge to Venice was now going to kill me. I was about to slide down the cliff and take that spike right up my ass from 70 feet. For the final 50 feet of the dive, I was a living dead man. I was experiencing the last fatal seconds of an airplane crash.

I stuck my feet down and closed my eyes, wondering if I would feel the pain or die on impact. Before my life had time to pass before my eyes, I slipped through the water and landed on a flat rock on the bottom of the channel. My chest was pounding so hard I thought I was going to have a heart attack.

I burst off the bottom, and every single person on the cliffs—Mexican, American, spectator, and official—was on their feet, whistling and cheering. I was too stunned to react. I looked back at where my bubbles were coming from and I'd missed the spike by less than 24 inches. I didn't even smile. It may have come off like I had a game face on and I'd laid down the gauntlet to all challengers, but I was in shock. Two seconds earlier I'd been dead.

Juan was the first one to greet me. "Incredible dive," he said. "I've never seen anything like that, and I've been diving here for 30 years!"

Bruce pulled me out of the water with a big smile. "That's showin' 'em!" he said. "That's fucking nuts, but that's showin' 'em!"

I'd tossed the biggest trick in my life, even bigger than the Mifflin Street 3½, but I wasn't the slightest bit relieved. I had to keep practicing the son of a bitch all week long.

Surviving 50 sea urchin spines in my foot, dripping blood up and down a cliff in Mexico, and being dead for a split second was enough of a day for me. I grabbed a towel and walked back up the cliff towards the hotel. I was still shaking from the dive and I needed to calm my nerves.

As I stepped into the hotel, sitting in front of me, watching the practice session, was my old mentor, and the greatest coach in the history of the sport, Hobie Billingsley. If I had sat down and prayed for one person on earth to be there—it would have been Hobie Billingsley. I hadn't seen him in seven years, and he hadn't coached me in twelve It didn't take more than one sentence out of my mouth for us to fall right back into the relationship. I walked up behind him, tapped him on the shoulder, and said, "Hey, Hobe! How's it goin', ya old coot?"

"Murdock," he said, "I thought that was you, but you can't ever tell unless you see a hurdle." For some reason I never understood, Hobie had always called me "Murdock." "What the hell are you doing here?" he said. "Haven't you gotten a job yet?"

Hanging with the great Hobie Billingsley in Acapulco. The diving gods could not have sent me a better blessing.

On top of being the greatest coach of all time, Hobie had been one of the greatest water show performers of all time. He'd done Florida shows with Esther Williams and barnstormed the country diving into small eight-foot-deep tanks. He, of all people, wasn't the person to tell me to get a job.

"I'll start working as soon as you do," I laughed. "You put on a tie lately?"

Cliff diving was a big stretch from competitive technical diving, and it was a huge relief to have the best in the business there at the contest. Hobie had been selected to judge the contest alongside Dr. Sammy Lee, a two-time Olympic champ and the man who got Greg Louganis interested in diving. Louganis, too, would be coming in to do the commentary on ESPN. WWP was pulling out all the stops.

"So, did you see that gainer double?" I asked.

"Sure did," Hobie said. "That doesn't look like an easy trick to put in the water. You sure you want to toss that in a contest?"

"I'm here to win the damn thing," I said. "If I put it in the water the DD [degree of difficulty] should put me over the top."

"We'll see about that," he said, "and don't forget to swing those arms all the way through, either. This isn't the time to slouch off on mechanics."

"That's all I'm thinking about, Hobe," I said. "Swing the arms through, then get my ankles above my head as soon as I can."

He joined me for a beer, and we caught up on where we'd been the last couple of years. He told me he'd retired from Indiana and was doing a little coaching on the side. That "coaching on the side" would lead to a gold medal three-meter springboard performance out of Mark Lindsay in the Barcelona Olympics. Not bad for a retired coach.

I told him I'd found a spot in France for the time being, and I was going to hold out there until it got boring.

"You studying the language?" he asked. "I hope you're not just wasting your time around a show tank. You don't want to be old and have nothing to show except a good photo album."

It was the first time a high diver ever advised me on anything besides diving. As jittery as I felt about getting the double gainer off the cliff, having Hobie there was the most reassuring thing I could ask for.

As the week went on, I tried to think of anything but the gainer double, but it was impossible to get out of my head. It dominated my conscious and subconscious. Not one night went by when I wasn't startled out of bed by a nightmare of my head crashing against the rocks. Jeremy said he, too, thought of the cliff all day and dreamt about it all night. There was no escaping it. We just wanted the contest over with so we could get some sleep.

The day before the preliminary contest, we had a meeting to go over the difficulty table. We sat in a room in the lobby, and Chip handed us copies of the proposed DD formula. I took one look at it and threw it on the floor.

"This is pure bullshit," I said. "I've got Mexicans telling me they've never seen anything like my dive before, and I'm getting the same difficulty as a required dive? You guys can't be serious!"

"We have to take the Mexicans into consideration," Chip said. "They're just tossing front dives, and they have to have a chance to win, too."

As it stood on the sheet, my gainer double was rated a 10.0, and a front dive was rated 9.8. I was getting a whopping two percent advantage for risking my life compared to the Mexicans who could easily do their swan dives in a drunken stupor. It chaffed me to think I'd trained my ass off and wasn't going to get any credit for it.

Before the TV finals, the American team had to trim down to eight from our original twelve. ESPN wanted to use our US trials as a practice round to get the production bugs out. No change was made to the DD table, but it was too late to change my dive even if I wanted to. The contest rules state you must practice the dive you were doing to the satisfaction of the judges before entering it in the contest. Even if I wanted to back down and toss a new dive, it was too late.

The worst-case scenario was coming true. I was trying to win the contest with a big trick, but they had taken difficulty out of the equation. The first round went by with everyone tossing easy tricks except for Jeremy, who tossed his back triple, and Roland, who stuck his triple half. Jeremy ripped his back triple, but he was short. The judges gave him a set of 5s when all the boys tossing flying fronts were getting 7s and 8s. Not only was he getting no credit for difficulty, but the judges also were judging his trick—which had never been done before—against a bunch of floaty soft dives.

I collected a bunch of 7s on my flying gainer and felt guilty I hadn't tossed a harder dive like Jeremy and Roland. After one dive I was stuck in the middle of the pack with my inconsequential "big trick" left in the bag. When it came time for the top level, much of the same happened. Jeremy again ripped his mid-turn triple short for a collection of 5s. Arguably the best high diver in the company was out of the TV finals.

When it was time for my gainer double, I was so pissed I couldn't see straight. In order to survive, I had to hit one of the toughest dives in the history of the contest as cleanly as everybody else's front somersault.

Louganis was doing a TV interview before each diver did his trick. He noted on my list of accomplishments that I was a high school state champion. He asked me if there were any similarities between high school diving and the Acapulco Cliff Diving Championships.

"Sure," I said, "just like any diving contest you have to block out all the surrounding distractions and concentrate on mechanics. It's just that here there are a lot more distractions."

He thought I was talking about the cliff and the water depth, but I was talking about getting completely ripped off by my employers. Two days earlier I'd gotten a great take-off, saw my spot on the water, and puffed the dive away without throwing a drop of water. That's the dive I needed to stay in the contest. I swung my arms through and got a decent take-off. I spun the first flip and saw that I was a little lower than I wanted to be but still okay. I tucked over the last flip and stood the dive up but threw some water. I came out of the water to see 5½s and 6s. I, too, was out of the contest.

I spent the next morning hanging out with a bunch of the Mexican divers who weren't selected for the team. We walked high above the city and blew a joint looking over the Pacific. Acapulco Bay was stretched out below us with The Love Boat docked in the harbor.

I was still smarting from the contest, but I couldn't let the experience go down as a failure. The 1,350-mile bike trip itself was a major win. Tossing the ballsiest trick in the contest was a win. Sitting up above the city of Acapulco with a fresh buzz was a win. Not being on the New Year's Eve ESPN telecast, however, was a major loss.

The Mexicans kicked our asses with Jeremy and me sitting on the sideline. I helped Hobie off the judging platform and asked him what he thought.

"You showed 'em too much, Murdock," he said. "People are already scared shitless over this thing, and you guys took it to a level they really didn't want to exploit. Hey, it was a great vacation, though, wasn't it?"

It took the genius of Hobie Billingsley to put it all into perspective. That night at the closing ceremony, Juan Obregon called Jeremy and me up to stand alongside him as he presented the awards. He doled out all the paychecks ($5,000 to the winner) and gave the diminutive David Reyes the first-place trophy that weighed more than he did. Jeremy and I didn't know why we were standing up there, but just before he finished, Juan gave us a special award.

"I have been diving off this cliff for 30 years," he said. "I have seen thousands of dives done by hundreds of divers from all over the world. These two divers are the bravest two I have ever seen. They truly pushed the limits of La Quebrada and the sport of cliff diving. I would like to present them with the Mas Bravos award."

All we got was a polite round of applause and a handshake from Juan, but the look in his eyes when he shook my hand was one of true admiration. I would have loved a paycheck, but that money would have been gone in just a couple of months. The look from Juan's eyes is mine forever.

•   •   •   •   •   •   •   •   •   •   •   •   •

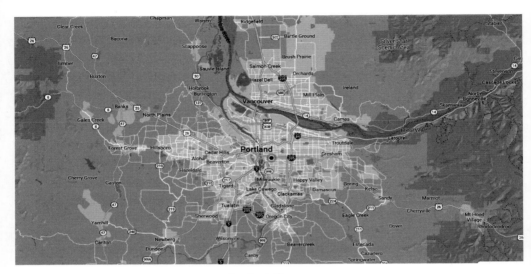

Portland, Oregon

Transition Before the Transition

One bad thing about circus work is that at some point, you have to pick up the tent and move on. I was so entrenched in my French lifestyle that I'd let that elephant in the room out the door and forgotten it even existed. I had a home, a job, and for the final two years of the contract, a girlfriend whom I would one day marry.

Rachel Weiner was a gymnastics prodigy from Shaker Heights, Ohio. She was forced into diving after breaking both her ankles so many times she'd lost count. She was doing back doubles on the floor as a 12-year-old and could actually hit the trick...most of the time. But at the ripe old age of 16, her ankles begrudgingly forced her into the pool. In no time at all she caught the eye of college scouts and eventually landed at the University of Virginia, where she was a silver medalist at the ACC Championships.

In 1989 she took a contract with WWP in Rust, Germany, where she earned the reputation as one of the finest high divers in the world. Maaike Leeuwenburgh, a Dutch diver for WWP, met her and relayed to me, "Tommy, Tommy—this Rachel! She's the one for you! She's the one for you!" For the next several months, every time I ran into Maaike, the first words out of her mouth were, "Tommy, Tommy—this Rachel—she's the one for you! We're gonna set you up! She's going to be on your team!"

Sure enough, in the spring of 1990, I drove to the train station in La Tour-du-Pin, the nearest city to Les Avenières, and set eyes on Rachel. Just like Maaike had reported, she was blonde, beautiful, and athletic. She also came equipped with a ton of spunk and took crap from no one.

I took Rachel to the park and introduced her to everybody in the office, who by this time were well aware Maaike was setting me up. After each introduction, Rachel would leave the room and I'd look back to see everyone making kissy-faces at me. To which I kindly responded with a smile and a polite fist with a slap on the bicep—the French equivalent of a middle finger.

Our courtship lasted all of one day. On her second day, I did an awkward high dive on an already aching knee and blew it out. There was a big scene at the park as paramedics hauled me into the ambulance. "Someone should go with him!" one of our teammates shouted—and then they all looked at

Rachel, who hopped in with me. I got a cast put on my entire left leg and made it back to the Platanes in time for happy hour. Drinks were already lined up, and I was in a lot of pain, so they went down easy. Everyone in the bar was matching me one-for-one. My injury, it seems, was the social event of the Les Avenières spring.

We made it back to our French farmhouse and Rachel helped me up to my room. She slid into bed alongside me and stayed there for a decade.

• • • • • • • • • • • • • •

By the time the curtain dropped on my high diving life, I'd been working and living abroad for seven years. With all the cycling I was doing, my body was never stronger. I felt like I could have kept going for seven more. But I'd stretched out the post-college lifestyle longer than anyone I knew. All my friends in the States were well into their careers. It was time to move on and I knew it. I even had a great partner with me to ease the transition.

One day in 1991, our show announcer Jean-Marie came backstage and told us Walibi had had enough of the diving show. We had been the number one attraction in the park for four straight years, but everyone in the region knew the comedy skit and it wasn't getting the explosive reaction it had gotten early on. We'd tried new bits in the past, but they just didn't work like the man-in-the-audience shtick. The writing was on the wall. On a chilly October afternoon, I did my final French comedy and a Mifflin Street Dive. I waved to the crowd knowing The Belle Epoch of Les Avenières had come to an end.

But we didn't go straight home. Rachel was keen to visit Asia before calling an end to our high diving careers. Our old teammate, Jerry Grimes, had started a new company in Australia and wanted us to perform for his show in downtown Sydney. We had four months to kill before arriving in Sydney, so we embarked on a global trek, the likes of which few travelers undertake. We started with a few weeks touring France with Rachel's parents, followed by a freezing cold hitchhiking adventure from Amsterdam to Poland and back to France.

While we were in Amsterdam, we bought plane tickets that let us make seven stops between Amsterdam and San Francisco. Over the next six months we hit Jordan, India, Nepal, Thailand, Malaysia, Singapore, Indonesia, Australia (where we stayed for two months to do the show), New Caledonia, New Zealand, and Tahiti. By the time we got to the airport in Tahiti, we were so burned out and cash-strapped we didn't even leave the airport. Tourists were arriving wide-eyed for the trip of a lifetime, but we just wanted to get on the next flight to San Francisco. The trip was a gigantic multi-stage magical experience that yielded enough sites and stories to last two lifetimes. We saw Everest and Machapuchare in Nepal. We parachuted off a mountain in New Zealand. We scaled Mt. Bromo on Java and snorkeled off the coast of Bali. I did the highest dive of my life, a 95-foot screamer, into Sydney's Darling Harbour, only to be topped the next day by Rachel, who did a 96-footer with a lower tide. Upon returning to the States, I had the feeling I was about to pay for the past seven years with a big hangover. I just didn't know how severe that hangover was going to be.

Rachel and I settled in Portland, Oregon. We are both from the Midwest, but our lives had been completely transformed by living in the Alps. We needed to live in mountains—our entire lifestyle was built around them. We looked at Colorado, San Diego, and a few other places, but Portland was an easy decision. Portland is full of Euro-trash hipsters like us, and Oregon has the added bonus of pristine Pacific beaches.

As much as I love Oregon now, at first it was rough sailing. My plan was to finish the last year of my master's program from Wisconsin, get certified, and start teaching and coaching in high school. Unfortunately, Oregon has some of the most rigid teaching standards in the country and I would have had to start a master's program from scratch. It was a three-year commitment and I just didn't have the money.

I spent two years waiting tables before I finally scored a dream job— working in event marketing for the sporting goods giant Adidas. Rachel had started working there six months earlier. I frequented Club 21, the Adidas watering hole, so often people assumed I worked there. Eventually, they took me in. Although the job would send me around the country working huge events (World Cup Soccer, Final Four, Boston Marathon) it paid little at the entry level. In order to move up the chain, I took a job buying bulk T-shirts from factories and making sure the final product got shipped to retail shops. It was a horrible job, where I had to spend 60 hours a week staring at spreadsheets. I was, however, learning the business, and saw a future that would send us abroad again; albeit to monitor factories, not jump off high dive ladders.

But it all came crumbling down one week when I was scapegoated and cut loose by a boss after a promotional T-shirt project went awry. It was a devastating blow, because Adidas wasn't just my job, it was my entire social structure. I spent nearly every waking hour at work, and the only social outlets I had involved going to sporting events or parties with people from work.

It was a classical Japanese, all-encompassing employment model, and I was devastated when it was gone. Rachel, of course, still worked there, and things between us started going south. I went from a guy who controlled a $15 million apparel inventory to an unemployed bum with a crumbling marriage.

But at least I had my health. Actually, it was a miracle I had it, because over the previous few years, I'd developed tendinitis in my right Achilles tendon, taking me off my bike and heavily restricting my physical activity. After I got fired, I decided to get back on my bike and either ride through the pain or rupture the tendon. For the first time since I started working at Adidas, the tendinitis subsided, and I became a bike rider again. In between job hunting I rode my bike miles and miles, taking on the highest climbs and the most scenic routes in northwest Oregon. I climbed the highest road in the state to Timberline Lodge; I rode miles along the Pacific Coast; and I spent hours discovering the Columbia Gorge.

This led me to my first job after Adidas—managing a small bike shop in northeast Portland. I was still looking for work at one of the big sports companies, but thinking more and more about working for a cycling company.

And then one bright Sunday morning, I went for a bike ride...

•   •   •   •   •   •   •   •   •   •   •   •   •

La Mappa dell Inferno Botticelli

Rebuilding the Mosaic

It was a sunny Sunday morning in September 1996 when I stuffed a foam cheese head in my backpack and rode out to meet some friends at a sports bar in downtown Portland. The Green Bay Packers were playing the Vikings, and the game wasn't carried on any of the West Coast affiliates. I may have left Wisconsin, but no matter where you move, your teams come with you.

I rode out of my house and turned right on Sandy Boulevard, one of Portland's major arteries. In the past, I'd ridden Sandy Boulevard during rush hour through driving rain, but on this sunny, 75-degree Sunday morning, it was clear sailing. It was a five-mile sprint to the sports bar, so after a short warmup, I dropped down on my handlebars and picked up my cadence.

Sandy Boulevard makes a big left curve as it approaches the Willamette River and drops from the neighborhoods of Northeast Portland into the commercial district along the banks of the Willamette. I'd out-pedaled my gears and got in a streamline crouch to drop the hill. I gauged the green lights, hoping to beat them before hopping the Hawthorne Bridge across the river to breakfast.

Suddenly a sedan driven by an elderly woman blew a stop sign and shot into the middle of Sandy Boulevard. I swerved left into the oncoming lane then jerked back, avoiding the grille of a Mazda. I turned and screamed at the woman then looked to the road ahead. The traffic light turned red, and I was flying. A 24-foot delivery truck entered the intersection and I made eye contact with the driver. We both hit our brakes as hard as we could. As he came to a screeching halt, I prepared to lay my bike under his trailer. Just as I started my skid, my rear brake cable snapped. My back wheel slid out, and I slammed my head into his front bumper. My helmet and the cheese head in my backpack saved my head and neck.

But my legs were toast.

Somebody had the sense to call 911, and the Portland paramedics came screaming to the scene. My feet were still clipped to the pedals, and I was leaning on my backpack stuffed with the cheese head. A paramedic asked me if I could unclip my cleats, and I told him I broke my back. He looked at the situation, nodded his head and said, "Maybe, I think you might be right, but let's not take any chances. This might just be a stinger." He had hope, but I had none. Stingers come from the neck. This thing was right around my waist. I was trying to be positive, but my confidence and self-esteem lay in a motionless heap below my pelvis.

They loosened my cleats, slipped my feet out, and pulled my mountain bike out from underneath me. Aside from the brake cable, there was nothing wrong with the bike. I watched a policeman roll it along the street and toss it in the trunk of his car. The wheels were still in true, and the fork was as solid as ever. The handlebars pointed straight ahead, and the paint didn't have a scrape on it.

They slid me into the ambulance, and I held on for a drive over the Willamette and up the switchbacks to the Oregon Health Science University in the Tualatin mountains overlooking the city. OHSU takes up some of the most expensive real estate in town, and its views of Mt. Hood and the Columbia Gorge are spectacular. Everyone else on the road was on a simple Sunday drive but I was on an adventure more harrowing than a zipline in the Himalayas. When I got to the emergency room, a doctor started some sensation tests.

"I've got some horrible news for you, sir," he said.

"I know," I said, "they're toast."

"Looks like it," he said. "Do you hurt anywhere else?"

"Nope," I replied. In fact, I didn't hurt at all. I couldn't feel my legs, and as far as I could tell, I hadn't taken a hit anywhere else. My helmet saved my brain, and I didn't even have as much as a cut on my entire body. I realized a couple days later that I'd bruised a rib, but that was it.

Although breaking your back is just about as unlucky as it gets, having a brother who is the director of the University of Michigan's Spine Center helps even the score. I told them to look in my bag for my address book. "Call my brother Andy," I said. I'd made this call a couple of times before, but this was a different deal. This wasn't a call from Taipei telling him I'd gotten in a car accident or calling from Les Avenières telling him I'd trashed my knee ligaments. This was the call he'd gotten from hundreds of people before, always dreading it would happen to one of us. Andy had just returned to his home in Ann Arbor from a conference when he picked up the phone.

"What's going on?" he asked.

"Hey, man," I started, "This is the big one."

"What kind of big?"

"I cracked my back. I'm toast."

"Fuck...Where's the crack?"

"They're not sure. T-11 to L-2 [11th thoracic to 2nd lumbar vertebrae]. Somewhere in there."

"You moving your fingers?"

"Just like Townshend."

"Toes?"

"Can't dance."

"What else? Are you bleeding. Anything internal?"

"Nope—not a scratch."

"They got you hooked up to some meds?"

"They gave me something, but it's just starting to suck."

"Jesus...Shit...try to relax—let me talk to the doc. I'm on my way."

Within an hour, the chronic pain that wrenches my abdomen to this day crept into my body and took a strong hold. When it became unbearable, they hooked me up to a morphine rig with a small plunger next to the nurse call button. I could zap myself once every 20 minutes with a big ol' hit of morphine. Of all the crap I've introduced into my body, morphine is the worst. It did nothing to relieve pain, but it made my brain too numb to respond. My body felt like a jalapeño: fiery red with pain, but a vegetable nonetheless.

A nurse came by and asked if I needed to call anyone else. Putting people on your Christmas card list is one thing. Being asked to prioritize everyone in your life to tell them that you'll never be the same is another. The list started out with my family. I left a string of messages, but nobody was home. Rachel and I were in the final stages of our divorce, but I needed her. She was out playing, too. I couldn't get a hold of anyone.

For the rest of the day, I zapped myself with doses of morphine and tried to watch football. Every 20 minutes or so, a nurse would pass me a phone, and I'd have to tell a close friend or relative I was going to fuck up their year. The evening turned into a morphine-soaked cauchemar. I couldn't distinguish minutes from hours, hours from days.

Eventually, most of the voices on the phone turned into faces at my bedside. My sister Sue was visiting friends in Seattle, and they sped down.

Rachel got the news from her roommate, and rushed over, only to pass out, pulling out an IV on her way to the floor.

My brothers Dan and Bagus flew in from San Francisco and stared in disbelief. The same man who had joined them at the summit of Mount St. Helens could no longer climb out of bed. Just two weeks earlier, I'd been roughhousing in a pool with my best friend Pat in Florida. Now he stood in front of me, afraid of what a touch might do. My mother, a former X-ray technician, came in with perfect bedside manner while my father, someone who passes out at the sight of blood but who had seen me through so many other scrapes, didn't even know where to start. My other two sisters Barb and Nari were told to stay put in Milwaukee with their kids. Their job would come later. This wasn't going to be a quick fix.

Finally, Andy arrived from Ann Arbor. He had been at a convention in Chicago and was only home long enough to kiss his wife, Brigit, and daughter Molly goodbye. He didn't have words to describe to seven-year-old Molly what was going on except that Uncle Tom was sick and things weren't going to be the same anymore.

On a professional level, he was the best person in the whole damn country, if not the world, to be there. Andy had created the Spine Program at the University of Michigan Medical School, and it was ranked first in the nation. His 27-page resume lists dozens of awards, published research, and high-ranking positions in international medical organizations. But even he felt helpless. Helpless to my legs, but invaluable in every other way. My family members wouldn't have to trust a newcomer to make the gravest decisions of our lives. As Andy surveyed the situation, I saw the OHSU doctors assume defensive postures. They were out of his league, and they knew it.

Meanwhile, my family and friends stood by my side, mustering up enough courage to stay and talk. After a while, I noticed they started coming in small groups. They'd stay in the room as long as they could support themselves, then sneak out and cry like babies while the next shift took over.

I was diagnosed as a T-12 paraplegic with 80 percent compromise of my spinal cord. I hadn't cut or broken the cord. In fact, it was only a small bruise. On any other part of the body, it would show up as a blemish. On the spinal cord it had permanently disabled me.

Andy spoke with the neurosurgeon, and they decided to fuse my spine between the second lumbar and eleventh thoracic vertebrae. A week earlier I didn't know how many vertebrae I had; now I only knew how many of them I had left. They were going to cut my back open and screw in a five-inch titanium clamp that would stabilize the region, help the bones heal, and ensure the bruise wouldn't spread. They also jacked me with a Sammy-Sosa-sized dose of steroids. While I was lying on the table I couldn't tell if I'd been in the hospital for a day, a week, or a year. I just knew I was losing consciousness and when I woke, I would never be the same.

As I regained consciousness, I discovered I was onstage again. The crowd was my parents, my brothers, my sister Sue, Rachel, her mom, Pat... who knows who else was there. It had been a couple years since I'd been onstage, but the sensation was familiar. I was out in front and everyone was watching. Once it was Tom Haig the state champion. Once it was Tom Haig the Acapulco cliff diver. For four glorious years it was Tom Haig le Plongeur de la Mort. Now I'd be onstage the rest of my life. Nobody would ever miss my act. Not the grocery store clerks, not the policemen, not the bosses, not even the geriatrics leaning against their walkers. From now on my act was, "Tom, the guy in the chair." The guy who needs help.

In order to sleep (or whatever you could call my nighttime activity), I was wedged into a fetal position with a pillow between my knees so I wouldn't get bedsores. Every four hours someone would come in, put in a catheter so I could pee, then turn me into the same pillow wedge on the other side. In the morning I was strapped back into a brace, which stayed on the entire day. At no time during the three months I was in the brace was I ever without piercing pain.

After the therapist strapped me in, she told me I was ready to sit up. I told her she was insane. She told me it would feel good to lift my head after lying down on drugs for four days. I put my arms around her neck and she lifted me up. It was the worst pain I'd ever experienced in my life.

After the accident and the surgery, my body had coughed up all the endorphins allotted in one single lifetime. Even though I was sedated on morphine, I could feel millions of neural endings slamming against the brick wall in the middle of my spinal cord. I've never passed out from pain before, but I could feel myself slipping away. My head swayed, my breathing accelerated, and I convulsed. The dry heaves were a trick my body was playing to distract me from the real situation. The therapist slid my legs off the bed and told me it was time to get into a wheelchair. If my pupils had lasers, she would have gone down like a stormtrooper. I couldn't get my breathing down well enough to speak, so I was unable to tell the soft-spoken therapist that she was Satan and I refused to do her evil will. She lined up a sliding board (a smooth skateboard without wheels) under my butt and told me to lean forward and grab around her neck.

"No…" I gagged, "no fucking way!"

She laughed, smiled and in an angelic tone said, "Oh, I think we're gonna do this. All we have to do is sit in the chair for a half an hour."

My head stilled, and the convulsions ceased. I looked around the room for Andy. I was sure he was going to back me up on this one. He wasn't there. "I'm not moving anywhere," I said. "Didn't they tell you I just got cut yesterday? Aren't I supposed to be in traction for six months or something?"

"No," she said. "As long as your back is fused, it's best to get the rest of you moving as soon as possible. We could drop you flat on your stomach, and it wouldn't change your level of injury."

"First day after surgery?" I asked. "I haven't even eaten yet."

"You can eat if you want, but it's not going to change the fact that you're gonna get in that chair before I leave."

I put my arms around her neck, and she slid me along the board into my first wheelchair. Emergency rooms have a pain chart ranging from cool blue to hot red. You're supposed to point to a color that describes your level of pain. If the therapist had shown me that chart, I would have lit it on fire.

At this point, I realized I'd forgotten how to cry. I was breathless and in shock, but crying from pain had been conditioned out of me years ago. I lost the ability while I was a catcher in Little League. I got bowled over by guys twice my size, but crying on the field just wasn't going to cut it. Since then, I'd been in car accidents, fallen from water towers, and landed flat on my back from 70-foot multiple somersaulting dives. No crying. I used to swear, jump up and down, and tell jokes, anything but cry. Now I wanted to cry. I had no physical outlets sufficient to relieve my pain. I was going to have to learn how to cry again, or I wasn't going to survive. Then again, I wasn't sure if I wanted to survive.

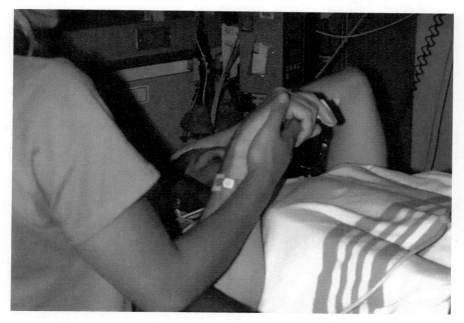

Rachel holding my hand the night of the bike wreck. I had no idea what I'd just signed up for.

After a week of watching family and friends come in and out of my room only to leave in fits of tears, it was decided I should move from Portland to Northwestern University's Rehabilitation Institute of Chicago (RIC). When I was at the University of Illinois, I used to visit Andy in Chicago where he was an RIC intern. Not only did he know the management and staff, he was a prized pupil of the founder of the RIC, the famed Dr. Henry B. Betts. Betts has a reputation as a tireless fundraiser with political connections so high it embarrasses him to mention them. At RIC I'd be getting celebrity treatment. I was in constant fear of my own body, and I wanted to be treated like a family member, not just the poor kid from Wisconsin who wiped out on Sandy Boulevard.

I assumed a medical air transfer was a fairly regular procedure, but we were taking a tremendous risk. If any of the nightmares that took place the following week had occurred on the plane, I could have died. I was off morphine, but only because it made me sick to my stomach and didn't curb the pain. Instead, I was jacked up on an oxycodone-drenched

Tylenol hybrid called Tylox. At 8:00 a.m., eight days after my accident, I was dressed by a nurse, slid onto a gurney, and loaded into an ambulance.

The ambulance rounded the switchbacks of Portland's West Hills, then merged onto the freeway through downtown and out toward the airport. I couldn't see where we were going, so I guessed, based on curves.

I nodded off and woke up thinking it was time for a 10:00 a.m. show for 3,000 Chinese school kids. But instead of jumping out of the van and beginning my stretching routine, I lifted my head and stared at my dead lower corpse. Three weeks earlier I'd been diving off cliffs in Hawaii with my brother, Bagus. The final dive of my life was a 50-foot flying gainer off the beachhead at Poipu on the island of Kauai. I ripped the snot out of it, not displacing more than a teaspoon of water. I was going to try another one that day, but I figured there were plenty more cliffs like that. Now six-inch curbs scared me.

The attendant lowered me out of the ambulance and rolled me into the airport. My next challenge was the flight.

Andy plopped my legs into a first-class seat, then he and my dad lifted me onto the transfer board over the handrail and into the seat. Even though the transfer was smooth, each small twinge was enough pain to roll my eyes back and take my breath away. Fourteen days earlier I was strong enough to pedal my Cannondale up 6,000 feet to Timberline Lodge on Mt. Hood. Now I was so weak I couldn't even hold my arms around Andy's neck. Once in the chair, Andy took my vitals and fed me some more Tylox while I tried to get comfortable. Comfort is a relative term that has changed dramatically since the wreck. I haven't been comfortable since.

It was a beautiful late summer day in Oregon, and the flight was magnificent as I crossed the country and went back in time to the Midwest. We swung around Mount St. Helens, where I peered into the active volcano we had climbed the week after my wedding. I started to describe the climb to Andy, then stopped, realizing we would never do monster hikes like that again.

We flew along the Columbia River, past Multnomah Falls, Larch Mountain, Dog Mountain, and Mount Adams. These were the main reasons I moved to the Northwest. What used to be monuments to conquer had turned to nothing more than pretty pictures. Mt. Hood was brilliant. I'd planned to summit it with my friend Aaron the next spring. Now I wondered if I would ever be healthy enough to climb the hills of East

Portland. As we passed over the Rockies, I spotted Yellowstone and the Grand Tetons. I could see Yellowstone Falls from the plane and traced the 10-mile hike I'd taken five years earlier. I remember being bluffed by some bison, who sent me scampering back into the forest. I imagined myself trying to escape a bison charge in a wheelchair. That scenario didn't end well, but at least it made me laugh. It was the first of many sardonic handicap jokes I would use to get through impossible situations. It was the first time I realized I'd become part of a special interest group. I had become a member of Handicap Nation. From now on I could laugh at all the cruel disability jokes. And I'd have to laugh to keep my sanity.

The plane landed and the worst period of my life began. The passengers deplaned while I took another hit of Tylox. We waited in the plane for 20 minutes before an attendant arrived with an aisle chair. Getting out of the plane seat was such a brutal experience I nearly passed out. Three people lifted me over the rail and slid me down the transfer board, where I landed with a thump on the thin aisle chair. The pain of the transfer hit with an acute crack that revisited me every few seconds in throbbing aftershock waves. Andy looked at my eyes and took my pulse before we moved. He'd seen me get as beat up as anyone, but I knew he'd never seen a look of helpless desperation in me before.

It was a full two hours before the ambulance finally showed up. I made one last transfer onto the gurney and lay back for the first time since leaving Portland. According to the doctors at OHSU, my seating tolerance was between 45 and 90 minutes. By the time I laid back in the gurney it had been seven hours. I thought I'd fall asleep as soon as I lay down, but the pain from the brace and the strain on my back kept me awake. I needed sleep more than ever, but it wasn't coming.

An hour later the ambulance pulled into the RIC. It felt like I'd landed in Shangri-La. One of Andy's best friends and oldest colleagues, Dr. David Chen, met us and showed us to my new room. They did a short intake and introduced me to the staff, many of whom were also Andy's old friends. I was transferred from the gurney to my bed, where they loosened my brace and jacked me full of pain pills. I dozed off, feeling like I'd landed at a luxury resort in Bali. But I woke up in a prison cell.

Every transfer I made was still a fiery ache-fest. I thought the change of venue was going to alter things, but I was still a fresh crip with plenty of agony. They rolled me down to X-ray where I glared at the chasm between my chair and the table. The X-ray tech called in a huge attendant who, without asking, grabbed my legs and swung them onto the table. Then he hoisted me by the armpits and dropped me on the table. My mother, an X-ray technician of 25 years, told me the walls of an X-ray room were made of lead to keep radiation from escaping. They also deafen the screams of mortally wounded patients. I'm sure my scream was heard far outside those walls.

They took a dozen films from several different angles and body positions. Each time they moved me I found another level of pain I'd never experienced before.

I chugged a Tylox, loosened my brace, and tried to drift to sleep. I almost made it when I felt the first twinge of nausea hit my stomach. I took a Zantac with a tall glass of water and tried to doze off again. For a while it worked. I fell into a deep sleep but experienced a paranoid nightmare like the kind I used to get from eating chloroquine pills in Thailand. I woke up with a start.

The nausea came back. I swallowed more water. I raised and lowered my bed. Finally, it got so bad I buzzed the nurse. The day nurse came into the room, followed by Andy and my parents. "Something's wrong," I said. "I'm sick to my stomach and I'm burning up."

"Jesus, Tommy," my mom said, "you're on fire."

"I'm ready to puke, too," I said. "But I can't get anything to come out."

Andy went over my chart and tried to figure out what was wrong. "Hey," he said, "when's the last time you've taken a crap?"

"I don't know," I said, "last Sunday as far as I can remember."

"Weren't they giving you a bowel program at OHSU?" he asked.

"What's that?" I asked.

Andy rolled his eyes and walked out of the room. He called OHSU and sure enough they had given me a "bowel program" but there were no results. Then I had to act the idiot and ask, "Hey, what the hell is a bowel program?"

For some reason hospital people find it very difficult to say the words "crap," "shit," "poop" and "dump." Instead, they use the term "bowel program." These people are sticking their fingers in us and ramming tubes into our bodies, but they're afraid to use the word "shit" in front of us. More than likely nobody wanted to be the one to tell me that for the rest of my life I was going to have to ram a pellet up my ass and stay on a toilet for an hour waiting for my bowel to empty. It gets even more fun than that. Every 15 minutes I have to put on a rubber glove and dig into my ass until all the shit drops out.

Andy looked at me and said, "Dude, you're F.O.S."

"What's that?" I asked.

My mother, Andy, and the nurse said in unison, "Full of Shit."

"So let's get that shit out of there," I said. "I'm sick as hell."

"We're gonna cram you full of laxatives," Andy said.

"How long's that gonna take?" I asked.

"About 24 hours," he said.

Andy's prediction of 24 hours was off by 24 hours. I lay in bed in fever-ish agony for two days until my bowels gave way to the jet fuel. Then, for the next 24 hours, I had the pleasure of erupting every four or five hours until I was cleaned out. When I lived in France, I read a book by Armand de Las Cuevas, who had to wade through cesspools while in a prison camp in Cuba. I never thought I would ever experience a low like that, but this one was worse. De Las Cuevas would leave his prison. I would never leave mine.

Over the next two weeks things got better as I regained the ability to leave bed by myself. A team of physical and occupational therapists put me on a weight-lifting regimen and tried to teach me the basics of living in a chair. None of them knew what they were talking about. I didn't real-ize this until months later, when my bones had healed and I had weaned myself from my brace. Some of the things they were asking me to do were impossible with the brace on, yet simple with the brace off. Dressing was the most obvious example. I couldn't reach down and tie my shoes, yet the therapists insisted this was easy and every one of their patients had learned it. I went through excruciating pain trying in vain to do it, whereas just three days after my brace was off, it became as simple a task as, well, tying your shoes.

They treated me like a baby and made me participate in games that wouldn't interest a worm. The worst of these games was balloon baseball. The therapist would make a ball out of an inflated surgical glove and we were supposed to play baseball with it. The diamond had eight-foot base paths, and we were supposed to slap a pitched ball and try to make it around the circuit. Each time someone made contact (which was every time) the ther-apist would cheer like a mother watching her kids at a t-ball game. "Run to first!" she would scream. I'd never felt so humiliated in my life.

Eventually they started letting us go for extended pushes. I was thrilled at the chance to get out into Chicago, but terrified at what I learned. Most sidewalks are tilted for drainage, making rolling on them especially difficult. If there is as much as a five percent incline, the chair will shoot towards the street. That means one arm does all the work while the other brakes in order to keep the chair straight. When you see someone in a wheelchair moving quickly along a sidewalk, they're working their ass off.

They started teaching us how to do wheelies, but they didn't know how important it was to hold a solid wheelie. Wheelie class was optional, when it is by far the most important thing they could teach us. The other skills (dressing, transferring, balance) would become second nature as soon as the brace was removed. Holding a wheelie allows a wheeler to jump off a curb and roll down a small set of stairs. It also allows a wheeler to bounce up on sidewalks, which is handy when there aren't any curb cuts or driveways. It allows wheelers to control speed when descending a hill. And once you get comfortable on two wheels, you can dance like a mutherfucker.

At night the staff gave lectures on things they had no business talking about. The most insane lecture was on sex. They separated us into boys' and girls' classes, then spoke to us as if we were 13-year-olds noticing our first sign of pubic hair. There's only one way to tell spinal cord injury patients (SCIs) about sex, and that's to have another SCI tell us the way it really is. If you ain't a crip, you don't want to know. If you are one, you need to hear it straight up.

In case you do want to know, here's the deal on sex: Regular, rip off the clothes and get busy sex is over. Period. The link between the brainstem and the penis is shot. There is no longer a connection between what you think and what you feel. You get erections when you're watching a baseball game, but you wouldn't be able to get a hard-on with a naked Pamela Anderson standing in front of you. You can take a hit of Viagra but you have to wait an hour for it to take effect. Once it's up, you can't ejaculate— and you never will.

This wreaks havoc with your brain and your self-esteem. The brain has been wired for millions of years to find a mate and reproduce, but something wrong is going on here. People assume it must be god-awful to live without standing up. To tell you the truth, legs are overrated. You can do pretty damn well without them. It's living without a functioning penis that drives male spinal cord patients insane.

Most SCIs can't handle that fact and repress it. Most SCIs repress everything. That's the one area where the RIC did well. I had a psychiatrist who knew what she was talking about. She dealt head on with frustration and suicide. She taught me one lesson I use daily. Once a high threshold of frustration has been met, you never go back to the old level. Once you've been suicidal, all it takes is a bad day to bring up suicidal thoughts. If you don't tone down your depression level, you're gonna kill yourself. After days where your frustration level goes well beyond 10, it's hard to bring it back to a 4. But if you evaluate each event individually, you're not as bad off as you think you are. Great in theory, but it took a few years to get there.

After four weeks of pain, confusion, frustration, and anger, the RIC decided to give me my walking, errr, "rolling" papers. The RIC had proved to be one major disappointment after another, and I needed to get the hell out of there. The doctors may have been the best in the country, but some of the therapists and night nurses were the cheapest money could buy. Even Andy and his colleagues were embarrassed when I told them of some of the lousy care the patients were given. I'd passed all the RIC's physical tests, and they decided I would be much better rehabbing at home. I was still in the brace and needed to be turned at night, but both the doctors and I agreed that the RIC wasn't doing me any good. It was time to try to live a real life again.

My parents drove down from Milwaukee and picked up my things, but I wasn't going straight home. The Who were in town, and it was high time I paid a visit to my high priest, Mr. Pete Townshend. If I was going to make it through this, I needed a refresher from the master. Most patients would have gone home and gone straight to bed. I was going to see the greatest rock and roll band on the planet.

My friend Shawn picked me up at the RIC and drove me to her apartment in Wrigleyville. Shawn is a Deadhead, and we'd gone to dozens of shows together over the years. We're concert pros, but we were both a little scared. The chair barely fit into her apartment, but once inside I had plenty of room to maneuver. If I was going to make it through the show, I was going to have to get some rest, so I transferred onto her couch. I sank deep into the pillows and fell against the back. I hadn't sat on a couch in over a month, so this was a new experience.

I never felt comfortable in the RIC bed, but the couch swallowed me up like an octopus securing its prey. I couldn't move, but I didn't care either.

Shawn drove us to the United Center, but we didn't have a handicapped placard. The attendants saw the chair and parked us up front anyway. The show was sold out and the lines getting in were endless, but being in a wheelchair was like Moses parting the Red Sea. Attendants came from every direction and cut me through every line. In just a few short minutes, we were at our seats listening to a horrible warm-up band.

A year earlier I'd pushed Rachel's paraplegic friend, Sarah, onto a platform at Portland Meadows to see Chuck Berry play with the Dead. I looked at all the people in chairs and imagined what a horrible world that must be. Now I was on that same platform. To the left of me was an obese quad with a finger control automatic chair, and to the right of me was a 30-something woman emaciated with multiple sclerosis. Farther down the aisle were two paraplegics who appeared to be a couple.

I turned to tell something to Shawn and, for the first time in our concert-going history, I was looking up at her. She stands barely five feet tall, and we've gone to tons of shows where she never even gets to see the band. I used to offer to lift her onto my shoulders, but she always insisted she was fine just hearing the tunes. Now I was the short one.

The last time I'd seen The Who had been in 1982 at the Milwaukee Arena. In those days I spent hours doing wild guitar windmills to Quadrophenia. At that point I couldn't play a lick of the stuff, but I had every Townshend mannerism down. Now I could play plenty of it, but I couldn't pull off the leaping windmill.

The lights dimmed and a mammoth diamond-vision screen illuminated English Channel waves crashing onto the shore in Brighton. A 15-piece orchestra started playing the *Quadrophenia* medley, and tension rose with each passing song reference. I was screaming with my arms in the air, but my legs were motionless. That morning I thought maybe when Pete hit the first chords of "Can You See the Real Me," my legs would bust through all the nonsense in my spine and jump into a mule kick. It would be all over, just a bad month. If anyone could get me out of this shit, it was Townshend. I'd punted Catholicism over what the guy was saying, and his message had rung true to me ever since. C'mon, Pete! Just one more time. Let me have just one more leap...

The band burst out onstage, and Pete smashed into the intro. Up to that point I—honest to God—thought I had a chance. My legs knew that cue better than they knew how to ride a bike or do a front dive. In fact, it would have been impossible to hear that cue and not spring into action. My ears took in the sound, my arms went for the power chord, my hips tensed up for the jump...But no response from the legs. Instead, I burst out in tears.

CAN YOU SEE THE REAL ME? DOCTOR! DOCTOR?

•   •   •   •   •   •   •   •   •   •   •   •   •

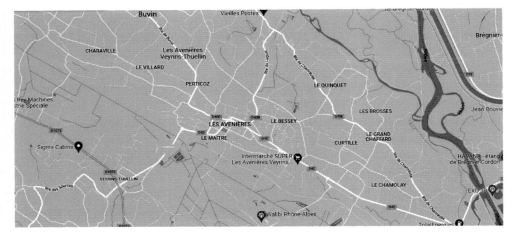

Les Avenieres

Allez à la Maison!

After two months of outpatient rehab and living with my sister Barb's family in Wisconsin, it was time to go back to Oregon and try to cobble together some kind of lifestyle. The broken vertebrae had healed, which meant I could take off the thoracic brace. Removing the brace moved everything from getting dressed to rolling uphill out of the "pure torture" category into the "feasible" category.

My body was still too messed up to think of getting a job, so school seemed to be an obvious solution. I was accepted at Oregon State University where my sister Sue was a biology professor. I took a French Business class, but having run an actual business in France, I could have taught it. I took Art History and Gothic Cathedral classes, but I had seen nearly every painting and visited most of the cathedrals. I took a World Geography class, but not only did I know the countries and their capitals, I was pretty familiar with their train schedules.

For the first time in my life, I was pulling straight As, but my new life in the chair was a living hell. I had to learn how to live with chronic abdominal pain, I was battling one urinary tract infection after another, and I rarely went a week without crapping my pants. I had a car with hand controls, but getting in and out of it required disassembling my chair and reassembling it every time I used it. The normal things people think would affect a paraplegic—stairs, bathrooms, curbs—were so far down my list of problems they didn't even register. For a few hours every day I could go to class and feel normal. The rest of the time I just wanted to put a gun to my head.

Then one day, for the first time since my accident, I felt excited about life. Although I hadn't seen them in almost six years, Jeanine and Jackie Couty from Les Avenières remained two of my closest friends. We would call each other over the holidays or whenever one of us had news about old Walibi friends. Over the years, when I talked to Jackie, we spoke as old friends and co-workers but with Jeanine, things were different. Jeanine, the woman who first greeted me by asking me if I'd ever "tasted" French girls, had become my surrogate mother. She didn't have a son, and when I lived in France, she (rightly so) thought I needed mothering. She washed my

167

clothes, questioned my choice of girlfriends, and told me to shape up after long nights at the Platanes. Their home was always open, their table always overflowing with food.

Jeanine called to invite me to her daughter Nadege's wedding. She offered to pay the airfare and all expenses. Nadege was a good friend of mine as well and if it were any other time in my life, I would have jumped at the chance. But this was different. My body was still reeling from the shock of the accident. Hopping on a plane for a quick weekend in France was out of the question.

When I told Jeanine I couldn't come, she didn't back down. "Why don't you come this summer?" she asked.

"That might work," I said. "My school's over in June. I'd love to come over for a week or two."

"A week or two!" she exclaimed, "What are you thinking? Why don't you stay all summer?"

"All summer?"

"Of course!" she said, "all summer!"

I looked at a calendar on the edge of my desk and contemplated the start of summer school. Then a wave of sobriety hit me. I don't have to go to summer school. Why not get back to France! "All summer it is!" I said.

With one short phone call, Jeanine gave me something to live for. I was heading home. Back to good old Les Avenières. The pain and frustration were still there, but for the first time since my accident, I saw a reason to live through it.

I did an Alta Vista search (pre-Google) on travel hints for handicapped people going abroad, but I came up empty. The only person I'd heard of who had traveled abroad in a wheelchair was the National Public Radio correspondent John Hockenberry. I found his email address and wrote to him, but his reply didn't come until the day I left, and it was only a series of questions. I was going to have to figure out international wheelchair travel on my own.

Since there were handicapped people in France, I didn't have to bring things like KY jelly for my catheters, or adult diapers in case I had an infection. I also knew Mr. Petit at the bike shop could help me with wheel spokes or parts if my chair started to break down.

What I was going to bring, however, was a brand-new hand cycle. The Nicolet High School alumni swimmers started a fund to get me back on track. So far I'd only used the money for tuition and putting hand controls in my car. But after trying a hand cycle at a handicap sports fair, I knew it was the toy for me. I bought an 18-speed hand-powered tricycle and we became best friends for the next twenty years.

It was a complicated piece of machinery with a poorly written assembly guide. It took me five hours to construct it, but in the end, I had a brand-new, lightweight hand cycle. I took it out for a couple of short runs and was amazed at what it could do. I could crank it up to 20 mph on the flats, and the brakes were as responsive as any road bike. For the first time since wrecking in September, I was thinking like a bike rider. Climbing was difficult, however, and the three-wheel composition of the bike made descending at high speeds harrowing. On even slight climbs, I was down to the lowest gear, working the pedals as hard as I could. It wasn't the fault of the bike; it's just the nature of the sport. Arms have about 60 percent of the power legs have. In my case, after years of springboard diving and cycling, I had huge thighs and average arms. Even though my thighs had atrophied, there was still a good chunk of heavy muscle mass left. That muscle mass used to propel me over Alpine passes, but now it was all dead weight. Even though I'd been working out in my chair in Corvallis, my arms were not in shape for long rides.

Two days after putting the hand cycle together, I had to tear it apart and put it back in the box. Another drawback of the hand cycle is that, unlike a regular bicycle, it is not easily portable. You can disassemble a bike and put it back together in minutes. The hand cycle took about an hour to take apart—and another three hours to reassemble in France. The wide seat also makes the bike box twice as wide as a regular bike box.

My flight was going through Chicago to Frankfurt, Germany. Before dropping down to Les Avenières, I was going to spend a little time with a couple of Adidas friends, J.D. and Kristina Burress, who had moved to the corporate offices in Herzogenaurach, just a few kilometers from Nuremberg. I'd only flown twice since breaking my back: once on the horrible adventure to RIC right after the accident, and again from Milwaukee to Oregon with my sister Sue. I had no idea what to expect from a solo transcontinental flight. Normally, I like to be the last person on an airplane and the first person off. The less time I spend in airports, the better. But for the rest of my life, I would always be first on and last off. They rolled out the thin aisle chair and strapped me in. But the plane transfer that had been a living nightmare on my previous flight to Chicago wasn't even a nuisance anymore.

There is a major train station underneath the Frankfurt airport so I could catch a train to Nuremberg without much hassle. I called for assistance with my bike box and three German rail workers rushed me through customs and navigated me down to the platforms. They upgraded my second-class ticket to first class and loaded me on a rapid inter-city train for Nuremberg. It was a cold, rainy day, but I was back on European soil, on an honest-to-goodness travel adventure. It had been six years since I'd last seen the tiny, twisted streets of Northern Europe. I could feel my attitude shifting. Just a few months earlier I didn't even want to see the outside of the operating theater.

Kristina met me at the train station with her son, Nicholas, and a one-week-old daughter, Alex. When I had heard Kristina had just given birth, I offered to stay at a hotel, but she and J.D. insisted I stay with them. Kristina's parents had also flown in, so the Burress household was packed. On top of that, their apartment was located on the third floor of a building with no elevator. Lifting me up and down the steps was a horrible chore, but everyone pitched in and we made the best of it. It got difficult one night when J.D. and I drank an aquarium of beer and tried to negotiate the steps ourselves. I pulled on a guardrail for dear life while J.D. gave himself a hernia trying to push. It was a new building, too. In America they never would have been able to build it without ramps and elevators.

I spent four days with the Burresses in Germany, which was capped off by a community fun run sponsored by Adidas and the Turnerschaft Herzogenaurach club. There were runs of 2K, 8K, and 15K. I lined up for the race with a group of school children and raced out of the track area only to discover I had started the wrong race. I was hauling ass with a bunch of sixth graders, until I came up on a sign that said, "2 km runners turn left." They all turned left, and I realized I did the start of the kiddie run. The race organizers were too polite to tell me I was in the wrong race. But my Adidas friends were doubled over in laughter when I rolled back over to their picnic.

Twenty minutes later I toed the line and blasted out of the gate for the 8K race with the Burresses giving me a Bronx cheer. I found a pack of joggers I could keep pace with and cruised in somewhere in the middle of the pack. When it was time for the awards presentation, the club realized they didn't have an official wheelchair competition, so they presented me with a small bathroom cup with the Turnerschaft logo emblazoned on the front. I was an international wheelchair racing champ! The cup still sits proudly on my mantle.

The next day Kristina dropped me off at the Nuremberg Bahnhof, for my long-anticipated train to Les Avenières. I went to get my bike box out of storage, but the concierge was locked, and my train to Lyon pulled out of the station without me. I had tickets to see B.B. King at the Jazz Festival in Vienne (south of Lyon—not Austria) and it looked like it was slipping away.

I found a train to Geneva leaving a half hour later, but it required three transfers, and I would have to call my old comedian friend, Pascal Chanal, and ask him to drive an hour out of his way to pick me up. Within the space of five minutes, I got Chanal on the phone, found someone to open the concierge locker, and arranged to have myself thrown into a luggage car to Geneva. I spent the first two hours in the baggage car before getting a regular seat in Ulm. When I got to the station in Tuttlingen, I only had ten minutes to make my connection to Basel, Switzerland. Unfortunately, nobody in Ulm told them I was coming, and they didn't have the transfer equipment ready for me. Most of the platforms in post–WWII train stations are at the same level as the wagon, but in the older stations, the platforms are at ground level. That left me with a four-foot jump and no legs to do it. I yelled for a conductor to help, but nobody came. A couple passengers helped me and my bike box out of the car, but they all had transfers to make.

The train to Basel was on an adjacent track. I saw the locomotive kick out a puff of steam and prepare to pull out of the station. Finally, an elderly bahnhof worker approached me with a luggage cart and helped me load my box. I pointed to the Basel train, but he pointed at his watch and shook his head, "Nein." "Ja bitte!" I screamed, and I bolted to the end of the platform to catch the attention of the Basel conductor.

The older train stations don't have elevators or ramps and the path between platforms is an inaccessible underground stairway. But, at the far end of each platform is a ramp luggage porters use to haul heavy baggage on carts. I raced 100 meters to the end of the platform with the bahnhof worker dragging my box and yelling "Halt!" I got the attention of the Basel conductor who put his hand out and waved me on. By the time I rolled up the ramp to the Basel platform there were three conductors ready to help me. They lifted my chair into a breezeway between two cars, and a few seconds later my box followed, squeezing me in. I looked out the tiny window in the breezeway and saw the old German bahnhof worker gasping for breath while at the same time reaching into his pocket for a smoke.

I suffered in the cramped breezeway for another two hours until the train pulled into Basel. This time the rail workers were ready for me and the transfer to the Geneva train went smoothly. My new Swiss train had spacious aisles, a delicious dining cart and even a functional handicapped bathroom. The Swiss don't cut corners on anything. They have the most beautiful country on Earth, and they do their best to make sure the beauty extends deeper than the mountains.

The final train took me from rolling hills into high mountains and along vineyards to Lac Leman and Geneva. Chanal was waiting on the platform to pick me up. Chanal and I had written over the years, but he hadn't heard of my accident until I'd called him a few months earlier. He couldn't believe it when I told him, but now he was taking my chair apart, stuffing it into the back of his Citroen, and heading south to Vienne.

The Theatre Antique in Vienne is one of the most spectacular places any musician ever gets to play. The 2,000-year-old Roman amphitheater overlooking the Rhone holds 10,000, but there are no seats, only original stone blocks. Topping off the theater is a medieval castle wall with a towering stone turret. In my four years in France, I'd seen (and bootlegged!) almost every living jazz great from that stage. It was as much a part of my life in France as Chanal was. Having them both in the same place after six long years was an incredible treat.

B.B. King was fresh off a plane from the Chicago Blues Festival and sat for most of his set. He was tired, but his band, most of them members of his extended family, took center stage and showed their stuff. At the end of the night, he got off his chair and finished the show with a flurry of greatest hits. He was twice my age and may have played more shows (300 a year!) than anyone in show business, so I was more than willing to let him work his jet lag off onstage. And, at the glorious Theatre Antique, one could watch Kathy Lee Gifford and have a great time.

The next morning, Chanal drove me along my old bike routes into the Alpine foothills of Isère through La Tour-du-Pin and finally back home to Les Avenières. Jeanine said most of my friends had moved on to Lyon or Grenoble, and I wouldn't recognize a face. But as we drove through town, I recognized at least a dozen faces, and some of them waved frantically when we made eye contact.

We pulled into the Walibi parking lot, and tears welled up in my eyes. Jean Marie Senna, my old show announcer, greeted me at the gate and brilliant memories poured over me. Walibi was the focal point of the greatest years of my life. When I was working at Adidas and money was tight, I wasn't sure if I would ever get back. Now I was back, but I'd gone from the most vital figure in the park to an invalid. I used to be the guy who did arm stand flips from the highest peak in the park. Now I needed help to get through the turnstile.

Chanal and I wheeled over to the haunted house, where Jackie and Jeanine jumped out to greet me. They welcomed me like a prodigal son with kisses and hugs. French people are quick to throw out kisses, but hugs are another thing altogether. Hugs are reserved only for close family members. I'd never been so honored in my life.

Jackie had rebuilt the ticket booth to the haunted house so I could wheel in and work. He opened up a sliding gate, and I took my old position next to Jeanine. We had years of catching up to do, and they needed to know just how immobile I was. When we were sitting in the booth, it all seemed like old times. Jackie and I watched sports, and Jeanine pointed out ridiculously dressed overweight farmers wobbling around the park. We laughed and told stories, and it seemed like absolutely nothing had changed. But when it was time to close up and leave, I turned into a crip again.

Closing time always meant putting on my bike shorts and knocking off 20 kilometers before hitting the Café des Platanes. Now I had to wait for Jackie to pile my chair into his car and drive the three kilometers to their house. I'd fallen into an easy, self-sufficient pattern in Corvallis, but here it was broken, and I felt helpless again. I despise needing help, and I'd put myself in a situation where I needed lots of help all the time.

For the first time since I started planning the trip, the depression returned. I was going to have to go into town and tell my story over and over to old friends listening with crestfallen faces. To the kids of Les Avenières, the divers had been role models and an integral part of the community. While we were there, Les Avenières had international cachet. Now those kids were in high school. Whenever I ran across one of them, they looked at me as if I were a ghost. As great as it was to return, I felt like crying whenever I saw a familiar face.

Jackie and Jeanine could sense my uneasiness, and they went beyond what I could imagine accommodating me. Jackie built two ramps into the house and turned a big closet into an accessible bathroom. Jeanine turned their living room into a bedroom. The fridge was packed with fruit, cheeses, and sausages, and they would get upset whenever I didn't gorge myself.

Their house was located on a ridge high above the village, and the views from my room were spectacular. To the east were the forested white cliffs that shoulder the Rhone and guide it through the Gorges de la Balme until it splits the Chat mountains, the first ridge of the Alps. To the west, I could look across the grande marée up to the rising slopes of Dolomieu, where I used to charge my Cannondale on the way to La Tour-du-Pin.

The problem with those views is they were just that: views, pretty pictures. When I had lived in Les Avenières, every mountain was an invitation to conquer. Now they were nothing more than fodder for my camera lens. I was living right in the middle of my beautiful France, but as close as I was to it, it all seemed even farther away.

That was until Jackie and Jeanine gave me their biggest gift of all. My bike box had been sitting in the train station in Geneva for a week before Jeanine's daughters picked it up and drove it to Les Avenières. When the box showed up, Jackie pulled out the pieces of the hand cycle and put his engineer's mind to the task. Jackie's been riding ever since he could walk and even rode on some tough regional teams. He knows a bicycle as well as any bike mechanic I've ever worked with. He pulled out the directions and said, "What is this shit? How are you supposed to figure it out from this?" I laughed and told him it wasn't a language problem. The directions were for shit, but the bike was great.

It took us all afternoon to assemble the bike, but when it was done, we were pretty damn psyched. Everyone except Jeanine. She thought it was too light and flimsy to take out on regular roads. She wasn't so sure about the brakes because they were on the front wheel—not the back. Jackie took it out for the first spin along the ridge and returned with a big grin on his face. "It's fine," he said. "And you're gonna look like Schwarzenegger after a couple weeks in this thing."

The next morning, I shot the long descent into town then headed east towards the Rhone. I remembered a flat 30K loop that would be a good test without wiping me out on the first day. I felt great on the roads in the valley, but even the slight rise of the Rhone bridges forced me into my lightest gear. By the time I returned to the base of the ascent up to the house, I was cooked. That's when I realized hand cycling is MUCH harder than cycling.

As I started up the mile-long climb, I was dropping one chain ring every two hand rotations. Before I was even at the tough part of the ascent, I was in lowest gear, pushing the handles one rotation at a time. I wasn't even halfway up before I had to stop and shake out my arms. I'd never stopped on a climb before in my life, and I'd never even considered this little ramp a climb before.

When I got to the house, I was so beat I could barely transfer back into my chair. Jeanine laid out lunch, and I inhaled it. I took a shower and a short nap, then wheeled down to Walibi nestled in the valley. Jackie let me into the ticket booth and asked me how it went. After all the work he'd put into it, I was afraid to tell him I didn't think I could tackle my old hills. "It rides great on the flats," I said. "Hills are a bitch."

"First day," he said. "You'll get 'em."

The next day, I went for a longer flat stretch to the north. Even though I was trying to stay along the valley floor I still had some nasty hills. And again, I never considered these roads to be hills before. They were just little bumps on the way to the big climbs. If I hit the hill hard and tried to keep up a tough gear, my arms would scream after just a few hundred yards. But I soon learned if I geared down earlier and kept up a cadence, I could last much longer.

I was about 20 clicks north of Les Avenières and ready to drop a short hill along the Rhone, when a car tried to pass a tractor over a tight lane on a bridge. I was dropping the hill around 45 km/hr when I had to make a sudden swerve to avoid the passing vehicles. I made a sharp turn, but the three-wheeled hand cycle couldn't take those speeds. I veered to the left and got myself up on two wheels. As soon as the third wheel hit the ground, the bike skidded out, then flipped over like a midget racing car.

After a helmet saved my life during the big crash, you would think I wouldn't go anywhere without one, but I wasn't wearing one. There was hardly any traffic on these roads, and I hadn't even owned a helmet when I lived in France. It never occurred to me I could wipe out all by myself and crack my skull open.

Sure enough, I slammed my head into the pavement and woke up a couple seconds later with blood gushing from my skull. The drivers of both cars pulled over and tried to revive me. Like every bike rider who's just been tossed, my first reaction was to get back on the bike. "I'm fine!" I announced and tried to slip back into the seat. As I reached for my legs and tried to put them back in their straps, one of the drivers was horrified, "Oh my god," she said, "you've broken your back! Don't move!"

As I was explaining my back was just fine, another gush of red clouded my vision and I got a splitting headache. "Please, sir," the other driver said, "I think it's best we wait for the paramedics."

I came to my senses and realized I had a concussion and a cut big enough to require a couple stitches. I leaned back on the seat and said, "Yeah, you're probably right. I'll just wait."

The paramedics showed up and took me to the local fire station, which the French also use as emergency medical clinics. They cleaned me up and called a doctor to give me stitches. I called Jackie at the haunted house and he dropped everything to pick me up. The firemen had to drive me to a doctor's house because the doctor was in a big hurry to catch a plane to Brussels. She took one look at me and started chewing me a new one for not wearing a helmet. She took me into a small viewing room next to her kitchen and started stitching me up. It only took her 20 minutes, but the entire time she kept bitching at me for not wearing a helmet and making her late for her flight. I wanted to tell her to shut the hell up and do her job, but she was the one with the needle in her hands, so I just took my medicine.

Jackie showed up and lifted his hand, gesturing he was going to slap me upside the head. "I thought something like this might happen," he said. "You need brakes on those rear wheels if you're going to be taking on these hills. Rear brakes will stop that thing cold."

I laid low the next few days until my headaches subsided. The Tour de France had started, and I wanted to put the bike away, watch the race, and work at the haunted house. What was I thinking, bringing a hand cycle into these hills?

But Jackie would have none of that. One day he came home with two wheels, two sets of brakes, and a couple slabs of iron. While Jeanine and I watched the race, Jackie was on the patio with a welding torch. I thought he was making a cart for his other business (French fast-food carts) but instead he was redesigning my entire bike.

He created a new rear axle with brakes on each wheel, both controlled from the same brake handle. As I rolled around to look at his design, he started to explain, "It's going to be a little bit heavier," he said, "but you'll be able to drop the hills at much higher speeds. If you're braking from the rear like this, there won't be any pressure on that front tire, and you won't swerve at all."

I'd given up, but he hadn't. "Let me try it first," he continued. "There's some kinks to work out."

I was all smiles, but Jeanine wasn't. "That's a death trap, you two!" she said. Jackie paid no attention and kept working.

After a few more trips to the bike shop, the hand cycle was better than ever; albeit ten pounds heavier, making the climbs that much more difficult. I hopped back on the bike and tried out the new braking system. I was able to let the bike drop faster, and when I put on the brakes, the bike would skid in a straight line. Now all I had to do was get a helmet and get in shape.

For the next three weeks, I went for a morning ride and made it back home for the Tour de France coverage. When I felt good, I'd drop down to the park to watch the race at the ticket booth, but more often than not I was pretty dead. I started out at 40K/day, but that increased to 50, then 60, then 70 (42 miles). As my arms got stronger and stronger, I was able to take on a couple of minor climbs. I bought a new copy of the Michelin map I had used when I rode these hills on my Cannondale. Every day I mapped out a

Jackie Couty rebuilding the wheel setup on my hand bike. He thought it was an interesting project—he didn't know he was saving my life.

course and marked the roads with a highlighter. The beauty of riding around Les Avenières was that there were hundreds of low-traffic roads leading to so many incredible vistas that you wanted to take them all. The rig was different, but I still wanted to color in as much of that map as I could.

Along the way I took in more of the passive, rural French life that seemed to assimilate modernity without changing any of its time-honored traditions. Floral-scarfed women rode bicycles with baguettes in their panniers and beret-headed farmers tinkered on tractors in the middle of golden Van Gogh sunflower fields. Each small village had a fountain in front of an ancient church with cafes, tabacs, and boulangeries crowding tightly cornered streets. I never had to go more than 10 kilometers between villages, but I rarely came upon a stoplight or stop sign. I kept riding and France seemed to flow around me like a river. I was drowning in it and I didn't want a lifeguard.

By the time Jan Ullrich had won the Tour de France in late July, I'd eaten up all the flat roads and had to make a choice. I could either stretch out my flat runs towards Lyon or point my bike to the east and start taking on some of the bigger climbs. I'd been riding for almost a month, and I was getting better and better at climbing the home ridge at the end of the day. When I first got to Les Avenières, I couldn't make it up without stopping; now I could make it without dropping into the lowest gear. I decided it was time to hit the big hills.

Over the next few weeks, I went for a couple of the bigger hills around town. If I found a good rhythm, I'd make it to the top. Climbs that used to take 20 minutes on the Cannondale would take over an hour on the hand cycle. But I'd get there.

The biggest climb in the immediate neighborhood was to the water tower overlooking the citadel town of Dolomieu. The road to the top was a 20K ride with the last seven kilometers rising 500 meters. It was 500 meters above the valley floor, but there were two huge dips leading up to the summit, putting on an additional 150 meters of climbing. It was a demanding climb on two strong legs. In the hand cycle, it was going to be a bitch.

I took off from the house with the water tower of Dolomieu far off in the distance. I slowly rode through Les Avenières, conserving all my energy for the climb. It was a sweltering day, and I made sure I was well-hydrated, but sweat began dripping into my eyes before I got to the base of the climb. I made my way up to the first dip three clicks into the climb, then shot into a small valley. The angle of the hill coming out of the valley was more severe than the earlier part of the climb, but I stuck to my plan and dug myself out. Five clicks into the climb I dropped into the second valley and again had to grind myself out of a big hole. I kept to my rhythm, and soon enough, the city was in sight. During the climb, I had Patrick Chêne, the Tour de France announcer, calling my progress in my head: "He's just passed under the three-kilometer banner—the city's in sight—he can see the water tower—this will be his greatest victory ever!"

As I wound through the tight switchbacks that slithered through the town, I imagined the shopkeepers and cafe dwellers cheering me on. Everybody gave me strange looks as I ground up the terrain in front of their homes, but only the town drunk, whom I recognized from seven years earlier, actually cheered. Once through town, the last passage was lined with farm fences and cattle. In my head, every curious stare from a cow turned into a roar from a would-be spectator.

I crested the hill at the water tower, and the giant sunflowers at the summit greeted me with a hero's welcome. I powered over a small flat then started to drop down into La Tour-du-Pin. I was flying at 60 km/hr, and my arms weren't even burning. My training was dead-on for the climb, and I was reaping its rewards. As I floated down the descent with Mount Blanc off in the distance, I felt like I was in a travelogue. I was living out a fantasy.

For the first time since the accident a year earlier, I felt alive. For the first time since September, I could feel the suicidal thoughts slipping into the abyss. I wanted to scream down Alpine roads on a bike more than I wanted death. It was a huge pain in the ass to get to where I was, but I wanted to get there as often as I could. I wanted to think of climbing and descending more than I wanted to think of putting a gun to my head. That was Jackie and Jeanine's gift to me. They gave me the gift of hope and life. A truck on Sandy Boulevard had taken that away, but as I was dropping into La Tour-du-Pin, hope and life were given back to me. I would live the rest of my life forever in the debt of Jackie and Jeanine Couty.

Before I left France, I had one last thing to accomplish. Now that I'd proved to myself I was in good enough shape to beat Dolomieu, I had to go out and tackle a bigger climb on a longer run. A week later, I packed a lunch and took off into the higher hills on the St. Benoit Mountains northeast of Les Avenières. In order to get to the highest road on the mountain, I had to make two separate climbs, both slightly easier than the Dolomieu climb.

The climb to the town of Prémeyzel was cut into the side of a Rhône cliff and slithered in and out of tunnels passing a three-stage waterfall. I skirted behind Prémeyzel and started on the second climb to the hamlet of Conzieu near the summit of Benoît. By this time, my arms were smooth metallic crankshafts, and I took in the two hours of climbing without much suffering. I'd already drained two water bottles, so I stopped at the town fountain in Conzieu and loaded up for the descent.

I was way up in the air, and I knew that I'd be gliding for a long time no matter what direction I took. I dropped through the town of Contrevoz, then joined the Rhône and flew for nearly 30 kilometers into Ambérieu. It was effortless pedaling with dazzling Alpine vistas in every direction. A few months earlier I couldn't find a reason to live, but for the second time in a week I was thinking life couldn't get much better.

Ambérieu is a fairly big town and not a great place to relax. I was running out of gas, but I knew of a nice place to stop in Lagnieu, just 15 clicks down the road. I made it to Lagnieu on an empty tank and devoured a baguette crammed full of ham and cheese. I soaked myself with water from the town fountain, then filled my water bottles and headed south towards the medieval town of Crémieu. The road was an open, flat uphill with hay fields on both sides. The side wind was piercing out of the south, making the flat ride more difficult than the climbs earlier in the day. Whereas sweat had poured out of my body on the climbs, hard salt plastered my face during the wind-swept flats.

By the time I hit Crémieu two hours later, I'd again drained my water and was hungry. I rolled up to a cafe in an ancient Roman market and asked them if they could make me a ham sandwich. The bartender gave it to me and refused my money. I thanked him and continued up a fairly steep climb towards the town of Trept. From Trept I could see far into the distance, and I knew I was up for a well-deserved descent. I shook out my arms and floated 20 kilometers into the town of Morestel, only 15 kilometers from Les Avenières. I was tired, but my arms felt like they had some more pedaling in them. Instead of heading to Les Avenières, I took a circular route back to Jackie and Jeanine's house. The wind was with me, and I doubled my speed from the wind-blown flats—nearly 20 mph.

My brain was fried and my arms were toast. It was getting towards 7:00 at night, and I'd been gone since 9:30 in the morning. I knew Jeanine would start to worry, so I bucked up and dug into the last few kilometers. I powered up the final hill, and then turned into the driveway to see Jeanine sitting on the porch.

"Hurry up," she said. "We're going out to dinner. And where the hell have you been?"

I looked down at my bike computer and poked at the button that would give me the final tally. I scrolled through the data until I got to the distance function. It read 164 kilometers—102 miles. Less than a year after my accident, I knocked off an Alpine century in a hand cycle. Those mountains weren't just pretty pictures anymore. I owned them again.

●　●　●　●　●　●　●　●　●　●　●　●　●

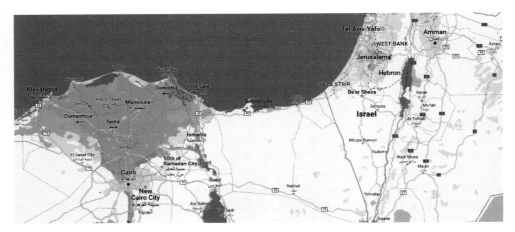

The Holy Lands

Holy Roller

Now that I'd gone back and conquered my section of the French Alps, I felt the full force of the Bridge to Venice coming back to me. The rules that pushed me through five continents and God knows how many crazy dives were the same rules I needed to rebuild my life in the wheelchair.

I had frequent flier miles to burn, and I could either use them back in the States or go somewhere from Europe. I couldn't just go home after conquering Les Avenières. As nervous as I was before I left, in retrospect it was about as soft an international landing as I could have hoped for. The Bridge to Venice said I had to push as far as I could go. I had to see if I could take on a developing country by myself in a wheelchair. The Middle East was just a stone's throw away, so it was an easy choice. I'd read plenty about Israel, and everyone needs to see the Egyptian pyramids before they die. But going to places I'd never been with nobody to meet me on the other side would have its challenges.

Before heading to the Middle East, I spent a week visiting cathedrals and museums in Florence and Siena with my friend, Pat. We were in our 30s, and we both loved this stuff, so we toured like two 70-year-old grandmas. I headed up north to Frankfurt where I spent a night kegeln (German bowling) with another old friend, Lawrence. The following morning, Lawrence dropped me off at the airport and I was off for Tel Aviv. After a five-hour flight on which we were serenaded the entire trip by an Israeli school group, the plane landed at Ben Gurion Airport. I knew I was going to be the last one off the plane, but the wait for assistance was ridiculous. The crew forgot to arrange for an aisle chair or ground transportation. I spent an hour on the plane with two elderly women waiting for chairs and a lift to the tarmac. A crewmember came along every five minutes until they became too embarrassed to look at me.

The string on my bag of patience had been loosened but was resecured with the arrival of the aisle chair and a lift to the concourse. A week earlier, I had tried to reserve a room at the Youth Hostel, the only accessible guesthouse in Jerusalem. I wanted to stay in a guesthouse not so much because it was cheap, but because I wanted to hang out with travelers as opposed to businessmen. They told me to call on my arrival to insure the reservation. I changed money, bought a phone card, and called the hostel to confirm my arrival.

"Hello, I'm Mr. Haig," I said. "The guy in the wheelchair who reserved the handicapped room."

"I'm sorry," the receptionist responded. "We had to give your room up. We've had people waiting since noon."

"You had someone in a chair waiting for that room since noon?" I asked.

"No, they were just students—but how could we know that you would show up?"

"But I told you I might be a little late. I'm not that late—it's only an hour after I said I'd call."

"I'm sorry sir, but this is a travelers' hostel, not a luxury hotel."

"Hey, ask the students if they'll move to another hostel, I'll pay for their room if they do." (it was only $10 a night.) "You guys have the only accessible room in Jerusalem…"

The receptionist hung up on me.

I went to a booking agency at the airport and they called five hotels, but nobody would take me. I looked in my Lonely Planet guide and found a bunch of guesthouses and hotels that weren't on the agency's list. I showed them the list, but they refused to call them, saying they were in East (Arab) Jerusalem. I told them I'd give it a shot. They handed me the phone and I hit pay dirt on my first call.

An American voice was on the other end. It was Homer, the caretaker of the Faisal Crusader Hostel just outside of the Old City. Homer was a Chicago Palestinian who assured me a wheelchair would be no trouble. I asked him if he had an elevator, and he told me not to worry. I hit the airport bathroom then found a minibus to the Damascus Gate in the Old City.

The drive to Jerusalem at sunset was everything I'd anticipated. I'd been reading about Israel all summer long, and the rugged, starched white terrain of the Bible came to life right in front of me. The further the sun dropped, the more the hills absorbed its penetrating red-orange glow. Wispy clouds in the desert sky sucked up the radiant light, leaving a psychedelic thunder dome for the bus to slither through.

Upon entering Jerusalem, I was taken aback by the saturation of Hassidic Jews, as well as the severity of the hills upon which the city has developed. When my books spoke of hills, I was thinking of the rolling hills of East Portland. But Jerusalem's hills were closer to the steep rises of San Francisco.

I was glad I'd piled up all those miles on my hand cycle, because it was going to be a tough week. The bus driver lived near the Damascus Gate on the east side of town and told me he would drop me off last. I was in Jerusalem's trance, and for all I cared, he could have driven me around all night.

The Faisal Crusader guesthouse was just across the street from the Damascus Gate to the Old City. The outdoor terrace at the Faisal hosted a hopping, lively cafe, but it was situated on the second floor. I tossed a couple of rocks up to announce my presence and was met by four hardened faces rushing to the edge of the balcony with rocks in their hands. Mistake No. 1: Never throw rocks in Jerusalem.

Homer saw me in the chair and called off his lions. The four of them came down to the front door and escorted me in.

"Where's the elevator?" I asked.

They laughed, rolled up their sleeves and pointed to their sizable biceps. There was no elevator, but Homer and his friends were powerlifters. They grabbed the corners of my chair and hoisted me up 24 steps to the Faisal. I dumped my bag off, and then joined them in the cafe for a beer and a couple of tokes off their apple hookah.

The Faisal was a working hostel where travelers found jobs and stayed for a couple of months at a time. Just as I was about to crash, a group of French and South African construction workers arrived and lit up the place. It was impossible to sleep in the congested dorm room that housed 16 people. I joined in the revelry until 4:00 a.m. when the lights finally went out. That was the schedule everyone kept, so it seemed reasonable to join in. I had no schedule at all.

I woke up at 10:00 and made my way into the shower room. What isn't a concern for an able-bodied person was a major worry for me. If I was going to stay healthy, I needed a place where I could sit on the toilet for an hour and get cleaned up afterward. Unbelievably, the Faisal had a private bath-shower with a door just wide enough to fit my chair. I did my duty while reading the Lonely Planet and planning my day. Except for a rude South African (who apologized profusely afterward), I was left alone. The biggest worry I had before taking off from Europe was finding an accessible bathroom. Aside from the 24 steps I had to negotiate each day, my worries were washed away.

After an egg and cheese sandwich, Homer and his assistant, David, carried me down the two flights of stairs, and I was on my way. My first task was to call the Israeli handicapped organization listed in the Lonely Planet guide. I'd gotten the impression from NPR correspondent John Hockenberry's autobiography that Jerusalem was a fairly accessible city. He said that due to the war, there were plenty of handicapped people. The hospitals were second to none, he'd written, and the sight of a young person in a wheelchair was nothing new to the average citizen of Jerusalem. The corollary, I assumed, was a fleet of handicapped buses along with ramps and elevators in the buildings. It couldn't have been further from the truth.

When I called the handicapped service, I received much the same treatment that I'd gotten from the youth hostel the day before. I asked if they had a list of accessible buses and the young female voice on the opposite end laughed at me. "This is Jerusalem," she scoffed, "not Chicago."

I told her I was just outside the old city and wanted to know where I could find the handicapped entrance to the Dome of the Rock. "Dome of the Rock?" she responded, "What is Dome of the Rock?"

The Dome of the Rock is the symbol of Jerusalem. It would be the same as asking someone in DC for directions to the Washington Monument. I assumed she didn't understand my English, so I repeated the question speeking ver-ee slow-lee.

"Where—are—the—wheel—chair—ramps—to—the—Dome—of—the—Rock?"

"What is this?" she said, "I don't understand."

"Dome of the Rock," I repeated, "The Temple Mount—The Western Wall…"

"I don't understand," she interrupted, "What is this you are talking of?"

"Look, I said I'm in a wheelchair and I'd like to get to the Dome of the Rock—how the hell do I get there without going through any steps?"

She sensed my anger and got a kick out of continuing, "Dome of the Rock? I have never heard of Dome of the Rock."

Assuming I'd gotten a wrong number, I hung up and called again. It wasn't a wrong number. They didn't want to offer their services to tourists—especially those who didn't speak Hebrew.

I was on my own so I decided to enter the Damascus Gate and see how far I could get. I saw people pushing carts through the gate, so I reasoned a wheelchair wouldn't be much different. I had a map of the old city showing several gates leading to the Temple Mount and the Dome of the Rock. The Dome is one of the biggest tourist destinations on Earth. One of those gates had to be accessible.

I dodged through a bewildering traffic maze on Suleiman Street across from the Faisal and rolled down a long stone ramp leading to the Damascus Gate. The Old City is encased in a medieval wall with only a few entrances. The Damascus Gate is the biggest and most ornate entrance, with a ramp leading to a lowered drawbridge. Hovering in a window above the doorway was one of the ever-present, armed Israeli guards. I crossed the gate with a crowd of veiled women, Arab men in thobe gowns, teenage Israeli girls wearing halter-tops, and wealthy American tourists dressed in their finest Miami Beach geriatric wear. I bumped down a step, then looked back to see if the step was low enough to hop over on the way back. It was about an eight-inch step, which is just an inch or two over my limit. I made a mental note that I would need some help on the way out.

The flow of people and carts pushed me through the gate into the old city. I tried to stop and take some pictures, but the crowd wouldn't allow it. They pushed like cattle until we came upon another curb, this one dropping not onto a flat surface but a ramp. I had no choice but to pop into a wheelie, drop the curb, and then catch myself before shooting down the incline. I'd been practicing wheelies for months, but this stretch of terrain was the ultimate test. I had to jump off one incline onto another incline six inches below, all while still holding my wheelie. At the angle I was on, if I'd lost my wheelie I would throw forward and go hurtling into the crowd, possibly breaking my wrist on the fall. For the next 200 feet, I stayed balanced on my two wheels while descending from ramp to ramp with six- to eight-inch drop-offs between them.

Dropping the ramps from the Damascus Gate was like shooting a black diamond ski run at Whistler. People were coming at me from all directions. An Arab pushing a cart stuck his front wheel right up against the back of my chair and tried to push me along. I turned to tell the guy to chill, but he snarled and motioned me on. The final 20 feet were the steepest of the set. They were two 30-degree declines with a 10-inch drop in between. I slipped off my grip on the final section and caught myself only a few inches from a face plant. It was one of the greatest athletic achievements of my life. The Arab with the cart blew by waving his fist in the air.

Once on solid ground, I passed by an army of vendors to get to the first bottle of water I could find. It was over 100 degrees, and I hadn't had a drink all day. I passed by a coffee house and saw an American woman and a French guy who had been up late with me at the Faisal. I sat down with them, and they ordered up some tea and a big pile of apple shish to fire up on the hookah.

"Shish" isn't hashish, opium, or anything psychoactive. In this case, it was strips of dried apple with burning coals placed on top of them. I sucked through the stem of the hookah and let the smooth cool smoke fill my lungs. The French guy could barely speak any English, but he was doing his best to hit on the American. I let him struggle for a while but soon enough it got annoying. I cut him off and told him he could speak to me in French if it was easier. A big sigh of relief passed over him, and he rattled away in French for fifteen minutes. He didn't want to talk about the wonders of the Old City; he just wanted to use me to get into the American's pants.

I passed on the opportunity to play Cyrano and continued on the Beit Habad path into the Christian Quarter of the Old City. The Old City is divided into quarters: the Muslim Quarter, the Christian Quarter, the Jewish Quarter and the Armenian Quarter. The Beit Habad isn't a road, but a semi-paved path lined with shops, covered overhead by large sheets stretched across the rooftops. The trail opened up at The Church of the Holy Sepulchre, where I stopped to take a few photos. Although discredited by scholars, legend has it that the Church of the Holy Sepulchre was built on top of Golgotha, the place where Christ was crucified. Not half a mile away was the Dome of the Rock, the site from which Muhammad was said to have ascended to heaven. That temple is supported by the Western Wall, or the Wailing Wall, the most sacred landmark in all of Judaism. If there was any wonder what the fighting is about, all anyone needs to do is walk a few blocks in the Old City and it becomes apparent.

I followed my map to a small alley that would take me to Herod's Gate, one of seven entrances to the Temple Mount. My map showed a path, but what it didn't show were the hundred long steps leading to the gate. I knew it was close to closing time and I had to hurry. I decided to risk hopping down the stairs assuming there would have to be an easy way out. I couldn't imagine millions of elderly tourists visiting the site every year without there being a ramp.

One by one I lined up and hopped the steps until I came to a small closed corridor just in front of Herod's Gate on the western side of the complex. A soldier guarded the portal where tourists entered.

"Four o'clock," he said. "Gate is closed."

"Quatre heure," I protested. (I'd decided to speak French as a matter of habit and not advertise that I was American.) "Mais j'ai toujours quinze minutes (but I still have 15 minutes)?" At this point, I wasn't going to try to take in the Dome of the Rock in 15 minutes—I just wanted to find a way out.

"Quatre heure," he repeated. "Revenez demain [come back tomorrow]."

In front of the Dome of the Rock in Jerusalem; a completely inaccessible site back in '97.

"S'il vous plaît," I said, "Je suis en fauteuil—je n'arriverais jamais de monter ces marches (Please sir, I'm in a wheelchair, I'll never be able to climb back up these steps)."

"Revenez demain," he said. With that he stepped through the portal and locked it behind him. I pounded on the door but there was no answer. I screamed through the small window in the portal, but again nobody came. I was screwed. There was no way I could get up one of the steps, let alone dozens of them.

After ten minutes of debating whether I should crawl back up the stairs, three Palestinian school kids chased a soccer ball down the stairs and saw me sitting there.

"Hey mister," one said. "You need some help?"

"Yeah," I said, breaking my French code, "do you think you guys could help me up?"

"Sure," he said. "20 shekels each" (about $5 US).

"I'll give you each one American dollar," I countered. In any other country that would have been a lock, but not in Israel. These kids knew the exchange rate.

"You're in bad shape," the leader said. "Five US apiece!"

Just then a skinny 40-year-old Palestinian man with a thin mustache and Western dress came down the stairs shooing the children away.

"I'm sorry," he said. "I'll help you up." He chased off the children and grabbed the back of my chair. "I have an old uncle, I do this thing all the time."

"Fucking Israelis," he said. "My name is Abdul. I'm a tourist guide here in Jerusalem. I know all the shortcuts."

Abdul helped me up about half the stairs, and then took me through a back alley up and down another few flights of stairs. We emerged from the bowels of the Old City onto the Via Dolorosa where he showed me one of the original Stations of the Cross, the monumental stopping points along Christ's last walk. He asked me if I wanted my picture taken. I handed him my camera and he took a picture of me in front of a carving of an ancient Jew handing Jesus water. He handed back my camera and I offered him my most sincere thanks for helping me out.

"No problem," he said, holding onto my chair. "No problem" are the first words any traveler learns in any language. Roughly translated it means, "You're in big trouble."

"No problem," he repeated, "Now being a tourist guide I do expect to be paid for my services. You did take me away from my job for a half an hour."

If he had said he was a little short of cash I would have bucked up. But this wasn't my first time in the Middle East, and I knew a con when I heard one. I looked around and sure enough he was surrounded by five Arab goons. They were going to take whatever cash I had on me. I was on their turf, and I didn't have a way out.

"Hey, my poor American friend," he said, "I can see you are a student. I charge adults 200 US dollars. For you, 100 is plenty."

I looked for an out, but there was none. "Listen, asshole," I said. "I've been in this chair for a year and you're the first scumbag who's ever tried to take advantage of me." Just then I felt a tug on my backpack. If they grabbed my pack with my meds and catheters I would be in deep shit. I reached down into my money pouch and pulled out a 100-shekel note—about $20. I threw it on the ground and tried to turn away. The man behind me grabbed my chair and made me face Abdul.

"Listen you dumb fuck piece of shit American," he said, "you are in Jerusalem. This is my fucking city and my fucking country. You're lucky I don't gash your throat right here. Now get the fuck out, you pathetic crippled piece of crap."

I had a pile of words ready for him, but I'd already said enough, and I didn't want them to rifle through my bag. I turned around, free from his henchman, and wheeled through the dust towards St. Stephens Gate on the east side of the Old City. They followed me for a few minutes then disappeared as I came upon a group of soldiers drinking tea. Ripped off again. Welcome back to the Middle East.

When I got back to the Faisal, I told Homer and his friends what had happened. They told me they would take me back into the Old City in the morning and get my money back. I told them the last thing I wanted to do was start a gang war in Jerusalem. Homer slammed his fist on the table.

"I hate when my people do this shit!" he said. "They fuck it up for the rest of us trying to do business—and even you in a wheelchair! And always in the name of Allah. In the end Allah will judge. And he is not blind." He went back into his kitchen and came out with a beer and some chips. "These are from the real Palestinian people," he said. "We are not thieves." I was inclined to believe Homer, but Jerusalem wasn't offering the best examples of Palestinian or Israeli hospitality. There's just too much hate in that city and too many people with major issues.

Aaron, a 25-year-old San Franciscan taking a break from studying Arabic in Tunisia, sat down with us and told me if I wanted to see real Palestinian culture, I should join him in the morning on a day trip to Hebron. All I'd ever heard about Hebron were reports of violent Palestinians counteracting Israeli rubber bullet attacks with rocks, burning tires, and Molotov cocktails. I thought Bethlehem might be more my speed. But when we turned on the TV, they announced Bethlehem was closed—because Palestinians were counteracting Israeli rubber bullet attacks with rocks, burning tires, and Molotov cocktails.

In the morning, Homer and Aaron helped me down the stairs where we found a van full of Palestinian women going to the market in Hebron. A thin Palestinian bus driver wearing a red-and-white shemagh took one look at me and told Aaron he couldn't take me. I told Aaron I could easily climb aboard and they could throw my chair on top. The van driver shrugged his head, and then agreed. I opened the door to the front seat and tried to climb aboard, but the driver ran over and stopped me. He spoke to Aaron, who looked at me and said, "You have to go to the back of the van, that seat is taken."

I opened the sliding side door to the van, got out of my chair, slid along the floor to the rear bench and hoisted myself up. In the West, nobody would ever let a handicapped person slide along a dirty floor, but this was Jerusalem. Sympathy just isn't part of the zeitgeist. ("You think you've got problems? Let me tell you about my two dead uncles and three maimed sons.") Seconds after I pulled myself up on the back bench, my chair was handed to me in three pieces. I spent the hour-long ride smashed between Aaron, the pieces of my chair, and one of the nastiest smelling human beings I've ever put a nostril to.

The windows on the van worked, so the pitted-out, festering onion body odor stench from my neighbor wafted behind me. After leaving the city limits of Jerusalem, we came upon an armed border check and were issued day visas to venture into the Palestinian West Bank. For an hour, we rolled along ancient terraced fields, passing rundown Palestinian villages and brand-new Israeli settlements.

As the van pulled into Hebron, the modern feel of Jerusalem vanished, and I saw and smelled the same kind of disheveled, impoverished city streets I'd seen in India six years earlier. Black exhaust poured out of vehicles right into the open windows of homes and stores. Trash lined the streets, which were bordered by open sewers. A spider web of power lines crisscrossed overhead between crumbling buildings. Fenced-in boulevards built on top of black and white striped curbs led to guard stations manned by beady-eyed soldiers.

Aaron helped put my chair together at the bus stop where, just like every impoverished city in Asia, our white faces meant only one thing: dollar bills. Aaron's Arabic got us through the first onslaught of young street hawkers, and soon enough we found the central marketplace. "Here's the deal with these people," Aaron said, "don't look at their forward behavior as being pushy. For the most part, they're just surprised to see you and want to talk. We're not in any hurry. You might as well just sit and talk with them."

We wound our way through an open market with shops selling everything from shoes and toys to fruit and rebar. As the road narrowed, the market flowed into a tunnel enclosed at first by reams of fabric and finally by a cement ceiling. It was cooler inside the tunnel, and that's where we found a grotesque display of skinned goats, cows, and even a flayed camel. The raw meat was covered with flies, but that didn't stop the shop owner from doing a brisk business. As I passed, he saw my gag reflex and shouted, "Camel good! I cook good for you!"

I smiled and said, "No thanks," and he and his two workers bent over in knee-slapping laughter. The tunnel slimmed down to a dark walkway leading to the back of the market. At the end of the tunnel was the Al-Haram Mosque, which locals claim is the birthplace of Abraham and even Adam. Dozens of stairs led to the entrance, so I told Aaron he should go on and I would roll around the perimeter and take pictures.

I rolled down the street to get a wide shot of the mosque when a squadron of Israeli storm troopers came screaming down the road with their sirens blaring. I ducked behind a fence and whipped out my camera ready to take a picture of whatever was going down. I looked at the far end of the street expecting to see a bunch of Palestinian youths in full riot mode, but nothing was happening. The storm troopers, carrying rifles and wearing full riot gear, bolted from their van and began to take the street one telephone pole at a time. The lead group scurried up to a front position, then looked back and waved on the followers. It looked like they were going to storm the mosque, and I was worried for Aaron's life. Suddenly they pulled their rifles off their backs and began firing rounds into the middle of the street.

But they were rounds of blanks. I was ready to take the most dramatic pictures I'd ever taken, but instead I was watching a training exercise. I hid my camera, hoping they hadn't seen it. If they had seen me taking pictures, they would have grabbed my roll of film that still had great shots of the Swiss Alps on it. When Aaron came out of the mosque, I told him what I'd just seen, and he very nonchalantly said, "Yeah, those raids are fucking noisy, aren't they?"

We turned back into the market and looked for a place to sit down for lunch. On the way I saw a 60-year-old Arab in a new sporty wheelchair. I asked him if he got the chair in Hebron, and he said, "My brother lives in Jersey." When I asked him what most Palestinians use for wheelchairs, he told me, "Most of them sit inside in a rocking chair and do nothing. Being handicapped is bad luck in this country." It's not good luck in any country, but living in the West Bank in a wheelchair would be a nightmare.

I needed to pee but there were no public bathrooms in sight. There were stairs everywhere, and I'm sure any bathroom around wouldn't be clean or accessible. Instead of searching one out, I found an empty alleyway, cleaned my hands with baby wipes, and cathed myself behind a dumpster. My urologist back in Portland would have died if he'd known I did that.

I came back into the market to find Aaron sitting down to tea with an elderly Arab. I joined them, and the three of us had a long talk about healthcare in America and Palestine. Before long the tea turned into a full-blown lunch, and we were served a couple of kabobs and figs. We offered to pay, but the man refused. He also told his son to come over and fix one of the handles on the back of my chair that had wiggled loose. I transferred onto a bench, and the man wheeled my chair into his shop just across the street. After my experience from the day before, I was a bit nervous giving my sole means of transport to a stranger, but then again, what would the man do with a stranded guy with a broken back sitting in his restaurant? In a couple of minutes, the son returned with my handle soldered into place.

After lunch we navigated back to the bus stop and found a van going back to the Damascus Gate. Once again, I was ushered into the back seat and spent the ride with my chair on my lap. There was a long line of buses at the border crossing and the guards were very thorough in their search. I'd been talking to a Palestinian businessman most of the way back to Jerusalem, but when the Israeli guards looked at his passport, they put him up on the hood, cuffed him and threw him into a paddy wagon. I have no idea what the guy was up to, and I didn't want the guards to know I was talking to him. The guards pulled my chair out and tapped all the tubes to make sure there was nothing hidden in them.

Two hours later, back in shiny West Jerusalem, I was eating an ice cream cone when traffic was halted on the street in front of me. A bomb squad rolled onto the scene, and a heavily padded soldier walked out of a shop carrying a small garbage can. For the second time in one day, I pulled out my camera thinking I was going to get a *New York Times* front-page photo (no cell phone cameras yet). The soldier tossed the can into a six-foot diameter bomb-squelching sphere, and a small explosion was muffled inside. I thought I was in the middle of a big news story, but when I looked around nobody on the street was nervous or even concerned—they were just annoyed. The bomb was holding up traffic. I raced back to the Faisal and told everyone what I'd just seen. The travelers were a bit shocked, but not Homer. He told me that the bomb squad detonates around 50 bombs a month. I'd been in Jerusalem for two days, and I'd been held up, caught in the middle of a SWAT team practice, and witnessed a bomb detonation. None of it surprised anyone.

I spent a week around Jerusalem and never once felt normal or comfortable. The museums and historical exhibits were the envy of any city in the world, but tension was ever-present and the paranoia that accompanies it was just.

I grabbed a bus to Tel Aviv, and when I arrived at the Ben Yehuda Hostel (an accessible hostel that kept my reservation), I read that two suicide bombers dressed as old Arab women sat next to two Israeli school children in the Jaffa Market and blew them to pieces. The day before I had eaten lunch at a bench not 50 feet from where it happened.

Tel Aviv, although nowhere near as interesting as Jerusalem, was much easier to enjoy. The beach stretches along the entire length of the city, and I couldn't go more than three pushes without passing some of the most beautiful women I'd ever seen. I needed a few days to get an Egyptian visa and arrange my travel to Egypt, so I found a pub along the strand, and Mulligans became my home for a few days. It proved to be a great place to find out what was going on in Tel Aviv and where to find the best travel deals. In between playing dozens of racks of snooker, I found a cheap bus across the Sinai and an accessible hotel in Cairo.

Nobody drives across the Sinai during the day, so at sunset of my last day in Tel Aviv, I threw down one last pint at Mulligan's and climbed aboard an air-conditioned bus to Cairo. The bus driver let me spread out across the first two seats, so I had a great view of the Mediterranean as we pulled out of town. A few hours later, we skirted the Gaza Strip and came to the Egyptian frontier. The bus driver helped me back into my chair, and I rolled into the customs office for one of the biggest security shakedowns of my life. The guards couldn't believe I was traveling by myself with nobody to see at the other end. I thought wanting to see the Pyramids was justification enough, but they were convinced I had something else up my sleeve. They made me get out of my chair, and they tapped each tube with an iron bar, listening for a non-hollow sound. I was in another room showing them my travel books and return tickets, trying to explain to them I was a simple tourist.

After a two-hour interrogation, they let me through and I rolled back to a bus full of people waiting for me to board. I apologized to everyone, but nobody was put off by the delay. It was par for the course when traveling in the Middle East.

We took off across the Sinai escorted by Egyptian jeeps in front and behind us. I thought they were just accompanying us to the highway, but they crossed the entire Sinai with us. It was a crystal-clear night, and in the middle of the desert, the only source of light was the Milky Way. I'd never seen stars like that anywhere on Earth.

The sun rose outside of the Suez crossing in Qantara, and the urban squalor of Cairo crept up on us. We passed thousands of people waking up, saying their prayers, and making their way to work or school. The closer we got to the city, the dirtier and dustier it became.

The center of Cairo was a gigantic grit bowl with plenty of activity, but nowhere near the energy of Paris or New York. I sat with a German traveler on the bus, and he told me the only way to get around Cairo was to get to know the subway system. It was cheap, and it goes a few blocks from anywhere in the city. As I crawled off the bus and got back in my chair, I followed everyone on the bus to the subway terminal. But, as I expected, there were stairs to the platforms. While the rest of the bus riders disappeared underground, I pulled out a map and tried to figure out where my hotel was.

When I called the hotel and asked them for directions, they told me they were full and they never got the reservation, which had been set up by the bus company in Tel Aviv. I was looking a little desperate when two other passengers from the bus came up behind me and asked me if I had a place to stay. They were homeless just like me. Together the three of us hailed a cab and we looked for hotels in the Lonely Planet Egypt guide.

There were plenty of rooms available, only they were up a few floors with no elevators. After driving around for an hour, my two new friends, Christian, a college student from Berlin, and Vasilly, a friend of his from Cyprus, told me we would take a room at the next place we stopped, regardless of how many floors they had to carry me. Luckily the next place, the Gresham

Hotel, only had eight stairs leading up to the foyer. Our rooms were on the fifth floor, but the building guard said he had an elevator. Unfortunately, the elevator door was so tight I had to pull off one of my wheels while either Christian or Vasilly held the back of my chair and pushed me in. The two of them were absolute troopers, and I felt guilty for slowing them down. They insisted it made their trip more interesting—and nobody in Cairo is in a hurry.

None of us slept on the bus, so after a quick lunch, we fell fast asleep. When I woke, Vasilly had already been on a walk and had scored some hash on the street. We rolled up a couple of big spleefs and prepared to take on the Pyramids freshly spiced. After another round of getting me into the elevator and lifting me down the stairs, we hailed a cab and navigated rush hour traffic south of the city to the Giza Plateau. We lit up in the cab and passed the spleef, with even the driver taking his turn. I asked the driver what the penalty was for hash in Cairo.

"For me, nothing," he said. "For you? Just pay the policeman 10 US dollars."

Over the next few days, I never went anywhere without a waft of secondary hash smoke filling up my nose. It was as ubiquitous in Egypt as the sands of the Sahara.

As we approached Giza, our eyes darted across the landscape looking for our first glimpse of the Pyramids. We turned a corner just inside the city of Giza, and the tip of Cheops peeked out above a pale yellow apartment complex. It disappeared as soon as I pointed to it, but the closer we got the more flashes we got. By the time we got to the plateau, we were so excited we forgot to pay the driver. We started walking towards them like lemmings to the sea when our patient driver honked his horn and shrugged his shoulders. Christian ran back and paid him, then we set our sights on the eye candy of the Sphinx and the Great Pyramids.

At first glance they seemed rather small, but I didn't realize how far away we were. Perfect structures tend to deceive the eye, as you can't differentiate a 500-foot pyramid from a 50-foot pyramid at a distance. But the pyramids grew larger with each approaching step. Those steps were easy for Christian and Vasilly, but next to impossible for me. My wheels were buried in sand and I couldn't move. Once again, they bucked up and helped me through the desert to a ramp that took us above the Sphinx.

We tried to take in the grandeur of the world's greatest monument, but souvenir hawkers and tour guides were on us like a Portland rain. We tried

Posing with a long-lost relative on the Giza Plateau.

to shoo them away, but as soon as one left, another one came. It was getting close to sunset, and we wanted to take in as much of the complex as we could, so we caved in and rented a couple of camels. I hopped into a small carriage with Vasilly while Christian rode on the back of a sleepy camel. Our pace wasn't much quicker than when we were on foot, but there's something special about checking out the pyramids via camel power.

The pollution of Cairo is intolerable, but it leads to crazy sunsets. We made it to the far end of the complex just in time to see the sun drop into the desert, drowning the pyramids in a bath of neon red light. The show was even more mind-blowing when you realize it's been playing every night for the better part of 4,500 years. Up until the Cathedral of Ulm was built in 1890, the pyramids were the world's tallest structures. That means the Burj Khalifa in Dubai, currently the tallest structure in the world, will have to stay up until the year 6,500 CE to be the tallest building in the world just as long.

I spent the next few days rolling around the streets of Old Cairo, haggling with shop owners and taking pictures of ancient mosques amidst new high rises. I'd always wanted to visit Jerusalem and Cairo, but there was a deeper reason for the trip. I wanted to see if I was capable of functioning in a country with almost zero disability infrastructure. Back when I was diving, the whole world had been my playground, so if I were now to be restricted to visiting only Europe, North America, and Australia, it would be just one more thing paralysis had stolen from me. But after dropping the ramps of the Damascus Gate and rolling through the hodgepodge of Cairo traffic, I felt just as comfortable as I did in Europe. Much of the business in Asia and Africa takes place on street level, so there is much less need for elevators and escalators. Wherever I encountered steps, there were plenty of people to help out.

The world had closed in on me in Oregon, but after four months in Europe and three weeks in the Middle East, it was busting wide open again. The Bridge to Venice was opening a new lane.

• • • • • • • • • • • •

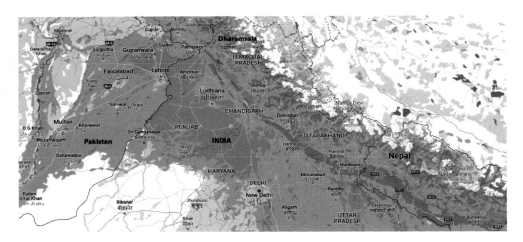

Dharamsala

High Roller

I made it back to Portland and began retooling my life. I was rehired by my old Adidas boss, Jay Edwards, to work in the new internal communications department. Adidas had quadrupled in size since I last worked there, and they could no longer rely on the old rumor mill for corporate information. Our department was a three-person outfit charged with getting everyone in the expanding enterprise on the same page. Our two main tools were a daily email news blast to the company and a monthly newspaper that ended up being one of the most effective communication devices in all of corporate America.

My responsibility was the newspaper. I had actually named the paper before I started working for Adidas in 1994. I was at "Club 21," the company's infamous watering hole, where anyone looking for a job would come to schmooze with a potential boss. I was sitting with Jay when he came up with the idea for a newspaper. If I could name the newspaper, they would have to hire me. I went into the bathroom, sat on the pot, and went through every letter of the alphabet, followed by "Adidas." When I came upon "L," I thought of how the French say Adidas—"AH-dee-Das." I put it together and it sounded like "Well La-Ti Da!" I came back to the table, Jay bought into "L'adidas," and a week later I was working for the Adidas World Cup '94.

In '94, L'adidas was just a fun little diversion, but four years later, it had become official corporate communication. Every month I had to fill up a four-page, 11 by 17-inch newspaper with industry news, internal programs, and profiles of Adidas athletes and teams. The thing that made our paper jump off the shelf (1,200 copies a month!) was the L'adidas Doer's Profile. The Doer's Profile lampooned a different employee each month. Adidas employees were ultra-competitive former athletes, so you had to have thick skin to work there. Being lampooned by the company paper meant you had made it in the Adidas corporate culture. It said you were tough enough to take it and could roll with the punches, which were as biting as we could legally make them.

For three years, I was the scribe of one of the loosest, most productive companies in the corporate world. I got to travel to dozens of Adidas events

201

including both the 1998 World Cup in France, and the 1999 Women's World Cup in Los Angeles (the Brandi Chastain game). We put in 60-hour work weeks and pushed the limits by partying at Adidas-sponsored events on the weekends. The closest thing I can compare the burgeoning Adidas America corporate culture to was our counterparts at ESPN. While reading James Andrew Miller's *Those Guys Have All the Fun*, I recognized all the hijinks as well as the corporate backstabbing. The two companies were mirror images of each other. I've been approached by former Adidas co-workers to write a tell-all book about the craziness of the early days of Adidas America, but I prefer to stay out of the courtroom.

After the accident, Rachel and I tried to make a go of it, but like most couples going through a disability crisis, we ended up divorced. Things weren't going well for us before my accident and, although we made an honest try, it just never felt normal again. We parted and are still good friends.

In 2000, Adidas announced they were dismantling our department because the German headquarters didn't want official company news coming out of their US subsidiary. The truth was nobody ever read a word of the slick, boring, glossy German corporate publications; everyone in the Adidas world read our newspaper cover to cover. I was invited to look for other positions in the company, but it was the age of the dot-com boom (though it was about to crash) and good jobs were still a dime a dozen. I checked around with my network and found that I had a better offer: I was going to work for the Dalai Lama.

Before 2000, my brother Dan, riding in his own lane on the Bridge to Venice, had made two trips to Dharamsala, India, the seat of the Tibetan government-in-exile and the home of the Dalai Lama. After meetings with the IT team at the Tibetan government complex, Dan organized a group of geeks from San Francisco to wire up their first computer network and build the original website for the Dalai Lama and the government-in-exile. While he was climbing trees like a monkey, stringing up cables in the Himalayas, his wife, Zoe, emailed, telling him she was pregnant. Now three years later, with their daughter Tashi still in diapers, the young family had decided to emigrate to India so Dan could work (volunteer full time, actually) for His Holiness and the Tibetan Computer Resource Center. It seemed the Bridge to Venice had built an offramp to Shambhala and I was going to take it.

Packing is my least favorite activity, and being in a wheelchair has multiplied that distaste a hundredfold. My body, which used to be of great use in transporting gear, had become just another piece of luggage for other people to carry. I had a duffel full of clothes, my guitar, a laptop computer, and a 3' x 3' x 2' box stuffed with six months' worth of toiletries, ten tubes of KY jelly for my catheters, five bags of baby wipes, ten boxes of rubber gloves, four extra wheel tubes, two extra caster wheels, and a toilet seat in case my room didn't have one.

It seems impossible now, but all that gear as well as my chair and back-pack didn't cost one extra dime to transport. It was, however, super difficult to haul around as I was making stops in Paris, Les Avenières, and London before getting to India. I could store the big box at my friend Pat's apartment in Paris while I boogied down to the Alps to hang with my old friends for a few weeks. But my flight to Delhi was out of Heathrow. When I left Paris to head to India, I had to pile everything into a cab, transfer it all to a Eurostar train, then take the Chunnel to London and store everything in a locker at Waterloo station—something you can no longer do because terrorists used the lockers to store bombs.

I found a guest house next to Waterloo station, but the only room they had was up a flight of stairs, across a courtyard, and down another flight of stairs. I had to pop out of my chair and climb both sets of stairs on my butt. I didn't sleep much thinking if there were a fire, I had no chance of escape. In the morning, I stuffed a cab with all my wares and got to Heathrow a full five hours before my flight. The cab from Waterloo to Heathrow cost more than the trains from Les Avenières to London.

I was exhausted before the trip even started and fell asleep before the flight took off. I woke up just in time to see the sunrise over the Himalayas. We flew over K-2 in Pakistan, and I knew somewhere off the other side of the plane was Dharamsala. As the 747 dropped over the Himalayas and tore across the flat plains of the Punjab, the squalor of Delhi emerged in the distance. I wasn't out of the plane before Indian poverty slapped me in the face. As the jet lowered, I saw a barefoot family of six squatting in the high grass along the runway. A few hundred yards behind them, a hamlet made of scrap wood and cardboard bordered a stagnant creek that served as both washbasin and toilet. It was a big reminder my main job here was to keep myself clean and infection-free.

It took more than an hour to deplane and go through customs, but Dan, who had already been in Dharamsala for six weeks, was sitting at the baggage claim with his friend, Greg, who was going to ride back with us. It had been a long, stressful journey, and when I saw Dan, I almost lost it. I was teary-eyed, but the pragmatics of the situation precluded the emotion, and it was time to get to work. Unfortunately, Dan's Indian driver decided to take a long lunch and left us sitting outside of baggage claim for more than an hour. Just as we were about to call another company, the driver pulled up. The five of us (Dan, Greg, digital security expert Locke Berkebile, myself, and the driver) packed our gear in the back, except for my chair, which they loaded on the roof. We pulled out of the airport and into the quagmire of Delhi traffic.

On my first trip to India, I traveled by train, so I never paid attention to how we were getting anywhere. This time, I sat in the front passenger seat looking drop-jawed at the circus taking place in front of me. Before I arrived in India, I thought we could have rented a car and done the driving ourselves. If we'd done that, we'd either be dead or still trying to find our way out of Delhi. I've lived in cities where the driving is crazy (Taipei tops that list), but for the most part the rules of the road are the same—red means stop; green means go; pass on the outside. India has a different system that is as complicated and mysterious as the country itself.

As we wove in between buses, motorcycles, cars, horse-drawn carriages, bicycles, auto rickshaws, bicycle rickshaws, and half-functional utility vehicles, our driver also had to make sure not to smack into an army of pedestrians, herds of goats, random cows, swinging monkeys, water buffalo, and hawkers selling everything from newspapers to coconuts.

We took a lunch break at a Tibetan compound in Delhi, then switched drivers and took off on the 12-hour trek to Dharamsala. Besides not knowing the code of the road, no matter how detailed a map you might have, you would get hopelessly lost. Drivers know Delhi by feel and landmark, not by street signs or highway indicators. About an hour after leaving the compound, we were on the outskirts of Delhi heading north through Haryana Province. We were traveling India's largest and most developed highway, but it was a chaotic hodgepodge of traffic.

None of our seatbelts worked, so I spent the first hour of the trip stiff-arming the dashboard, assuming at any moment I might face-plant the windshield. The saving grace of India's traffic is that nobody is ever going very fast and everyone (aside from us) understands the language of the road. Even with a huge bus and a rickshaw coming at us in the wrong lane, the driver just honked a few times, made some arm signals, and the bedlam magically cleared.

Five hours outside of Delhi, traffic subsided and the driver got the jeep up to 50 mph. We crossed into the Punjab at Ambala, where the driver had to bribe an officer with 100 rupees ($2) to let his cargo of Westerners through the state checkpoint. For the most part, the police in India are absent; but when they do get in the way, a small "tariff" will let you slide. We made our way through the confusing mess of Chandigarh (capital city of both Punjab and Haryana provinces), where night fell, changing the language of the road from honking and hand signals to flashing headlights. Darkness, however, did not signal the end of the diversity of traffic. Cyclists continued to ride in the middle of oncoming traffic without a light, bell, or reflector. To this day, after three subsequent trips, I have still never seen a rider in the Indian subcontinent wearing a bike helmet.

As we passed into the state of Himachal Pradesh, the road thinned to a barely passable two-lane trail, and the driver's speed dropped back to 25 mph. When big trucks clogged the road, another confusing Indian driving protocol went into effect. Drivers flashed their brights and flipped the lights on and off to dictate who was making the move and when it would take place. The mountain roads, however, are less confusing than their urban counterparts, because there aren't many places to go except the city at the end of the trail. It was also comforting to once again be in the mountains instead of the plains.

At our first switchback, we were 40 miles as the crow flies from Dharamsala. But it took four hours of winding along sliver-thin cliff roads before we reached Kotwali Bazaar, the main market of the city. The driver took an abrupt right at the base of the 3,000-foot climb to McLeod Ganj, the home of the Dalai Lama, and started up a semi-paved pathway that proved to be the most insane road I'd ever traversed. The Library Road (so named because it is the road to the Tibetan National Archives; it has since been resurfaced and renamed "Potala Road") cuts about 20 minutes out of the drive to McLeod Ganj, but the switchbacks are so tight I swear I could see the back of the jeep on the bottom half of the switch as I was on the top.

For many of the turns, I could not see the surface of the next level before making the turn. The road was rarely wider than 15 feet, and the price of an error could be a 1,000-foot roll into the adjacent valley. At a few points along the road, landslides had wiped out the pavement, leaving a drooping pile of gravel that had to be taken at good speed or the jeep would plummet over the side. The road continued like this for three miles, until we reached our hotel at the summit of McLeod Ganj. Later I would learn this mountain path was a major thoroughfare from Dharamsala to McLeod Ganj. In the middle of the day, there were even traffic jams on it.

It was 4:00 a.m. when we arrived at the Pema Thang Guest House and I dropped dead in my bed. Ten hours later, I woke up to find myself perched at nearly 7,000 feet looking down at the Tibetan government compound and the residence and temple of the Dalai Lama. Maroon-robed bald monks sat in a circle listening to a geshe ("geshe" is basically a doctorate in divinity) while a teeming vegetable market bustled just a few hundred feet away. The cliff I was on was so severe I could have hit the bottom of the valley 3,000 feet below with a good overhand Frisbee huck. Off in the distance lay the plains of the Punjab, and behind me lay the Dhauladhar range, a 15,500-foot block of granite separating Dharamsala from Kashmir. My parents were worried because we were so close to the constant fighting in Kashmir. But with the nearly complete lack of infrastructure north of us, it would have taken weeks for an army to make their way into Dharamsala.

Jet lag and the enormity of the trip were weighing heavily on me when my three-year-old niece, Tashi, knocked on my door and entered smiling so widely I forgot I was perched above the world like an eagle. Tashi was followed by Dan's wife, Zoe, who brought us samosas (spicy deep-fried potato pastries) for lunch. Tashi thought my big box was a present for her and was a little disappointed when she was told she wasn't allowed to play with anything in it. Instead, I pulled out my new digital camera, and we took pictures of everything in sight. When I opened them up on the computer screen, her eyes lit up and she said, "It's Tashi! It's Tashi!" For the next four months, we had a toy that just wouldn't quit.

As an Oregonian I've seen as much rain as anyone in the United States. It's part of our culture and something we all learn to deal with to live in one of the most beautiful places in America. Before going to India, I looked at a climate map of Northern India and discovered I would be arriving during the monsoon season. How bad could that be?

Weeks after arriving in McLeod Ganj, I had yet to go through one single day without a terrific downpour. In the Northwest, we have nice clean sprinkles that rarely require a raincoat. The monsoon of the Indian Himalaya comes in like ocean waves on the Pacific coastline, one enormous cloudburst after another. At times, it is accompanied by roaring winds, deafening thunderbolts, and golf-ball sized hail. Losing electricity

Dropping down the Library Road to the Tibetan government-in-exile complex in Dharamsala, India.

was a daily occurrence. Sometimes the power grid would go out for five minutes. Often it would be out all day.

I'd moved from the Pema Thang overlooking the Dalai Lama's residence to the Hotel Tibet right in the center of McLeod Ganj. The Hotel Tibet was run by the Tibetan government, so the rooms were spotless and the food delicious. Zoe scouted out hotels before I came and found it to be the closest thing to an accessible hotel in the city. I could roll into my room and the dining room, but there was still an annoying stair going into my bathroom. The only time I washed my hands was after I'd spent one of my hour-long sessions on the toilet. I had to park my chair at the bottom of the step, throw myself onto the bathroom floor, slide myself across the tile, pull myself onto the toilet and start my defecation routine. An hour later, I would lower myself to the floor and slide to the shower drain a few feet away. The shower consisted of a faucet and a couple buckets of water. Half the time there was some hot water to be had from an electric heating unit on the wall, but often enough the power would go out and I would have to endure an ice-bucket-challenge shower.

I went for weeks without leaving the Hotel Tibet except for an occasional meal with DZT (Dan, Zoe, Tashi). I started writing this very book, and it consumed me for days on end. My writing breaks came courtesy of the army of monkeys patrolling the city. My room overlooked a busy courtyard of guesthouses and restaurants, where every day the monkeys performed the most incredible athletic feats I've ever seen. They would swing from balcony to balcony and jump across rooftops, looking for open windows. If someone left a door or window open, the monkeys were sure to find it and walk away with a prize. One time a group of visiting monks left their doors open, and a band of five monkeys had a field day. One by one, they entered the open doors, and each one exited with a different treasure. The first four came out with fruit, but the king came out wearing a pair of maroon underwear on his head. When Tashi stopped in for visits, she would run to the window and try to get them to come over and play. Occasionally one would gallop past our windowsill, and Tashi and I would scream for joy, then laugh until we hurt. I'd learned about monkeys from Curious George. Tashi was learning about them the same way American kids know about squirrels.

I rarely left the hotel because the streets of McLeod Ganj turned into mud rivers stained by hundreds of cow pies. Rolling around in a wheelchair was the same as walking through it on my hands. I'd brought a couple pairs of gloves, but there was no way to keep the bio-mud off my hands. I had to keep my hands sterile because I was inserting a catheter five times a day to urinate. As much as I fought to keep my hands clean, I was still exposed to way too many bacteria. I ended up fighting off constant infections, and in the end, it drove me back home.

After eight weeks of confinement in my room, the sun broke through and, for the first time, the Bagsu Road in front of the Hotel Tibet dried up. I rolled out to see a colorful market dominated by the snow-capped peaks of the Himalayas. The outdoor cafes opened, and the chai stalls just down the street from the Hotel Tibet came to life. McLeod Ganj is roughly composed of 1/3 Indians, 1/3 Tibetans and 1/3 travelers. The locals may refer to the foreigners as tourists, but these people were not the same breed that frequents the beaches of Florida. These are travelers in the truest sense of the world. Rarely did anyone stay for less than a few weeks, and it wasn't uncommon to speak with Westerners and Israelis who ended up moving there permanently.

Along with the Tibetan Government and the Dalai Lama, Dharamsala was crowded with experts willing to both teach and learn. People studied Hindi, Tibetan, tabla (Indian drums), sitar, herbal medicine, Indian and Tibetan cooking, and any number of crafts. Although there were organized classes, most of the teaching was done in small groups or one-on-one. When people gathered at the chai stands at the end of the day, the conversation was the most interesting and informative I've ever heard. Then again, sometimes it would just be gossip, the lifeline of Tibetan society.

Aside from watching the monkeys, I always took a break to play some guitar. For years I'd been playing Grateful Dead, Beatles, and Pink Floyd covers, but rarely sat down to write my own material. In the few months before I left, I began to polish up a few song ideas I had banging around my head. Once in India, all those ideas went down on paper and became finished songs. Then Zoe, an aspiring writer and poet, teamed up with a Tibetan couple who owned Tea O'Clock, a teahouse located right in the hub of McLeod Ganj, and started Poetry Across the Planet, an open mic night for music and poetry. They had a guitar, a mic, and a stereo; an expat friend had left a bass with Dan to go stateside for a long visit back home. A couple of amps materialized... and we had a band!

Our first Saturday night attracted a handful of people, but word quickly spread, and soon the tight room upstairs at Tea O'Clock was the place to be on Saturday nights. There wasn't a lot of electric music being played in the Indian Himalayas, so we often had people standing outside the teahouse aching to get in. Dan and I always played short solo sets before turning over the "stage," or sitting in with whoever wanted to jam. People from around the world would show up to play, and we ended up having a steady house band consisting of Oren, an Israeli guitar player; Ult Mundane, an American didgeridoo player; Pascal, a German trumpet player; and Ngödrup, a Tibetan flute player from Nepal. We called ourselves the Himalayan Avalanche Orchestra and we were the toast of the town. It was also the first time I'd ever played out on a consistent basis and the first time I'd ever been known as a musician. It was the first time I'd ever had any recognition outside of being an athlete. It beat the hell out of being known as the handicapped guy.

As the streets dried and the sun became a constant, I began exploring my neighborhood. People at the chai stands talked about the neighboring villages, but I hadn't been anywhere. I was getting a lot of writing done, but I didn't travel to India just to sit in a room. As I ventured away from McLeod Ganj, I realized what an island the place was. McLeod Ganj comprises six roads meeting at the center bus stop outside of Tea O'Clock. You can't go more than a half-mile in any direction without encountering a huge hill. As the weather cleared, I started waking up early and going for morning workouts. Although I'd lost a lot of weight living on a rice diet, I hadn't been in any kind of shape in over a year. My first few days felt almost as though I was coming back from an injury. I didn't have any energy, and I struggled on all the inclines. After the first week, however, the stiffness went away, and I started feeling stronger.

Each day I ventured from the Hotel Tibet, India became more and more alive. The first town I hit was Forsyth Ganj, a mile away on the far side of a massive ravine that separates it from the Dalai Lama's temple. The road to Forsyth started at the McLeod Ganj bus stop and dropped into a densely wooded section. As I navigated the potholes, and cow pies away from the town, I realized I was surrounded by a lush forest. McLeod may be a tiny village in northern India, but India is so densely populated that the noise level of even the smallest town can rival a busy street in New York City. Long, blaring horn blasts are constant and the whizzing of poorly maintained motorcycles dims the senses. Politicians love to blare over loudspeakers as do any merchants who can afford a sound system. Here in the forest, though, I could listen to rustling leaves, trickling waterfalls, and foraging birds. It was the first place in all my travels of India where I found a peaceful spot. Strange, as so many Westerners come to India to find serenity.

I woke up one morning with a knock on my door, and a smiley three-foot ball of energy bounced into my room to look for monkeys. Dan and Tashi were on a morning walk and stopped in to see if I wanted some breakfast. The three of us walked down the Bagsu Road until we came upon a large gathering next to the neighborhood chai stand. One of the Tibetan government buildings had a line of Westerners reaching out into the street. The line was for registration for a public audience with the Dalai Lama. Although Dan worked for the Dalai Lama and had had a few meetings with him, I had only seen his residence. Dan stood in line for tickets while Tashi and I played with some newborn puppies. Tashi and the puppies drew the second biggest crowd in town, after the line to register for the Dalai Lama.

The audience was scheduled for 7:30 a.m. the next day. I got up for an early breakfast, then rolled down the steep hill towards the temple. It was a festive day in McLeod Ganj, with vendors hawking white silk khata scarves to present to the Dalai Lama for his blessing. The town lepers were at their posts along the temple road, cashing in on one of the bigger days of the year.

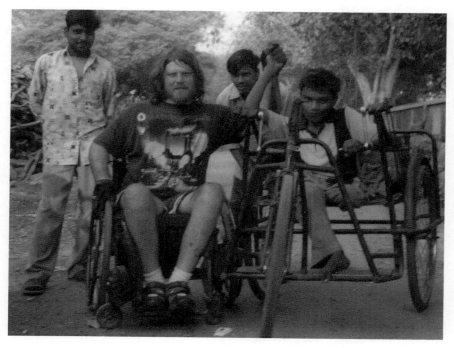

Just after a chair race with a fellow wheeler in Delhi

There were ten or so lepers who hung out in McLeod Ganj, and they were as much a part of the neighborhood as the shopkeepers. A few were missing their legs, one had stubs for hands, and several were mothers who walked the streets with their children. They slept on wide benches along the road in the center of town and manned their posts early in the day. Most of the lepers in India work for crime bosses who take a cut for protection and assign the most disabled people into the densest tourist areas. I was told the Tibetans made sure these local lepers begged for themselves. It is virtually impossible for a leper to find work in India. Even if they could get the education or skills and their leprosy weren't contagious, they were untouchables, and nobody would ever hire one.

The line to the security checkpoint went up a long set of stairs I couldn't navigate, so I pushed my way up a steep path towards a closed-off entrance. I'd been to the temple several times for teachings, and the guards knew me by now. After all, I was the only white guy in a wheelchair in the whole town. I thought an audience with the Dalai Lama would be somewhat of a small gathering, but that wasn't the case. I was herded into a courtyard with about 300 other Westerners waiting to clear security. Once everyone was checked, we were sent in a single file line up a steep hill to the Dalai Lama's residence. The Dalai Lama stood in front of his residence and greeted everybody in line by blessing their articles. It was more a receiving line than an audience.

For some people in line, it was the culmination of a life-long spiritual quest, and for others it was just a chance to check something off their bucket list: "Taj Mahal: check. India Gate: check. Dalai Lama: check." While I've never claimed to be a Buddhist, I've leaned in that direction ever since my disappointing dissolution with the Catholic Church. The Church was all formality and structure with little flexibility to incorporate social change. On top of that, I just couldn't believe Jesus Christ was a godhead any more than Muhammad or Sun Myung Moon for that matter. I see Jesus as a great rallying cry for poor people to overcome tyranny. But like Townshend says in the song "Won't Get Fooled Again," the new establishment took power and behaved just like the old. Jesus Christ became the power behind the aristocracy, and horrible deeds were done in his name. I went from a loyal altar boy in grade school to a committed agnostic in college. Religion was bunk, but spirituality had merit. In the end, I'm just hoping a collective consciousness serves as some kind of universal, cosmic glue.

I had heard the Dalai Lama speak in Madison, Wisconsin just after he received the 1989 Nobel Peace Prize. I found him to be incredibly sincere and downright funny. People showed up hoping to be wowed, but instead they left laughing. He was nothing like the Catholic priests I grew up with. In fact, he didn't even want you to join his religion. He just wanted you to listen to what he had to say and see if it applied to your daily life—which of course it uncannily does.

I was in line on the hill when I was swept up and rolled to the front of the line by a monk. Normally I'd take offense to someone grabbing me and taking me somewhere, but it was a long line, and nobody cared if I was cutting as long as a monk escorted me. He wheeled me to the fourth or fifth position in line and continued to guide me as I approached the Dalai Lama. The traditional way to greet the Dalai Lama is to fold your hands and touch the three upper chakras: your forehead, your throat, and your heart. Before I put my hands to my throat, the Dalai Lama went to one knee, put his hands on my legs, closed his eyes, and offered up a short but intense prayer.

When he rose, he spoke to one of his attendants, who translated for me, "His Holiness would like to know if there is anything he can do for you." I was taken aback by his question, as nobody in line got anything more than a handshake. Most people would have freaked and not known what to say, but I came prepared with a request.

"Actually, there is something you can do for me," I said. "There is a monk in the monastery with a broken back. He lives on the second floor, and he needs to move to someplace where there are no stairs."

After the attendant translated my request to the Dalai Lama, his eyes grew, and he looked me straight in the eye. "Here?" he asked. "Namgyal Monastery?"

"Yes," I said, "his name is Lobsang, and he lives on the second floor..."

A few weeks earlier, I'd been introduced to Lobsang, a 30-year-old thangka (Buddhist iconography painter), who had broken his back falling from a tree while hanging prayer flags. He was a paraplegic, like me, but had enough motor skills to get around using a walker. He couldn't get down the twenty steps from his room to the monastery courtyard however, so he spent his time sequestered in his room.

The Dalai Lama motioned one of his attendants over to me. "His Holiness would like you to take me to this man," he said. Before I could say anything, the attendant grabbed my handles and whisked me away towards the monastery. The attendant was going so fast he would have thrown me out of my chair if we'd hit a rock. I told him to let me navigate it, and he let go of my handles. I popped into a wheelie and made my way down a hill past hundreds of Tibetans who were waiting for the Westerners to finish their morning audience.

The monastery courtyard has few visitors, but for the audience there were over 1,000 Tibetan, East Asian, and Western pilgrims. Between the gathering at the audience and the crowd in the courtyard, I'd seen just about everyone I knew in McLeod Ganj. I wheeled over to the temple steps and gave the attendant the directions to Lobsang's room. While I waited at the bottom of the steps, the people who had been in line with me made their way out and asked about my conversation with the Dalai Lama. I recounted the story and told them I was waiting to find out if Lobsang's room could be changed. I waited for a half hour and even sent some people up to Lobsang's room, but neither Lobsang nor the attendant could be found.

Two weeks later, I found out what happened. I ran into Lobsang's Israeli friend who took care of him. She studied Buddhism and had a true heart, but she had become an enabler, allowing Lobsang to wallow in his depression instead of fighting it.

"Hello, Tom," she said, stopping me on my way to the Hotel Tibet. "I heard about your conversation with His Holiness. Lobsang sends his eternal thanks."

"So he got a room!" I said. "He's off the second floor!"

"No," she said. "Lobsang likes his room. It's peaceful and quiet there. He can spend lots of time with his teacher."

"But he's a prisoner up there," I said. "He can't do anything by himself up there."

"Tom," she said, "you have to understand that Lobsang is a monk. He is not the same as you. He doesn't need to race around Dharamsala in a wheel-chair. He just wants to read and paint."

"What about going for a walk?" I said. "What about going to a book-store? What about going for a cup of chai? He's a prisoner up there. We've got to get him out of there!"

"Tom," she said, "you only know one part of Lobsang's life. The rest of his life is very different from yours. If he wants a book, I can get it. If he wants to go out, all he has to do is ask and I will arrange it. He doesn't ask for much."

At this point I was infuriated. "Okay," I said, "you go sit in that cafe over there and I'll give you a phone. Every time you want something just give me a call. I'll be right over with it. Just don't leave that cafe...What do you call that? I call it prison. What if the power goes out? What if I'm not around for you to call? What the hell do you do then?"

"Tom," she said in a calm voice, "we know it's not like that. Lobsang has..."

"He's got an enabler," I said. "And you're killing him."

This was my first encounter with disability hovering, something crushing the future of persons with disability all over the world. They are getting loved to the point where they become insignificant parts of their own society. In the West, we are trying for global solutions like ramps, wide bathroom doors, and accessible buses. In most of Asia they are still relying on a family member to assist. It sounds like that would be better than nothing, but it's not. It's much worse than nothing. It's a ticket backwards.

● ● ● ● ● ● ● ● ● ● ● ●

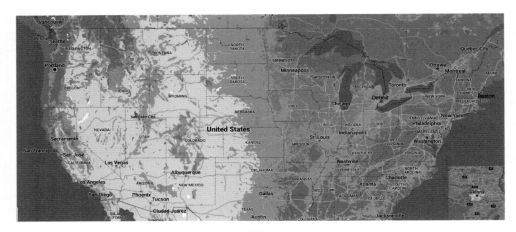

USA

Rolling and Rocking

I'd planned to stay in Dharamsala for the better part of a year, but the filthy streets and the lack of a sink in my room led to a series of urinary tract infections I couldn't beat. After only four months, I was forced to return to America. I called Virgin Airlines to change my flight and faced some horrible disability discrimination. They asked why I was changing my flight and I told them I had to fly to the States for medical reasons. They said they could change my ticket, but due to my disability and my medical condition, they would not allow me on their aircraft unless I was accompanied by a doctor. I was dumbfounded and there was nothing I could do about it. I tried hanging up and calling again, assuming I would get another ticket agent, but my itinerary was already flagged.

I had no choice but to eat the ticket and buy a one-way ticket on another airline to get back to the States. I spent a week shopping at Internet cafés in Delhi until I found a super cheap $450 one-way ticket on Aeroflot. It ended up being a piece of great luck as I was allowed to get off the plane in Moscow for the weekend. When I left Delhi it was 90 degrees, but when I arrived in Moscow it was 28. Seeing as I was only granted a transit visa, I was at the whim of the airline, who told me where I had to stay and what I could do. They put me up in a hotel 20 miles from the city center in a neighborhood of high-rise rent-controlled apartment buildings. I told them I wanted to see Red Square and the Kremlin, and they told me they could arrange a guided tour. I told them I wanted to wander by myself and they insisted I be accompanied by an official travel agent. They put me in a car to the center where I was supposed to meet my guide. But as soon as I was out of the car, I told the driver to meet me at the same spot at 6 o'clock. He didn't speak any English, but he got the message.

I played around the city center all day visiting the tourist spots before drifting a few miles off the beaten track to a flea market selling old Soviet-era knickknacks. Amazingly enough there was a handicap-equipped bus, so I avoided freezing my fingers rolling back to the Kremlin. I found a sports bar showing a hockey game and settled in to a few beers and some schnitzel. When the sun dropped out of the sky, the temperature dropped to 10

217

degrees; I was ill-equipped to handle that kind of cold. I hurried back to the spot where the driver dropped me off and found him asleep behind the wheel with an empty vodka flask on the front seat. You can't expect a guy to wait all day without a drink, can ya?

A few days later I arrived back in Chicago and recovered my van, which had been sitting in my parents' driveway in Wisconsin. I spent the holidays in Milwaukee then took off on a six-week roadie, visiting a dozen National Parks and everyone I knew west of the Mississippi. For most people it would be the trip of a lifetime, but I was just procrastinating because I didn't know what I was going to do with my life once I got back to Oregon.

While I was in India, I'd learned the basics of website construction and I already knew how to create professional-looking print pieces from my work at Adidas. I hung a shingle and offered my services to anyone who needed print brochures, boutique web sites, or copy writing. I loved doing the work, but operating your own business is 10 percent work and 90 percent sales. I hate sales with a passion, so I was barely able to pay my rent.

But I had two major passions keeping me entertained over the next several years. I was a jock, and I was a musician.

Before I left Adidas, my boss, Jay Edwards, challenged me to compete in the wheelchair division of the Boston Marathon. He bought me a lightweight, three-wheel aluminum racing wheelchair. After three weeks of training on it, I entered the 1998 Boston Marathon. I'd been training in my daily chair for four months; it just took that long to get the custom racing chair ordered and built. I had a few training sessions to figure out how to get the new chair to work, but in just two weeks, I'd dropped my 20-mile time in half. When I got to Boston, I found the course difficult, but much easier than my training rides in Portland.

As luck would have it, I finished just ahead of the women's champion Fatuma Roba. Unbeknownst to me, she was just a few meters behind me as I arrived on the final stretch down Boylston St. The crowd was cheering like crazy and I assumed they just loved wheelchair racers. I spent the rest of the day thinking the people of Boston were the best wheelchair spectators in the world! Then I saw the TV finish with Roba on my tail and it all made sense.

In 2001 I entered the New York City Marathon. Shortly thereafter I sat dumbfounded watching the scenes unfold on television on September 11th. I saw the course covered in caustic dust from the heinous terrorist strikes on the World Trade Center. I sent a volley of emails to my friend, Adam Freifeld, who was to be my host for the race. The final post he sent read, "Dude, two F-15s just flew by my window..." I told him I'd get the hell out of the office and go sit in the park. I didn't hear back from Adam for more than a week.

With the world in turmoil and New York City looking like it had been hit by a nuclear bomb, I assumed the race would be cancelled. But just a few weeks after the attacks, the New York Athletic Club sent out an email saying the race was on! Just six weeks after the United States had been attacked, I found myself on the starting line of one of the most poignant sporting events in American history.

The Paralyzed Veterans of America always have a big presence at wheelchair events, but they stood out even stronger at this race. There were tears as 30,000 runners sang the Star-Spangled Banner, then Mayor Giuliani shot off the starting gun and 150 chairs sprinted across the Verrazano Narrows Bridge. I settled into a pack well behind the leaders, but still in the top 20. The course wound its way through Brooklyn, then crossed the 51st St. Bridge (yes, the Simon and Garfunkel Bridge) and dropped me onto the First Avenue drag strip that became a seven-mile thunder dome of applause.

I'd been knocking off riders, but I had no idea where I was in the standings. The course jumped in and out of the Bronx then rose up a steady and arm-crushing ramp to Central Park, which is a monster climb at the toughest part of the course. I crossed the finish line in 3:03 and ended up taking a respectable 12th place.

As I recovered with Adam and my brother, Bagus, we watched the army of finishers flow through the finishing chute, collapsing in the arms of loved ones. Squad members of first responders who had died in the attacks ran in place of their fallen comrades with their friends' faces emblazoned on their shirts. One firefighter's nipples had chafed to the point of bleeding; the image of his partner's bloody face on his T-shirt will forever remind me of the grotesque stain September 11, 2001, left on me.

I got a lot of dap for finishing Boston, New York, and my first few Portland Marathons, but training in a wheelchair was torture. To get to the optimal position, the wheeler needs to kneel on the seat and spend the entire training session with their chest flattened to their thighs and their eyes staring right at the ground. I was putting in hours and hours on bike paths and I couldn't even see the landscape I was passing. It was dangerous, too. The brakes on racing wheelchairs are more or less a prop. Although there are brakes on the front wheel, all of the power is coming from punching the rims on the two large rear wheels. You can brake the tiny front wheel and it will freeze, but it doesn't stop the chair. That made training on the open roadway too dangerous. I couldn't see traffic and I couldn't stop even if I wanted to.

But I still had the trusty hand cycle that guided me through the French Alps. On the hand cycle I could sit upright and see everything. The brakes are fixed to the large front wheel generating the power. When I hit those brakes, the bike stops cold. Living in a wheelchair was a giant pain, so I didn't want to spend hours a day training in discomfort.

When I returned from Dharamsala, I was training in the racing chair for four out of five workouts. By the end of the summer, I was training almost exclusively on the hand cycle, pulling out the racing chair for a few workouts before a big race.

And there were lots of big races. Over the next few years, I competed in a dozen local short races and several big-city marathons. The more I trained in the hand cycle, the more it became MY sport. I was a cyclist, after all. Cycling got me into this mess and now cycling was the thing that gave me the most pleasure.

Pulling for all I've got at the 2002 Portland Marathon—which I won!

When I did the New York Marathon, I noticed there were more than 50 entrants using hand cycles. At the time, I thought they were cheating, but the more I trained on my hand cycle, the less I cared. I put in thousands of miles training and I put every ounce of force I could into those handles. After one great 50-mile training ride, I decided I was going to do the Portland Marathon in a hand cycle.

When I came up to the line for the 2002 Portland Marathon, I saw I wasn't the only one who thought that way. More than half the wheelers were in hand cycles. The gun went off and I peeled off the line, only to have my front wheel dislodge from its mounting. While my competition was running away from me, I was sitting on wet pavement trying to get my power wheel (hand cycles are pulled from the front, not the rear like normal bikes) back in the fork. By the time I was up and going, I was in a sea of thousands of runners and my competition was nowhere in sight.

I was already out of breath as I weaved my way through the densely packed field of 10,000 runners. I kept screaming, "Chair!" as I tried to pick up speed, but I had to come to a dead stop a dozen times. As I got to the third mile, I was amongst a much thinner group of elite runners and I was able to get up to speed and pass them. The fifth mile was a long descent into downtown Portland, and I was able to catch my breath and get some rhythm. I'd put in more than 2,000 miles training for this race and most of my workouts were more than 20 miles. I was in the best shape of my life and I knew it. I geared up and worked the handles as if they were acid I had to push away from me. Before long, I started catching up to the slower riders and I had the leading riders in sight. I caught the second-to-last chair on the steep ascent of the St. John's bridge and finally caught Jerry Martin, the greatest wheelchair racer in Portland Marathon history, with six miles to go.

I breezed to victory but was quick to disqualify myself for riding in a hand cycle. When Jerry Martin finished, he came up to me in protest, but I just shook his hand and told him he was the winner. So while I had disqualified myself from the wheelchair competition, there was no regulation against me competing in the hand cycle. I was declared the winner of the Portland Marathon—and Jerry was declared the winner of the wheelchair division. It took a few months to sort it all out, but in the end we both got victory plaques.

But the dam had been broken. The next year when we toed the starting line nearly everyone was in a hand cycle. I'd been training like a fool ever since the rains subsided in April and had even gone on a crash Atkins diet, losing

10 pounds before the race. When the gun went off, I shot off to an early lead and never looked back. I'd tapered my workouts like swimmers do before their championship meets, so even the three big hills on the course passed under my wheels as minor obstacles. I finished the course in just under an hour and fifty minutes and was officially crowned the Portland Marathon champion.

It was my biggest win since the 1980 Wisconsin state diving championship. I'd pumped every ounce of force I had into those handles and I was as sore as any of the runners. But unlike them I didn't need my arms to support my body weight, so I recovered in just a few days. I kept my form for another month, then traveled up to Seattle where I placed second in their marathon, which had a much bigger field (and a much hillier course!).

I never won another Portland Marathon but finished on the podium on all but one of the next dozen races. When I had the money, I traveled to other marathons and had top 10 finishes in the Washington DC and Detroit marathons—both races having more than 100 riders. For runners, the marathon distance is long, but for the hand cyclist, you need to be riding nearly 20 miles a day just to be competitive. You also have to push some extra long rides as well. Over the years, I've cranked out more than 100 rides of 30 miles or more and had one glorious 93-mile grind through the Oregon Coast Range with my training and guitar partner Bill Crabtree.

Which brings me to the other thing I was doing in the 2000s. I played a ton of guitar.

I came home from Dharamsala with a dozen songs in my satchel and the confidence to go out and play them. I began playing open mics every weekend and developed the chops to sit in with local musicians and play lead guitar. For some reason, playing in a seated position made me concentrate more on how chords and scales worked together on the guitar. I wasn't just responsible for knowing how the song goes—I needed to know how to play the song in every key, on the fly, without practicing it in that key. I needed to be able run major, minor, or blues scales throughout a song, hitting the key change at the same time the song changed chords—and again in any key.

Being a Deadhead, I was well-versed in improvisation, but I needed to work on structuring improvisation over the right parts of the guitar at the right moments. I started recording my songs on a four-track analog recorder and it cleaned up my playing as well as my song writing. I wasn't just leaving open spaces between verses. I wrote licks and kept everything tight.

My brothers Dan and Bagus had been playing in bands since college and had tolerated my playing in the past, but now I was shedding wood and catching up. They came up to Portland to play two benefit gigs for a disability group I helped fund in India. Eighty percent of what we played was our original material. Aside from not having a professional quality vocalist, we sounded like a bona-fide, honest-to-god rock and roll outfit.

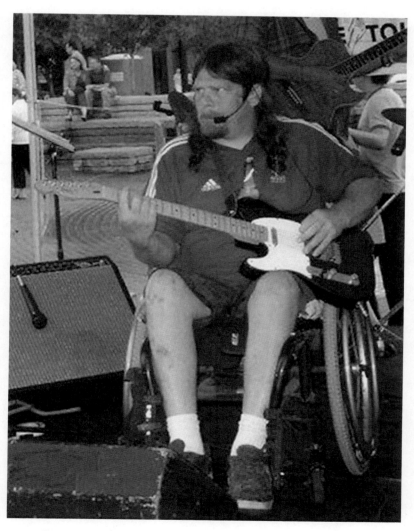

Sound check at Bastille Day 2004 in Portland. We rocked the joint!

Whenever we found ourselves back in Milwaukee, we got together with some of our oldest friends (Karl Landwehr [Toys], John Goldthwaite, Jon Bodner, Michael Bathke) who had also picked up their musical game in their 30s and 40s. We formed a group called The Khampas. (Khampas are the tribes from the eastern Tibetan province of Kham; proud, fierce, and independent.) In 2004 we pulled off a Midwest college tour in support of the Students for a Free Tibet organization.

Our finest hour came when the entire group met in to Portland and played more than five hours at the Portland Bastille Day Festival. (We split the 7-member Khampas into 2 bands, but basically it was all of us.) There was a roaming downtown crowd of 2,000 at the festival and we (along with our old high school friend Lance Halvorson's band) kept the Frenchies entertained all day. I'd kept my French together over the years and was the bilingual festival MC as well as the entertainment director, lead guitar player, and singer of the main act. It was an exhausting weekend, with two days of intensive rehearsals and a downtown rooftop gig the night before Bastille Day to warm up, but one we'll take with us to our graves.

During this time, I had a musical bucket list moment that I didn't even know happened until it was over—and it was an absolute fluke it happened at all. My best friend, Pat, had been living in Paris for most of his adult life and his wife planned a big 40th birthday party for him. I was invited, but my business was crap, and as much as I was dying to go back to France, I just didn't have the scratch to pop over to the continent.

Just a few weeks before the party, Pat's mother called from Milwaukee and asked me if I was going to the party. I told her I was broke and couldn't swing the ticket, but she told me she would buy it for me. After 40 years she had already given him every present she could think of, so she might as well just send me!

It was the nicest gift I've ever gotten in my life. We agreed to keep it a secret. I contacted Badou and Sophie Faye, old friends of ours, who would keep me hidden in Paris until the party. (I later lived with Badou and Sophie in Dakar.) I flew into Paris and hopped a Metro train into town, where Badou picked me up at the station. I crashed at his apartment for a few hours waiting for the party to start, then we headed over. There were two flights of stairs up to Pat's condo, so we needed help to get me up. Badou went upstairs and told Pat he needed help with a keg of beer. Pat came down the stairs to discover I was his keg of beer.

It was a most awesome surprise, followed by an incredible international bash that lasted long and loud until the sun came up. Pat had business in Amsterdam the following Monday, so we couldn't hang out long. But that fit into my plans, as my brother, Andy, was on sabbatical in Vienna. I could have flown but instead took a train to Geneva and spent a few days with the Couty family from Les Avenières. From there I hopped on one of Europe's most glorious train rides through Switzerland and Austria.

Andy and his family picked me up in Vienna and we spent the next few days exploring downtown Vienna and the Schönbrunn Gardens, a massive public park that used to be the home of Austrian royalty. For the first time in his adult life, Andy's schedule allowed for some free time. Being a fulltime doctor, medical school professor, father, and husband doesn't lend to an open schedule. But in Vienna, he just had to do daily rounds and a few lectures.

It allowed us one unencumbered night of clubbing, which ended up being one of the most memorable nights of my life. I searched the Internet to see if there were any shows in town and stumbled across a website for Jazzland, an underground club resurrected from the guts of a medieval wine cellar. The club was booked for the entire week by a trumpet player named Oscar Klein. Reviews of Jazzland rated it the number one jazz spot in all of Vienna. Legend says you don't ask someone in Vienna *if* they play an instrument; you ask them what instrument they play. If somebody could keep that place full for an entire week, they had to be something special.

We arrived at Jazzland, on Vienna's outer ring, only to discover there were more than twenty stairs down to the club level. Andy and the doorman went into the club for help and came back with two robust Austrians in a spirited mood after having downed a few glasses of the club's merlot. Jazzland waived the entrance fee and seated us at a table eight rows back from the stage. The venue looked like Liverpool's Cavern Club, which I'd visited fifteen years earlier. On that trip I experienced a religious epiphany as I looked upon the stage where The Beatles, my musical and cultural heroes, cut their teeth. I'd had long hair and was wearing a tie dye as a nod to the revolution that had taken place in that very club. But while that visit was a nostalgic revelation, this night would put me onstage with greatness.

The club was embarrassed they had no accessible entrance, so the first few pours were on the house. We took our first few sips but were taken aback by Oscar Klein and his "Country Blues Band." They were a five-piece squeezed tightly on a tiny stage underneath a cobblestone arch. The first row of long tables were pushed right to the edge of the stage, nearly putting those patrons in the middle of the band.

The 71-year-old Oscar Klein directed the band from underneath his sea captain hat, and let his young understudies steal the show. His drummer, Henri Altbart, was the dominant force in the band, and one of the greatest drummers I've ever seen. Not only was he lightning quick, but he also had a lyrical musicality to his playing, just like Keith Moon of the Who. Just before the set break, he filled the wine glasses of the front row patrons to different heights and played songs on them as if he were playing a xylophone. He played a ten-minute solo that rivaled anything John Bonham of Led Zeppelin ever did, then finished it off by juggling three sticks and playing at the same time—without missing a beat. When the rest of the band jumped back in, Jazzland exploded, with Andy and me leading the screams.

They finished their first set to a standing ovation and announced they would be back after a short break. I needed to hit the loo, but the bathrooms were down yet another ten steps. Luckily there were more than enough volunteers to get me down the stairs which led, amazingly enough, to an accessible bathroom—albeit thirty stairs from street level.

I did my business then rolled back to a team of patrons who carried me back up the stairs. Missing from that group was Andy, but that was because he was sitting at the bar—talking to Oscar Klein!

I rolled up to them and Oscar addressed me, "Your brother says you are a great guitar player—let's see what you've got!"

With that, Katie Kern, the lead singer and songwriter for the group, handed me her guitar.

"Hey, you guys," I said. "I can play, but I'm left-handed. I can make a go of it with this, but it's really not my jam."

I flipped the guitar upside down and whipped off a couple of blues progressions to show I knew what I was doing. I was in the process of handing the guitar back when Oscar said, "Nonsense! You play terrific! You're coming up onstage with us!"

Before I had a chance to question it, the band members were pushing back the front-row tables and clearing room for me on the stage. The path to the stage was so tight my chair didn't fit. I had to pull off my wheels while the band lifted me up and tucked me in between Katie Kern and the bassist, Jan Jankaje. I snapped my wheels back in, but I was jammed into a tiny box on the stage. I couldn't even turn around. Katie handed me her beautiful hollow-body Gibson and I dialed in a clean sound through a Marshall amp.

Oscar got on the microphone and addressed the crowd, who were more than a bit curious. "Good evening again, ladies and gentlemen…" (he was speaking in English now whereas he'd been addressing the crowd in German earlier in the night), "I want to introduce you to a young American who has a very strange talent. This is Tom Haig from Portland, Oregon and he will be playing rhythm guitar for us this evening, but he will be playing left-handed and upside down!"

One thing I've picked up in going to jazz clubs and festivals is they tend to be filled not with music fans but with actual musicians. Although there was some nice applause, I also looked over the audience to see a number of players with skeptical looks on their faces.

I tuned them out, then Oscar whispered to me, "Blues in C—a dirty C." I listened to the first loop of the song so I could tell what the progression was, then slid into the 12-bar blues they were laying down. As soon as I played the first chord, the crowd applauded, which shocked me, but I closed my eyes and just let the music pull me through.

The hours of working on progressions in every key was paying off, because this group was all over the place. It was all blues, but lots of it was much more complicated than a simple three-chord run-around. During one song, Oscar pointed to each member of the band and they had to pull a solo. Playing chords upside down is one thing, but ripping out a lick is a different trick. He pointed to me and I hit a smooth blues scale, trying to be clean rather than fast. I sweated it out for the entire progression then looked back at Oscar with a panic in my eyes that said, "Dude, get me out of here!"

Oscar signaled the group back in and we finished off with a flurry. The crowd went crazy, led by Andy, who was beaming ear to ear.

The purpose of the week-long stand was not to showcase Oscar, but Katie, who had just released her CD, *Pick-A-Blues*. Towards the end of the set, one by one, the band members stepped off stage until only Katie and I were left. Normally it was her solo slot, but since I couldn't get off stage, I backed her up and even sang some vocals. As long as I wasn't making bad noises, it all worked out great.

Katie took her final bow and the crowd gave her a nice hand while she walked off the stage. The show was over, but I was stuck onstage with 100 people staring at me! "I'm done, too!" I announced. It got a good laugh from the crowd followed by another nice round of applause as the band helped me off the stage and back to the bar where Andy was chatting it up with Heini Altbart.

I rolled over to Oscar, who gave me a big hug and told me I'd done great. I told him I wish I had my left-handed guitar so I could toss in some nice runs, but he said, "Nonsense! The crowd didn't leave, did they?"

Oscar was struggling to come up with English words, so I asked him if he spoke any French. As it turned out he'd spent decades in France and had played with all the jazz greats of the day. We stayed at the bar chatting frogspeak for two hours, swapping stories about the places we'd been, the shows we'd done, and the difficulties we'd overcome.

Oscar had overcome incredible odds in his lifetime. Being a Jew, he was interned in a Yugoslavian concentration camp where he saved his family's life with his trumpet. As a 14-year-old boy, he would play outside the barracks at night and it caught the attention of Romano Mussolini, an officer in the camp and the son of the Italian dictator. Romano was a schooled musician and had no interest in his father's fascist nightmare. He put Oscar's family into protected quarters, saving their lives. The two became lifelong friends and played music together for more than 50 years.

The next day, one of Andy's colleagues invited us to a wine tasting in the hills just south of Vienna. We were both a bit hungover from the night at Jazzland and Andy explained to his colleague why we were reluctant to dig into the offerings. "Jazzland!" his colleague said, "I know it well! I've seen all the greats play there."

Andy proudly interrupted, "Tom was able to get up and play with the band last night too! It was really fun."

"Who was playing?" the doctor asked.

"A local guy," I said, "Oscar Klein."

The doctor gave us a stunned look, "You mean THE Oscar Klein? THE OSCAR KLEIN!"

"Yeah," I said, "I think that's his name—that's right…Oscar Klein."

"You don't know who he is, do you?" the doctor said. "Oscar Klein is one of our national treasures. Oscar Klein is the father of Austrian Jazz. He is our Louis Armstrong. In Vienna you learn Mozart, Schubert, and Mahler, but you listen to Joe Zawinul and Oscar Klein!"

On the one hand I was stunned, but on the other hand, I was glad we didn't know beforehand, or I never would have gone up on stage!

* * * * * * * * * * * * *

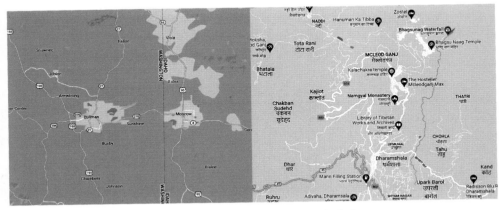

Pullman, Washington, and Dharamsala, India

Becoming a Journalist

Although I was keeping myself entertained in the 2000s, my business was not happening. I had enough cash to pay for room and board, but I was always looking at an empty bank account at the end of each month. I liked working on websites and print graphics, but I had no interest in drumming up business. I'd already hit up most of my friends for contracts and I began to feel like a pariah whenever I'd go to a BBQ or a party. I also realized my digital skill set was not keeping up with the industry. I became very skilled at HTML and Photoshop, but the mega-geeks were flying by me at lightning speed. I know the aptitude of people who are successful in the web-coding business and I was not that kind of person. They were in love with computers and could spend hours upon hours learning new code systems and backend database interfaces. I just liked it when my pages worked and looked cool. Something had to change.

In the spring of 2006, the most precious thing in my life, my 12-year-old golden retriever Sydney, was diagnosed with terminal cancer and I had to put her down. Dogs have always been mythical gods in my family and Sydney was the queen. As a pup she was so damn beautiful she stopped traffic. Cars would stop in the middle of the street and gawk at her. She knew she was a supermodel, too. When she was young and I was traveling quite a bit with Adidas, she liked to run away from home just as I was taking off for the airport. One time a family called to say they found her. When I went to pick her up, the three young kids in the family were in tears as she left. Sydney just hopped in the car and gave me a look that said, "See, I can get this kinda love anywhere."

But after I broke my back she completely changed. She knew I was messed up and she protected me like a soldier. I no longer had to walk her on a leash, and she would sprint to me whenever I called. Even when she grew older and her hearing and eyesight went south, she would still bound like a pup after a tennis ball. The end came suddenly as she went from an elegant old woman to a cancer survivor to her grave in less than one week.

Following her last vet checkup, I called my parents to tell them Sydney was on her last days. Mom and Dad loved her like a grandkid and cried on

231

the phone. The day before I had to put her down, Dad flew in from Milwaukee and said I shouldn't have to go through this alone. Rachel, who had always been a doting dog mom, Dad, and I took her to the vet, and we held her paws while the vet injected the now emaciated pooch with the sleeping serum. I'd never been so crushed in my life.

Her passing allowed me to gain some clarity. My apartment was eerily silent as Dad packed up his bag for the airport. Before he left he asked me if I was happy—did I think I was doing what I should? I told him I was barely staying afloat working for myself and had been applying for corporate jobs more than looking for contracts. Then he asked me, "If you could do anything, what would it be?"

"I guess I'd like to be a real journalist," I said. "Working for the Adidas paper was the best job I ever had, aside from diving."

"Then let's work on that," he said. "Why don't you start looking at schools? We'll find the money."

I began looking for journalism schools but was coming up against a brick wall. The print industry had begun its severe decline and newspapers all over the country were laying off staff or folding altogether. The only way to become a journalist was to become a broadcaster. Unfortunately, none of the schools in Oregon offered a broadcast sequence.

I put the idea away until one night I went to watch a West Virginia football game with Scott Fogarty, an old friend and a Mountaineer alumnus. While we were tossing down beers, I got into a conversation with a guy at an adjacent table about conditioning. I mentioned something about average joes not knowing anything about real athletic training like college athletes do. He said he'd played Division I basketball and he knew what I was talking about. I asked him where he played, and he said, "Washington State!"

The conversation drifted until I told Scott I was thinking of going back to school, but there weren't any broadcast programs in Oregon. "Dude!" he said. "You gotta check out Wazzu! We've got the best broadcasting school in the Northwest—maybe even America!"

He opened up his laptop to show me the page for The Edward R. Murrow College of Communication at Washington State University. I surfed my way around the site and it became obvious: Wazzu was the perfect place for me. I never saw that basketball player again, but eight weeks later, my apartment was packed up and I was driving along the Columbia River towards Pullman, eastern Washington, and Washington State University.

Had I actually visited Pullman, I might not have ever applied. Pullman is a citadel campus with San Francisco–sized hills leading up to the classrooms. My sister, Sue, took a week off and drove a U-Haul truck with my belongings over the frozen landscape to Pullman, which on January 2nd looked more like an Arctic research facility than a Pac-12 school.

I was accepted into the Murrow College, but I didn't have a major or even a place to live. I drove my van up to campus to get my academic program settled while Sue scoured Pullman looking for an accessible living situation. The frozen roads up to the Murrow Building were so steep and slippery I had to approach it from three different routes before I found one my van could climb. Getting around this campus in a wheelchair was going to be a nightmare.

I met with an academic advisor who told me I had been accepted into the graduate program for communication studies. I asked her what that meant, and she said it was a two-year program where I would do academic research on technical communication issues like linguistics and end-user data. I asked her when I would start reading the news and she told me the broadcasting program was an undergraduate degree.

"Can I just transfer into that program?" I asked.

"You can," she said, "But you've been accepted into a master's program. It's one of the best in the country. But if you're set on being a journalist..."

I was set. I dropped out of the master's program and signed up for the undergraduate broadcast journalism sequence. Since I already had a degree and more than sixty additional credits, I would only have to go to school for two years and change.

Out-of-state tuition was more than $17,000 a year, which was much more than my Dad had expected when he suggested I go back to school. He came up with money for the first semester, but I found a way to pay for the rest. I did research on disability athletic scholarships and came across the Swim with Mike Foundation (SWM) out of USC. SWM was organized by friends and teammates of Mike Nyeholt, a three-time All-American swimmer who had been paralyzed from the chest down in a motorcycle accident. What started out as a one-time fundraiser from his college teammates had blossomed into a massive non-profit putting dozens of disabled athletes through college. I'd applied for the scholarship before I got to Pullman and just a few weeks into my first semester, I got the call I'd been accepted. A full four-year athletic scholarship—and I didn't even have to go to practice!

My living situation at Washington State University ended up being the premise for a sit-com. In the steep hills of Pullman, there was no accessible off-campus housing. Every apartment had steps or driveways too steep for a wheelchair. After three days of searching, Sue found what ended up being the cheapest and nicest housing of all—the Pullman Retirement Home. I had an accessible three-room apartment—bigger than my apartment in Portland—and I was only paying $200 a month because of my disability. The catch was the youngest person in the apartment complex was in their 70s. That meant I would spend all day in school with kids in their early 20s, then come home and live with geriatrics. The only people who were my age were my professors—and I couldn't exactly ask them out for beers.

After college, everyone gets the dream where they are back in school freaking out because they haven't studied for their final. For the next three years, I was living that very dream, except for the part about showing up for the final unprepared. Seeing as I had no social life, I studied like I never had before. When I took the two semesters at Oregon State, I aced them, but that was because I had as much experience with the subjects as the professors. My coursework in Pullman, however, was all fresh information, so I had to study.

My first year I had to take a lot of pre-reqs to qualify for the broadcast news sequence. There was a technical sequence, a writing sequence, and a few broadcast history courses. None of it was difficult, but if you missed class you could get in trouble in a hurry. At first, getting around campus was difficult, but soon enough I discovered accessible parking spots hidden behind campus buildings. I also found I could enter buildings on the bottom floor from the lower campus and take elevators to the top floor—which, because of the severe hills, also had ground level access to the main campus on top of the hills. Despite the weather and the hills, in my five semesters at Wazzu I missed zero classes.

While I didn't have much of a social life, I wasn't exactly living like a monk either. I hooked up with Cable 8 productions, the Wazzu student-run TV station, and became a main contributor for After Hours, a weekly 30-minute sketch comedy show. Aside from playing music, I hadn't done any kind of performing since I quit high diving. By the end of my stay in France I'd become a good diving show clown and I missed that as much as I did the diving. I peaked as a diver, but I was still learning how to work a crowd. I hadn't been onstage for 15 years, but I felt right at home on After Hours. For two years I, along with a fantastic group of young comedy writers and performers (Dan Paris, Joey Clift, Dom Bonny, Ben Foley, Joanna Favali, Lacey Faught) created some of the funniest sketches I've ever seen. My chef-d'oeuvre was Captain Crip, a superhero parody where the hero happens to be in a wheelchair. We even got Glenn Johnson, who was not only our broadcasting professor but the actual mayor of Pullman, to do a cameo for us. Working on that show made me feel more alive than I had since leaving India.

Because my major was broadcast news, I was able to take a handful of eclectic electives to fill out the degree requirements. These classes ended up being absolute jewels taught by some of the most interesting people I've ever met. The best of these were in US History: Baseball, The History of Rock and Roll, Entertainment Management (we had George Takei for a lecture!) and Modern Popular Culture. At Illinois I never read the extracurricular reading list for any college course, but for these four I read everything I could get my hands on.

As I moved into the final semester in Pullman, I spent all my time working on Cable 8 nightly news. Each student was required to do every facet of the broadcast at least once—everything from writing sports, to manning the camera, to dancing around the weather maps. We also had to learn how to use the cameras and the video editing equipment. After two semesters of producing the news, I was picked by Glenn Johnson as a teaching assistant to teach the news.

We were also responsible for the content of KUGR, the campus radio station. We wrote and read daily newscasts, took turns doing DJ shifts and got to call sports for online broadcasts. My basketball partner Alex Haight and I felt like we were Dick Enberg and Al McGuire. In 2009, the Cougs were on an historically great run that saw them reach the NCAA Sweet 16. That brought national prominence to the program and Brent Musburger came in to call the game against our rival University of Washington Huskies. After the game, Musburger hung around to answer questions from students. When it was time to leave, I started pushing myself up the steep ramp to get out of Beasley Coliseum. I felt someone grab my handles and give me a push. Before I could say, "Hey, I got this!" I turned to see who it was. It was Musburger. I let him push.

Thirty months after I moved to Pullman, I graduated from the Edward R. Murrow College of Communication with a BA in Broadcast News. I four-pointed my final two semesters and graduated cum laude. It was a far cry from my B average at Illinois. I also won All-Campus awards as the Best News Writer, the Most Inspirational News Writer, the Best Soccer Play-by-Play Commentator, and the Best Basketball Color Commentator.

Old students ROCK! I barely escaped Illinois with a degree, but rolled out of Washington State's Murrow College of Communication, cum laude.

Had I been a 22-year-old graduate, the offers would have come pouring in for me. But as much as I was told my age wouldn't make a difference, it did. While many of my classmates were picked up by small market TV stations, my job applications went in the dustbin. One local news director who had assured me my age would be a great asset instead hired one of my students with whom I'd spent hours because she wrote poorly and couldn't edit video. I knew this going in, but it was tough to face after all the success I'd had in Pullman.

I went back to Portland and returned to coding websites and doing small print jobs, until I got an offer that nobody in my graduating class would ever see or consider. In the fall of 2009, I had been training hard for the

Washington DC Marine Corps Marathon, the biggest wheelchair race in the world. I had taken second in the Portland Marathon, but didn't even taper my training for it. I was all in for DC. Since I hadn't found work and could maintain my web clients from the road, I packed my bike in my van and drove from Portland to my brother's house in Charlottesville, Virginia. I had just cracked the Idaho border when Dan called, asking me if I wanted to go back to Dharamsala and help put a radio station on the air. Before he got the word "air" out of his mouth, I said, "Oh hells yeah!"

I was going back to Dharamsala to start a Tibetan radio station. The Tibetan Children's Village (TCV), founded by Mrs. Tsering Dolma Takla, the older sister of the Dalai Lama, is one of the best K-12 schools in India. For more than three years they had been working on getting a license to start a "community radio station," much like a "Pacifica" station in the United States. The paperwork had finally gone through, but they didn't know how to run a radio station. Their communications director, Phuntsok Dorjee, had reached out to Dan for help. I was to be the deus ex machina.

Before 2000, Indian radio was state-run, with one station taking up as much as 30 percent of the FM dial. But since 2000, at the insistence of some major players in the global communications industry, the Indian government has been selling radio frequencies for huge sums of cash. By 2010, the new radio giant, Big FM, owned 20,000-watt stations in all the big cities: Delhi, Calcutta, Mumbai, Madras, and Bangalore. They came in with plenty of capital and expertise and it's been a tremendous success.

But in the rural regions of the country there was no one to create and broadcast local content. This left significant populations lacking in health, agriculture, and legal information. So in 2006 the government opened up licensing to local non-profit agencies. If they could come up with enough gear to open a station and wade through the tedious Indian bureaucracy (locals call it "license raj"), they could operate a community radio station.

The first time I went to Dharamsala, I packed a huge box full of medical supplies. But in the ten years I'd been gone, Dharamsala had become much more sophisticated, with plenty of hospitals, pharmacies, and medical supply stores. All the medical supplies I had to pack in 2000 were now available in town.

By now I was a seasoned India traveler, so when I arrived in Delhi, I ignored the army of rickshaw drivers selling hotel rooms I knew were inaccessible. I had reserved a room in the Vivek Hotel right in the middle of my old Paharganj neighborhood.

When I went for my first stroll in the main bazaar of Paharganj, I noticed the street was unfamiliarly clean—or at least there wasn't trash piled next to store fronts. The cows were still there and I had to be careful not to roll over chunks of their biocrud, but the rotting piles of filth were much less ubiquitous than they had been in 1991. A lot of the shops and restaurants had changed owners, and my favorite restaurant was gone. There was also a large military presence monitoring metal detectors at the entrance to the main bazaar. I sat down at a pizza place and asked the owner what the deal was with all the soldiers.

"2010 Commonwealth Games," he said. "Everything in the city is changing. Much cleaner; new Metro. The army is here to drive the mafia out of Paharganj. Many of the buildings are coming down—the street will be repaved—maybe Delhi will get the Olympics if things go well."

In 1991, the thought of Delhi hosting the Olympics was kind of like Green Bay getting the Oscars. The country seemed to be one big unemployed open sewer. But that's the kind of transformation India has gone through over the past twenty years. Although there is still a population the size of the United States living in poverty, the loosening up of archaic English banking laws has created a more favorable business climate. The Indian call centers that we hate in the US are leading to new cars, wide screen TVs, cell phones, washing machines, and better medicine. In 1991 I couldn't go ten feet without crossing a heavily maimed beggar. But in 2010, after two days of roaming Old Delhi, I hadn't run into one.

Just across from the Vivek was a restaurant I used to hang at back in 2000. The same owner was there, and the same gaggle of Westerners were sitting in benches sipping Kingfisher Strong Beer. I bounced down two stairs to the floor and ordered a Kingfisher. I sat next to a Belgian named Jan who was riding a motorcycle to Goa for the annual Christmas debauchery. Jan had also been to India twice before, and we were marveling at the changes. Goodbye American Express Cheques, hello ATM. Goodbye telephone and telegraph office; hello WiFi. Jan's first trip to India was in 1991, just like mine. Then he said he'd be spending his birthday in India next week.

"Me too," I said. "How old are you gonna be?"

"48," he said.

"Me too," I said. "What day?"

"Monday the 21st," he said.

"Me too," I said.

I was staring at a guy who had spent almost the exact same number of minutes on this planet as I had—and both of us were thousands of miles away from home having never met each other. We sat back and sized each other up, then Jan laughed and said, "Shit like this happens in India all the time."

Four days later I was at the Delhi local airport climbing up stairs to a Kingfisher flight on my butt because they didn't have any way to get me on the plane. I sat in the last seat of a 40-seat commuter flight and gobbled up a suspect

The pipes broke in Paharganj, India during construction for the 2010 Commonwealth games. Every disease in the world is swimming in that puddle behind me.

chicken sandwich as we ventured north towards the Himalayas. I had made the same trip on the ground four times before, but I wanted to see the Himalayas from the air. Unfortunately, clouds blocked all but the highest peaks and I wouldn't get to see that full panorama until I passed by them again in 2016.

I'd only been gone from Dharamsala for ten years, but the metamorphosis of the village was mind blowing. I didn't even recognize where I was until the van dropped me off at the Pema Thang Guest House high above the Dalai Lama's temple.

As one makes their way down one of the six streets of McLeod Ganj, you notice the town is as international as New York, Dubai, Hong Kong, or London. You are just as likely to run into someone from Taipei as someone from Cedar Rapids. The majority of the town is Indian, but there is a large minority of Tibetan refugees and a smaller, but very noticeable, group of Westerners. (Noticeable because no other town of its size in the Indian Himalayas has more than a few lost white folks. Dharamsala and the surrounding area have more than a thousand.)

The only negative effect I noticed from the growth spurt was that many of the buildings had added two or three stories, which left the narrow streets sunless in the middle of the day. The other growth effects made the place much more palatable. The streets had been paved and effective drainage kept puddles and creeks at bay. For someone in a wheelchair, this was a godsend. Although the opportunity to teach broadcasting to the kids at the Tibetan Children's Village was something I couldn't pass up, in the back of my mind was the fact that I didn't survive my first stay in McLeod Ganj. In 2000, after two months of rolling along muddy roads chock-full of cow/dog/monkey/human urine and feces, I'd developed an infection that even powerful antibiotics could not cure.

As I took my first stroll into town, I caught a most welcome sight—a garbage truck. Back in 2000, shop and restaurant owners tossed their trash into the street or out their back window down a ravine. One of the main entrances to the town was a festering garbage heap that gagged even the Indians who grew up next to it. It has since been replaced by the new McLeod Ganj bus terminal with (gulp) an accessible ATM! The hillsides that had a grating skin of plastic trash on them have been cleaned up and the old pockets of dump-funk air had been minimized.

Ever since my first visit to a foreign hospital in Taiwan, one of the major goals of any trip I take is to not have to visit the hospital. On this trip the dream lasted less than 48 hours. Before I even made it back to the Pema Thang my stomach was rumbling with the awful sensation of Delhi belly. I ate a plate of white rice and drank gallons of bottled water to flush the bugs, but it didn't work. By the time the sun rose, I had a 101 degree fever, I hadn't slept a wink, and I'd worn a path to the bathroom—which was up a step and had no hot water.

I was supposed to start work, but when Phuntsok Dorjee, my new boss, came to take me to the Tashi Delek FM studios, he took one whiff of the room and knew I was sick. He looked at me with a puzzled frown, extended his hand and asked me if I wanted to start the next day. In my condition, all I could say was, "Yeah, that'd be great…"

Five full days later, my symptoms had cleared (or so I thought!) and it was time to get to work. I hadn't even left my room since my first stroll and couldn't be happier when the TCV jeep came up to the Pema Thang to take me up to the radio studio. The driver's name was Rajesh and he became my pilot for the next six months. I considered Rajesh a coworker; we would eventually go on some

Blown away by the Taj Mahal. The most beautiful man-made thing I've ever seen.

long drives to obtain materials for my wheelchair and the studio, but I could never get him to call me "Tom." I saw him every day for six months, yet he continued to call me "sir."

The three-mile drive from McLeod Ganj to the TCV took me through a dense forest, past the hamlet of Forsyth Ganj, then rose above the valley around sacred Dal Lake to an auditorium looking over the TCV football grounds. Rajesh helped me out of the jeep, where I was met by my new coworker Kalsang Tsewang. Kalsang was a local musician and the technical expert behind Tashi Delek FM. He was a man of few words, which would prove awkward when the power would go out, but he was a brilliant guy who kept the station on the air.

Kalsang told me to wait while he gathered up some friends to carry me up four big steps to the foyer of the auditorium. That would have been enough of a daily challenge, but I was soon to discover the studio was up another two flights of stairs. By the time they carried me up there, the four of us were exhausted. I gave Kalsang a worried look and asked, "Is the studio staying up here? Are we going to have to do this up and down every day?" He just shrugged and said, "It's no big deal."

Kalsang opened the door to a tiny studio thirty feet long but with four feet of space between the desks and the wall. There was a long desk with a row of computers and a single microphone mounted in a stand. Kalsang turned on the power and waited for the computers to boot up. Then he flipped on a light switch connected to the 50-watt radio tower perched on a ridge 500 feet above us. He opened his iTunes account and started a random playlist of Tibetan classical and folk songs.

And that was Tashi Delek FM.

The next few weeks were glorious in Dharamsala as we began staffing Tashi Delek FM and working on dividing Dharamsala into news beats. We planned to cover health, government, music, sports, social events, and the Dalai Lama Temple. One thing they didn't tell me was Indian radio is not allowed to cover politics. This was a stunning revelation, as the entire reason the Tibetans are in India is political. I had planned at least an hour a day for interviews with local leaders on the Tibetan struggle for independence, but we weren't allowed to cover it. Indian TV and the Internet were ripe with these stories, but radio was not allowed to cover them. The Indian government was afraid of splinter or terrorist groups running small radio stations, so they banned politics. Again, it was India being extreme.

Our second week in operation we had our first celebrity interview. Alice Walker, the author of *The Color Purple*, was on a humanitarian tour of India and the Middle East and was going to speak with the Dalai Lama. We weren't allowed to cover the actual meeting, but we were allowed to follow her around the TCV and even conduct a full hour interview with her. It was the first time I'd ever interviewed a non-athlete celebrity, so I prepped heavily. Phuntsok was interviewing with me so he would cover Tibetan issues while I took on more global themes. We set up our remote recording equipment (it was all equipment from the States—computer, two microphones with stands, and a tiny mixing board donated by my bandmate, Goother) at Ms. Walker's hotel and had an unforgettable conversation with one of the most influential women in US history. In the end, it wasn't the context of our discussion that stayed with me. It was her calm demeanor discussing the inevitability of her actions. She was visiting His Holiness for a few days, then flying to Jerusalem to head up an illegal march in support of Palestine. Her life could be on the line, but she spoke of it almost as if it were merely a personal matter. Just something she had to do, even though thousands would be following her.

We spent January building playlists and preparing for the students to return to the TCV so I could begin teaching them much of the same content I'd learned at WSU. Then one of the worst nightmares a paraplegic can ever come across nearly cost me my leg. Although the days in January were warm and sunny (50–60 degrees F), at night temperatures dropped below freezing. I'd moved to the picturesque village of Bhagsunag, which sits at 7,000 feet above sea level. When the sun dropped below the mountains in early evening, the temperature shot down 20 degrees in a matter of minutes.

When I got home from work, I would put my laptop on a wooden platform and set the platform on my knees. I bought a cheap double-filament Chinese heater and placed it below the platform to warm my legs, which were often freezing after sitting in the cold studio all day. There was no heat in my hotel, so that small Chinese firetrap was my only source of warmth. Just days after I bought the heater, one of the filaments burned out and I hadn't had time to replace it. One night while I sat at my makeshift desk, I felt the wooden platform warming up. I lifted the platform and saw the burned-out filament blazing away. It had a bad connection that randomly reconnected.

I felt down my left leg and discovered my pants were nearly on fire. I lifted the pant leg and saw a gigantic blister along my shin. It was ten inches long and

Kalsang Tsewang, Phuntsok Dorjee and I pose with Alice Walker after our interview with her for Tibetan radio.

four inches wide. The skin was red and bubbling. There was no ice in the hotel and no snow on the ground, so all I could do was pour cold water on my burn. The colors kept changing from red to white to pink to purple. I swallowed a handful of aspirin, drank two liters of water and went to bed.

When I woke up, the skin had ballooned into a gigantic bubble filled with fluid. It covered the entire outside of my lower left leg. I showed it to the owner of my hotel, and he looked at me as if I were going to die. We wrapped it in gauze and waited for Suresh to pick me up. Suresh took one look at it and drove me straight to the Tibetan hospital on the road to Lower Dharamsala.

When the doctors saw me, they freaked out. They'd never seen a burn like it in their lives. This wasn't a sear from wood or boiling water. This wound was slow-cooked. Anyone who could feel their leg would have pulled it away from the heat source immediately. But I had let it sit there for an hour.

The doctors debrided my wound, gave me a jug of antibiotics, and told me I had to get a new sterile dressing every day for the next two to three months. Big burns are notorious for being almost healed, then getting infected to the point where one could lose a limb. Everything was going so well in Dharamsala and then WHAM! I was stuck in another life-changing medical crisis.

For the next three months, I went to the TCV clinic every day before work. Suresh pushed me up a super steep 50-foot ramp, then a doctor would debride my wound and change the dressing. But just as the first doctor predicted, 6 weeks into healing, the wound became infected and I was rushed off to the Indian hospital 45 minutes away in Kangra. Kangra had a burn unit and their doctor nearly flipped out when he saw my wound. Instead of showing concern and comforting me, he began yelling at me!

"How could you do this to yourself?! What were you thinking?! Don't you know you can burn yourself in your condition?!"

He was super angry and he began to scare me a bit. I sheepishly looked at him and said, "Doctor, you realize I can't feel my leg, right?" I was hoping the guy actually knew what a spinal cord injury was.

In the end, he debrided the wound and cut out quite a bit of infected tissue. He told me I needed a skin graft or I would most likely lose my leg. I asked him if Indian skin would work with my white skin and he furrowed his brow and gave me the Indian non-committal head shake.

I was hooked up to intravenous antibiotics, then shelved in a dark room with ten empty cots. I couldn't sleep, and unfortunately, I'd finished my book the day before, so I didn't have anything to read. All I could do was stare at the cracked walls in a dark, dirty hospital room with a leg I might lose any day. If there is a hell, I'd like to at least take a peek at it and compare.

Eventually I was moved into a ward with five large beds. None of the other patients spoke English, but just being around people took my thoughts away from my circumstance. Each patient had at least one other family member sitting on the edge of their beds playing cards or reading magazines or snacking. Anytime anyone pulled out food, they came over to my bed to offer some. Every time someone opened a bottle, they offered it to me first. They could see I was in a state of panic and they did everything they could to comfort me—and they weren't even staff.

Shortly before dark, a doctor took a peek under my dressing and said I could go home. I called Rajesh and he sent Kalsang over with the jeep. Kalsang took me to the pharmacy for more antibiotics then dropped me off at my hotel. Before leaving he looked at me and said, "Maybe you should stay home a few days?"

I took a week off and changed the dressing every day. I kept the leg elevated and never let any of the damaged skin touch my chair or my bed. Every day either Phuntsok or Rajesh would stop by to see how I was doing. After five days, I could see the wound was healing and I decided I could try going back to work. I continued the daily debriding for another month, until scabs began to form and skin began to grow underneath it. As you can imagine, there is quite a scar. While that story is quite harrowing, as it turns out, I never felt any pain and was able to be productive the entire time.

Phuntsok gave us four TCV employees who wanted to learn how to write news, so I sent them out to cover the town. I hung out in cafes all over McLeod Ganj and Bhagsunag looking for local musicians to put on the radio. I started a Saturday night open mic series, Dharamsalad, at a local restaurant called Nick's Italian Kitchen. Dharamsala is full of musicians, so I recorded as many as I could and put the best ones on Tashi Delek FM.

Just as my leg became manageable, another catastrophe occurred. I was riding up the long hill from McLeod Ganj to Bhagsunag when I hit a rock and was tossed onto the road. A bunch of people helped me back onto my chair, but after a few pushes I noticed something was wrong. I looked down at my front caster wheels and saw one of them was missing! It had torn clear off—I had become a three-wheeled bandit! Amazingly, my Quickie wheelchair was so well balanced I got full traction on three wheels. But transferring was difficult, and it put lots of strain on the remaining caster wheel. When I got home, I grabbed a brick from one of the construction projects (there were dozens of them) and used it to steady my chair for transfers. I rode like this for three days until Suresh drove me out to Kangra to find an aluminum welder. They welded my chair and I thought my problems were over. But only two weeks later, I hit a rut going up a hill and the wheel cracked off again. This time I put the wheel in my backpack and just kept going.

I spent my last two months in Dharamsala on three wheels. I ended up being the baddest wheelie rider that town had ever seen. I climbed the five-mile, 2,500-ft. rise from Kotwali Bazaar in Lower Dharamsala to my hotel in Bhagsunag on three wheels. I was damned if I was going to let a chair foible destroy my last few months in the Himalayas, especially after a Chinese heater had destroyed the previous two months. I pushed like hell on the uphills and rode like a circus rider on the descents. One night on my way home I was chased by a pimp who tried to sell me a sex worker. I told him to take his shit show out of town and he took great offense to that. He chased me on his motorcycle all the way to Bhagsunag, twice trying to knock me off the road. At one point I almost lost it down the side of a steep embankment, but I was able to spin away and stay on the road, controlling my careening chair by grabbing the spinning wheels. Not only were my wheelies solid, but my hands were tough as leather.

I also played as much guitar as I ever had in my life. My musical goal before I left was to write an album from scratch. Over the course of the six months, I wrote eight new songs, which are still in my playing repertoire. When I arrived in Dharamsala in 2000, I was a basic chord-strumming side man. But ten years later, I'd become one of the best players in town. The music scene in Dharamsala was fickle, as cafes got popular and faded depending on their proximity to the guest house of the next good musician who passed through town. After a few months, the cafe owners knew that if I was playing, it would draw in more musicians and lots of paying customers. By my last month in town, I was booked every Friday and Saturday night. I refused their money because it was usually the equivalent of two or three dollars—but I didn't have to pay for food or beer!

Thank God I was booked for those final weekends, because Tashi Delek FM had nearly fallen apart. The road up to the TCV Auditorium went under construction and it became impossible for me to access the studio. Up to that point, I was doing eight newscasts a day and still coming up with new music and podcasts. But the grand opening kept getting put off. When the road construction started, the station went right back to the way it was before I came—just recorded music. Without me there, the students were too embarrassed to read the news. Many of them thought the big voice of the radio was too loud a mouthpiece for a simple student.

There was also no firm date for the grand opening—or more accurately, I was not informed of the date of the grand opening. The people at the TCV knew the Dalai Lama was coming to the station for its inauguration, but he was scheduled to come on June 3rd—one day after my plane left for France. Nobody had the heart to tell me. Once I wasn't at the station every day, they just pretended I wasn't around anymore. But when I got to France and looked at the Dharamsala news feeds, I saw a picture of a full auditorium, with His Holiness the Dalai Lama putting khata scarves on my students and everyone who worked at the station I helped build.

The disappointment was overwhelming.

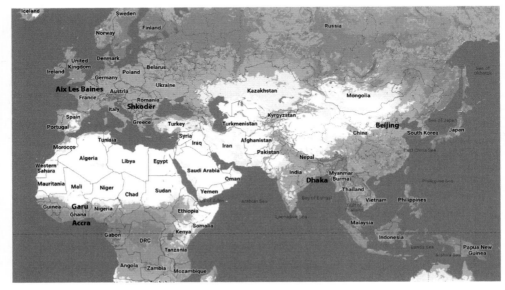

Making Movies

Making Movies

I returned to Portland and cobbled together a life doing disability seminars and volunteering at Oregon Public Broadcasting. I sent out reams of resumes to TV stations all over the country, but I wasn't even getting rejection letters in return. I thought graduating cum laude from one of the nation's most respected journalism schools and starting a radio station in the Himalayas from scratch would surely draw some attention. But alas, TV news is entertainment, and there was no place for a 50-year-old rookie.

While TV stations were not interested in me, the rehabilitation medicine community was. In 2003, my brother Andy and I started the International Rehabilitation Forum (IRF), a group of rehabilitation doctors working in low-resource countries. Over the next decade, we'd made great strides in connecting doctors in poor areas with cutting-edge physicians in wealthier nations. We'd organized some fantastic meetings in Turkey and Puerto Rico and had built an eager group of doctors, nurses, and therapists who wanted to work in challenging areas outside of their countries.

The most useful skill I acquired from my time at the Murrow College was editing audio and video. It was daunting at first because we were using old, clumsy Avid equipment. It was more difficult loading the video into the software than editing the video. But once I slogged through the process and started editing video on a daily basis, ideas sprung into my head that I couldn't ignore. I wanted to travel to the hospitals where our IRF colleagues worked and make documentaries about their struggles and successes.

I'd proposed the film idea to the IRF board, which they pondered for the better part of two years. I never got a "no," but I didn't get the magic "yes" either. Seeing as this was a virtual group that didn't meet often, it was an idea on the back burner until we would come together at a medical conference and get enthused about it again.

One day I got a message on my Facebook feed, from someone I didn't know, asking me if I was friends with a name I didn't recognize. Normally I would have just flushed it, but it was written from Aix-les-Bains, France, just 30 kilometers from Les Avenières. I clicked on the name of the second person and was stunned to see the face of Hélène (pronounced "L-N"), a

249

woman I dated in France nearly 20 years earlier. I replied to the post saying, "Of course I remember Hélène!" Two days later I got an email from her. And thus began a dreamy, whirlwind two-year period that, unfortunately, was a dream I would have to wake up from.

Hélène had two older kids and had been divorced for a few years before we reconnected. She had fallen into some money and decided she wanted to go out and see the world. The last time she had been to America was in 1988 when she traveled from Montreal to Milwaukee with my brother Dan and me. She said she was thinking of coming back to America and wanted to know where I thought she should visit.

I only had to show her a few pictures of Oregon and she was convinced. She wouldn't be coming for several months, and that gave us some time to rediscover each other. Eventually she arrived in Portland and I was smitten. I showed her around town and took her on some stunning day trips into the Cascades. Hélène said she wanted to fly to Los Angeles to visit Jennifer Kelly, another one of our old Les Avenières teammates with whom she'd also reconnected. I suggested we forego the flight and drive down south in my van, stopping at all the national parks along the way. Needless to say, by the end of that trip we were together. After a month in the States, Hélène asked me if I could come to France and try to make a go of it. It was the quickest "yes" I've ever uttered in my life.

In December of 2013, the IRF hosted its third World Congress in Dhaka, Bangladesh, in conjunction with the Bangladesh Society of Physical Medicine and Rehabilitation. The IRF popped for a ticket, but I requested it go through Geneva on my way to Dhaka. On the return, I was getting off the plane in Geneva, but I wasn't getting back on. I was moving to Aix-les-Bains.

But before I returned to the Alps, the IRF had a meeting to run. I had a new task at this convention. I'd purchased a Canon camcorder and began filming events at the conference as well as back-roll (B-roll) shots all around Dhaka. The bustling streets of downtown Dhaka were full of buses, taxis, and plenty of high-end new cars—a surprising contrast to the preconceived image Americans have of Bangladesh. But when we traveled into the twisted neighborhoods of old Dhaka, bicycle rickshaws took the place of taxis and bells replaced the ubiquitous blaring South Asian cab claxon. We visited massive public gardens, and Andy popped me up the 23 steps to the porch of the Asahn Manzil, or "Pink Palace," which used to house the local rulers.

Over the next four days, we were privy to one of the rarest medical conventions an American could ever attend. There were presentations on rehab due to torture, rehab for Islamic prayer positions, and how to build rehab clinics with little or no money. My presentation was on the effect of social media in global rehabilitation medicine. Much of my presentation required me to be hooked up to the Internet, so I was in a bit of trouble when I discovered there was no Internet at my conference room—and much of YouTube in Bangladesh is censored. I reworked my presentation and got it ready just in time to speak to an eager and attentive crowd of 30 physicians.

While the presentations are novel and exciting, the best part of these meetings is getting to know doctors from around the globe who tackle great hardships just to keep their practices alive. Many of the Bangladesh doctors had to postpone their medical schooling because the country was involved in a civil war for years and the medical schools were shut down. One doctor told me he kept his anatomy textbook in his backpack while he carried a gun on the front lines of the conflict that gave birth to their country.

When I was living in India, I met Javed Abidi, the president of Disabled Persons International (DPI), a group that champions disability rights all over the world. The IRF flew Javed in for a keynote address on how he got the Indians with Disabilities Act pushed through the immensely bureaucratic Indian Parliament.

At the end of his talk, the two of us fielded questions about disability rights in our respective countries. But when one question centered on Nepal, a diminutive figure walking on canes emerged from the crowd to answer it. Dr. Raju Dhakal and I met that day and have been very close ever since. There was something about his demeanor that told me he was much more than just a doctor. Raju is a fantastic guitar player and an astute observer of the disability world, both a physician and a person with a disability. At the time, Nepal did not have any practicing rehabilitation doctors. Raju was studying in Dhaka so he could return to Kathmandu as the leader of Nepalese rehabilitation medicine. In just a few years' time, Raju would send my life in yet another astounding direction.

As the conference came down to its last day, Dr. Taslim Udin, the president of the Bangladesh Society of Rehab Medicine, informed us of a labor strike the following morning that might force the final presentations to be canceled. Dr. Udin and the hotel manager (who was legally in charge of our safety) told us they would not be comfortable with us leaving the hotel in the morning.

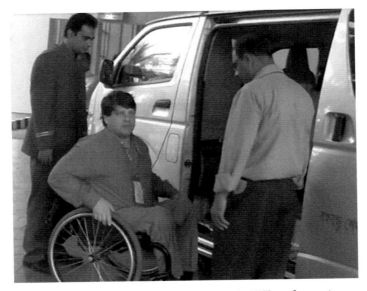

Avoiding rioters by taking an ambulance to the IRF conference in Dhaka, Bangladesh.

We went to bed a bit nervous, but the Bangabandhu Sheikh Mujib Medical University hosting the conference was only a quarter mile away. We couldn't imagine not being able to sneak across the street for final presentations and the closing ceremony. But in the morning, when I turned on the TV, I saw images of violent demonstrations all over the capital. This was a full-blown riot, or "hartal" as it's called in Dhaka. Cars were overturned, buses were set on fire, and riot squads marched on demonstrators all over the city. We were not allowed on the street, but we could see and hear the violence from our hotel rooms.

We met for breakfast and once again, the hotel manager told us we would not be safe crossing the street. Something close to martial law had gone into effect and all the streets were closed. But Dr. Udin had a great idea. The only vehicles allowed on the street were police cars, fire trucks, and ambulances. Dr. Udin looked up at us and said, "Hey! We've got plenty of ambulances!"

Twenty minutes later, the IRF board members were loaded into two ambulances in front of the hotel and ferried down the road under police escort to the conference at the medical school. When we exited the ambulances, we were greeted with cheers and directed through a back entrance to the conference hall. It felt a little bit like being a Beatle.

The conference ended up being a huge success and a great feather in the cap of the IRF. The Bangladesh PM&R Society is the largest society of any developing country in the world and it was amazing to be a part of it. Andy and I even got up onstage during their talent show and played a few numbers backed by a band of Bangladesh PM&R doctors!

I flew back to Geneva and it didn't take me more than a few days to feel right at home in Aix-les-Bains. I found old friends from the high-diving days and got to know Hélène's friends and family. My French was a little stiff at first, but after a week I left English behind and didn't even use it for my internal dialogue. Hélène was a masseuse at an exclusive spa an hour away in Geneva, so when she was gone, I sat at my computer doing work for the few clients I still had from my web business.

On the weekends, we ventured all over the French Alps visiting friends and family who lived in Shangri-La locations. I reconnected with my French parents, Jackie and Jeanine, as well as the Fabbri and Vermaut families from Les Avenières who have taken me in on more than a dozen occasions. I'd spent parts of nine different summers in the Alps, but the last time I spent a winter there was on my very first trip to Europe in 1986. In all my time in the Alps I'd never even skied there. I made up for lost time by joining Handisport Savoie, a handicap ski club that had outings at the best ski stations in France.

But the coolest part was spending a Christmas among towering snow-covered peaks. Hélène used to own a restaurant high in the Bauges Mountains at the base of the Aillon-le-Jeune resort. I had Christmas dinner there with her kids, deep in an Alpine valley.

I had to get to work, so I got busy shooting and editing video. It took a few weeks to put together a 20-minute documentary for the Bangladesh conference, and then another week to dub it in French. Once that project was done, I started shooting video all over town. I interviewed locals and made an English-friendly travel video of Aix-les-Bains that got picked up by the local Chamber of Commerce. I got friendly with the Aix Maurienne professional basketball team and shot a piece on their two American stars. I even took the camera up to film the Handisport Savoie Slalom Ski championships.

After a few months I had to leave the country for visa reasons, so Hélène and I took a trip to London to see my friend, Pat, and his family. I shot video the whole trip and cobbled together a comedy piece featuring every major monument in the city. When we got back to France, things started to get a bit tense, as it was clear I wasn't going to be able to stay for the summer. I'd stretched the visa regulations as far as they could go, and after several attempts to get a long-stay visa, I was told I had to leave France for at least six months before returning. The news was devastating, but there was nothing I could do. I had to go; failure to comply could easily result in a multi-year ban. In order to get a long-stay visa, I had to apply from the United States, not France. I know all sorts of games to cheat on visas, but if I was going to make a go with Hélène, we had to go by the book.

Seeing as I was already on the other side of the world, I wasn't going directly back to Oregon. I'd been shooting and editing video on a daily basis for six months and the idea of visiting the clinics of IRF doctors to make documentaries was more present than ever. Andy and I were planning an IRF global session at the International Society of Physical and Rehabilitation Medicine (ISPRM) conference in Beijing in mid-July. That gave me six weeks to shoot video anywhere in the world between France and China. I'd been in close contact with Germano Pestelli, the vice president of the Italian PM&R federation. He begged me to go to a small clinic in Albania where they had spinal cord patients who rarely left their bed. I'd also been asked by Gifty Gnyante, a physical therapy professor from Ghana, to shoot video in Africa. With the French government saying, "You don't gotta go home, but you gotta get up outta here!" I booked my ticket: Lyon—> Istanbul—> Tirana, Albania—> Istanbul—> Accra, Ghana—> Cairo—> Beijing—> Chicago. I'd figure out how to get back to Portland after I got back to the States.

After a tearful goodbye with Hélène in Lyon, I took the first step of what would prove to be the most difficult yet rewarding trip of my life. It started off in stunning fashion as the Turkish Air A330 Airbus swung north out of Lyon then angled off to the east, flying past every place I love in France. I could see the cliffs I used to stare at before launching 75-foot high dives. On the other side of those cliffs lay Aix-les-Bains, where I'd spent the last six months, and the Lac du Bourget, where I trained on my hand bike. I traced the bike paths back to my apartment but had to look away, as it was a bit too painful to think I no longer lived there.

Once past Aix the flight veered over the Savoyarde capital of Chambéry and headed to the French Alps, where I spotted my friend Vincent's house just outside of the Olympic city of Albertville. Next came the big Alpine peaks, including Mt. Blanc, the Eiger, and the Matterhorn. The plane drifted south over Italy, where I had a clear view of the Milan Cathedral. Just a few minutes later I traced the long bridge that led to the funky fisheye at the end of the Bridge to Venice—the genesis of everything my life was about.

Before the sun set, I caught reflections of the Adriatic along the Dalmatian Coast, where in 1986 my brother Dan and I spent five chilling January nights incarcerated in a Ford Escort. An hour later the pilot circled the Bosphorus Strait, where a crescent moon, the symbol of Turkey, was blazing in the distance.

After an overnight turnaround in Istanbul, I landed in Albania. Albania is Europe's poorest and most secluded country and, up until recently, traffic jams would have been impossible. But now the streets were full of everything from antique Russian cars and horse carts to brand new BMWs. Not two minutes after arriving in a surprisingly accessible hotel in the center of Tirana, I was deep in REM sleep.

I woke up six hours later, not sure if I wasn't still dreaming. The Madonnina del Grappa, the clinic where I would be filming, was 90 minutes north in the town of Shkodër, an ancient Adriatic city that is equal parts Muslim and Catholic. I was picked up at my hotel by Fabrizio Nocchi, the clinic manager, who told me he was putting me to work every day of my stay. I was listening, but my eyes were drawn toward the incredible landscape that went from high mountains down to the Adriatic coastline. The national highway wasn't anything like an interstate, but was instead a four-lane rural road. As we approached cities and villages, the road became the main street of each little town, then turned back into a highway as we exited.

As we got further from the capital, I saw more traditional dress, more bike commuters, and even some livestock on the roads. Although I saw plenty of late-model cars on the road, there were also an abundance of abandoned vehicles in ditches. I later learned that Albania has more stolen vehicles than any country in Europe. Thieves go to rich countries and steal cars, but don't have enough money to fix them once they are back in Albania, so they are left on the roadside.

When we got to Shkodër, the center of town was undergoing a massive makeover with new cobblestone streets and sidewalks, curb cuts, and the occasional ramp. The street markets were full, and cafes were getting ready to receive happy hour crowds. The 2014 scene was quite different from the country that had been isolated for decades under the dictator Enver Hoxha. Hoxha killed tens of thousands in his quest to make Albanian communism the purest form of communism in the world. He broke off ties with the

Soviet Union at one point because they weren't communist enough. So while the rest of the Balkans became Tito's Yugoslavia, Albania aligned itself with Mao and stayed an isolated nation like North Korea, completely closed off from the rest of the world.

Globally there are two Albanian icons: John Belushi and Mother Teresa. In between you will find the full range of Albanian personalities. In my two weeks in Shkodër, I saw just as many drunks as I did orthodox Muslims. One morning I met the surgeon general of the country, and later that afternoon I met a man so traumatized by a gunshot wound that he never left his home. That was the normal range for a typical day in Shkodër.

I checked into my hotel in the city center, then Fabrizio drove me through a tight labyrinth to the Madonnina del Grappa clinic, which would be the base of my operations. I'd shot a little video along the way and wanted to recharge my battery, so I found an outlet and plugged in my charger. This would prove to be a grave mistake—one of the many made over the course of the next six weeks that could have ended the entire project.

Fabrizio introduced me to several physical therapists who, through varying competencies in English and French, said they had people they wanted me to meet and things they wanted me to film. After having almost no schedule for six months, I would be booked nearly every hour for the next two weeks.

Fabrizio made his rounds, then asked me if I was ready for dinner. I told him I was famished, but I had to pack up my battery charger. I rolled into the small office where I'd plugged in the battery charger and smelled the acrid scent of electrical burn. I yanked out my charger only to discover it was fried, taking both of my two-hour batteries with it. That left me with one 45-minute battery I could only charge from the camera—which was slow going at best. I hadn't even shot my first interview and I was already without a backup battery. One sacred rule I learned from the Murrow College is to always have a backup. I asked Fabrizio if there were camera shops in town, but he looked at my camera and said he doubted they would have my battery—not for such a new camera.

I went back to my hotel and unpacked my bag. Sitting on the bottom of my bag was the brand-new tripod Hélène bought me before leaving Aix-les-Bains. I pulled it out of its sheath and slid the legs out only to discover the airlines had destroyed two of the three legs. Instead of having unlimited battery power and a stable shooting platform, I would spend the next six weeks shooting off a one-foot-high guerilla tripod and constantly searching for electrical outlets in two countries where electricity could not be taken for granted. On top of that, the camera's power cord had gotten bent and the battery wouldn't charge unless I wrapped the cord tightly and jammed the camera between two immovable objects. When I left France, I was worried about finding interview subjects. Now I was worried about turning my camera on.

The next morning, I gingerly packed my camera gear and rolled over some rough cobbles to the clinic. I was introduced to the first of two incredible women who would save me over the next six weeks. Linda Cenaj was a local language student whom Dr. Pestelli had hired to translate. Linda was smart and assertive, and I never had to explain anything to her twice. I explained the project and she just nodded her head and asked to look at my day planner. She made notes in her schedule and told me there were a few times she couldn't join me, but for the most part she was on board. On the very last day I discovered the reason she couldn't join me was that she was in the middle of her finals! I remember not even being able to think straight during college finals, but she was working on a major film project all day and studying at night!

The other thing Linda was used to was stuff breaking down. I explained how screwed up my camera equipment had become, and she just shrugged it off and said, "It's Albania. That's normal here." She learned how to work the camera and took it upon herself to find places to charge the camera—many of which were too high for me to reach or behind things I couldn't move. The battery was always in the back of our minds, but it was no longer the debilitating issue I feared it would be.

The project was limping, but it was time to shoot interviews. The doctors, clinicians, and local leaders spoke good English, so I could handle those, but many of the patients needed Linda to translate. I would ask the questions and they would nod as if they understood, but then look at Linda, who would make sense of it.

The clinic allowed us to go on house calls to see the full spectrum of spinal cord patients. On one morning we spoke with Olympic judokan and quadriplegic Anton Shkoza, who owned and operated his own gym. Then an hour later, we talked to a close neighbor, a paraplegic who was too depressed to leave the house. Unfortunately, there were many more of the latter than the former. Disability awareness was nearly non-existent in Albania and I realized Dr. Pestelli had been invited not so much to film, but to be an example of someone who wouldn't let disability get in the way.

Word got out I was making a documentary and all kinds of people jumped on board. I interviewed Dr. Astrit Beci, the former surgeon general of Albania, and Linda scored her best coup by interviewing Lorenc Luka, the mayor of Shkodër. By pure luck we were able to interview Albanian autism advocate Alma Topalli Prendi, who would soon be named one of the most influential women in the country. We also had the tables turned on us when Radio Pulla, the local rock station, had us on for one of their morning broadcasts.

I'd almost forgotten about the equipment snafus when one morning I suffered another devastating setback. I was rolling over some rough cobbles when my left front wheel snapped out of its mooring and swung loosely in its place. Something like this happened the week before I left France, but I thought I'd secured it. I hopped out of the chair, pulled out the wrench I used in France (luckily it wasn't confiscated at the airports like it would have been in the US!) and tightened it down. That lasted for about a half a mile before the constant jarring of the cobbles loosened it again. Now, on top of my camera and tripod being a mess, I was a mess. And I hadn't even gotten to Africa yet.

We made it to the clinic, where a wheelchair expert secured the wheel. But it was far from a permanent fix. There are adjustment grooves in the mounting and those grooves had been worn thin from inexact placement. Instead of having the strength of being locked into the grooves, I only had the force of my elbow grease and a large screw. Thank God I was working at a rehab clinic with chair experts. They could get me through my stay in Albania, but I was getting ready for a month in Africa. If I'd been making the trip directly from the States, I might have canceled until I could get a new chair. I repressed my anxiety and pushed the rest of my stay in Albania in a wheelie—just like

Radio publicity with production assistant, Linda Cenaj and a local DJ at Radio Pula, Shkodër, Albania.

I had the last two months in Dharamsala. Hopefully the roads in Ghana would be flatter than the rugged cobblestones of Shkodër.

After two weeks, during which I made friends for life, it was time to wrap up the gig in Albania. I spoke to a class of physiotherapy students at the Madonnina del Grappa and was invited to their weekly activity night where therapists, students and patients get together to play volleyball, dance, and do art projects. One thing I've noticed everywhere I go is people who work around persons with disabilities are the nicest, funniest, and most caring people I've ever met. From ski instructors in Oregon to therapists working on severe cognitive issues in Albania, you can't find a rat among the bunch. My experience in Shkodër left me pining to stay in Albania much, much longer. Some people can't stand being away from home for more than a week. I can't stand being in a new country for less than four months!

This next leg to Ghana would be my third trip to Africa, but my first with an actual business purpose. Knowing someone was going to meet me at the airport took a lot of stress out of the flight. I let go of my equipment anxieties and watched the Mediterranean pass under my feet. Soon enough we crossed into Egyptian air space and in minutes I was flying over open desert. Flying over the Sahara is the closest thing to space travel I'll ever experience. It's so enormous and empty that you realize whatever is on the other side can't be anything like the place you just left. I was in the air for over an hour when I saw a small hamlet around an oil rig. It was another full two hours before I saw any other man-made structure. I followed a long dirt road extending from one end of the horizon to another, but nobody was on it. At one point I flew over an intersection of two such dirt roads and wondered what would happen if you missed your turnoff. Occasionally the desert grew into enormous mountains with stunning red cliffs—but again, no trace of human life at all. It was like I was looking at an undiscovered Grand Canyon.

As night fell, I arrived at Kotoka International Airport in Accra and was surprised to be greeted at the gate by a brand-new airport transfer chair. After passing through customs, I was escorted to the waiting area where I hoped to find my friend, Gifty Gnyante, a physical therapy professor I'd met twice while working with the IRF. Gifty is the hardest working person I've ever met in my life and every single minute of her life is booked. So it shouldn't have surprised me she wasn't there to greet me at the airport. But I wasn't allowed into the country without my sponsor.

Ghanaian visas are difficult, cumbersome, and expensive for US citizens. In order to get one, not only did I have to take several medical exams while I was in France, but I also had to have an official invitation from a sponsor. Fortunately, one of our IRF connections was the retired head of the Physical Therapy Department at Korle Bu Teaching Hospital and had enough juice to invite me. Even though my paperwork was in order, they were not giving a "sick" person (paraplegic) access to their country unless I was properly escorted out of the airport.

I wasn't allowed to roam the airport, and I had an armed guard with me the whole time. This may paint Ghana as a rugged African country, but that couldn't be further from the truth. Ghana is one of the most sophisticated countries on the African continent and its educational standards are superior to most of the States. But they have strict arrival rules, and I wasn't getting through. I found an Internet cafe and pulled up my correspondence with Gifty. The police read them and could see there was a mix-up. As my guard wandered to find his captain and explain the situation, a Canadian relief worker picking up someone from her NGO approached me and asked me if I wanted her to pretend she was my contact. We made quick plans and as the guard returned, I introduced her to him and she told him she was taking me to the university. He let me go, the two of us hopped in a cab, and she took me to the hotel where her group was staying. The hotel had Internet access, so I could drop an email to Gifty and tell her where I was. It wasn't an ideal landing, but I was in bed on African soil.

At 6 a.m. (which I found out is the equivalent of 8 a.m. in the States) Gifty knocked on my door, apologized profusely, then took me to the Monrose Guest House in the Adenta neighborhood north of Accra. Whereas Linda was my savior in Albania, Gifty was an absolute miracle worker in Ghana. The Monrose is a super-friendly place with a car ramp leading up to the front door. It was almost accessible except for the 10-inch step to my room. I told the manager I'd pay to have a carpenter build a ramp, but he'd already hired one. In less than an hour, the ramp was built and I was lying on a huge raft of a bed in an air-conditioned room. The bathroom door was just a little tight for me, so we yanked it out and replaced it with a curtain, making the Monrose a 100 percent accessible African guest house!

The first full day in Accra, Gifty set up an audience with Rev. Michael Ntumy, the former head of the five-million-member Church of the Pentecost. Rev. Ntumy had a severe case of cervical stenosis (shrinking of the spine in the neck area). Surgery to relieve the condition has left him a quadriplegic. He was the current head of the German branch of the Church of the Pentecost and was visiting Accra as a guest lecturer. As happens in many areas of the world, the only time any action takes place on disability is when someone in a high position is affected. Since his surgery four years earlier, Rev. Ntumy had been an active voice in the disability community and was instrumental in the ongoing process of turning one of the pastors' residences into a physical therapy and rehab ward. I wished I could have been in the country a bit earlier before such an important interview, so I would have been able to ask more pertinent questions to such a high-level figure. But Ntumy was extremely gracious and his responses to my basic questions filled in the gaps.

Since I was staying in Ghana for a month, my schedule wasn't as jam-packed as it was in Albania. That gave me time to relax and roll around my new neighborhood. The streets of Adenta were some of the liveliest I've ever seen. Women wore colorful patterned dresses and vendors roamed the streets selling everything from fruit to fertility drugs.

Everyone warns Westerners about eating from food shacks and street carts in Africa, but I had no issue with it. If I saw a guy bring a chicken into his restaurant, then pluck it and put it on the grill, I knew it was fresh! Otherwise, I stuck to eating pineapple and bananas (and anything that looked like them) and never used any of the sauces unless I saw a working refrigerator in the shack. I'm pretty sure I was paying more than the average customer, but I knew they were going to be extra careful to not feed me questionable food.

With everything from elderly women to livestock to Mercedes Benzes sharing the same road, rush-hour traffic was insane—and the main cause of spinal cord injury in the country. Although there were traffic signals, stop signs, and cops, they were routinely ignored; people tried to get where they were going as fast as they could. There were few paved streets, so the major arteries were painfully clogged for hours each day. During rush hour the major freeway turned into an open market with vendors walking in between idling cars and buses.

I was only a quarter mile from the highway connecting Adenta to Accra, but the road from the Monrose to the highway was often impassable. When it rained, the road turned into a series of muddy puddles that were more like small lakes. Early in my stay I found a trustworthy taxi driver, and I used him the entire month. On days when the road was impassable, I had to call him just to get a ride to the stores along the highway. He would carry me 400 yards, wait for me to do my shopping, then take me back 400 yards. On the highway, there were hundreds of ride-share mini-buses that would stop for anyone who put their hand out—except someone in a wheelchair. The cost of a round trip into Accra was $2 for an able-bodied person in the van and up to $50 for a disabled person in the taxi. The price of that commute is out of reach even by Western standards.

When I didn't feel like venturing out, there was plenty of entertainment on my own block. There was a soccer field next to the Monrose that was in use every daylight hour. It was a red-dirt pitch, 80 yards by 30 with tiny 18 by 36-inch cages on either end. Everyone from youth leagues to semi-pro teams trained on the pitch, but the most intense games were the pickup matches on Friday night. For these games, the best players showed up and the skill level was higher than any university game I've seen in Oregon. It was the biggest social event in the neighborhood, and I ended up meeting people with disabilities who came out because their family members told them I was making a documentary. Ghana is a word-of-mouth country and not much gets done without it.

My first weekend in town, Gifty and I were invited to attend the Accra chapter meeting of the Ghanaian Society of the Physically Disabled (GSPD). It was held outdoors in a courtyard surrounded by dozens of wheelchairs, three-wheeled vehicles, and both handmade and contemporary adaptive devices. About 70 people showed up for a tightly run meeting focusing on how the organization would spend their annual budget. Their budget, according to the newly passed Ghanaian Disability Act, was a staggering two percent of the city's annual budget. Having come from Albania, where there was almost no governmental help for the disabled, it was amazing to see how organized the Ghanaian disability community had become. The GSPD is an official government organization with chapters in every town in the country. I interviewed the Accra chapter president, the representative to the government, and the sporting director, who also happened to be the African hand cycle champion. The positive vibe from this group was infectious and I ended up hanging out with them the whole time I was in Ghana.

But the person I hung out most with was Gifty. Gifty's schedule was so insane that I can't believe she had five minutes for me the entire time. Being a physical therapy professor at Korle Bu Teaching Hospital in the center of

Accra, she was up at 3:30 a.m. to prepare her lessons. At 4:30 her husband and three children woke up, so she made them breakfast and got them ready for school and work. By 6:00 she was fighting the awful Accra traffic to get to work, where she taught all morning long. In the afternoon, she was either working on her Ph.D. thesis, helping me with the documentary, or working on any of the dozen international committees she was on. After work, she hurried home to get dinner ready for her family. Being an elder in the Pentecostal church, she attended services after dinner on Tuesdays and Thursdays, and prepared for the three-hour Sunday services. She and her husband also ran a successful event catering company on the side. Somehow, she not only squeezed in my project, but she also made contacts for me to visit at hospitals all over the country and drove me to most of my meetings. I seriously do not know if the woman slept.

Sunday was Gifty's church day, so at 6 a.m. she and her four kids escorted me to the Lion of Judah Pentecostal church, a fire-and-brimstone charismatic Christian church. Gifty saw I was playing guitar every time she picked me up, so she asked me if I wanted to sit in with the church band. I was thrilled. Three hours of church can be mighty long to an agnostic, but put a guitar in my hand and it becomes one big concert. In the beginning, they were playing structured church songs I hadn't heard since I was in 8th grade. I wasn't sure what to play, but I've learned along the road that one bad note can destroy all the good ones. I kept my axe pretty quiet unless I knew where the music was going. Two and a half hours into the ceremony the parish lined up for communion and we played a somber instrumental while the flock received bread and wine. But as soon as the last person received communion, the band leader picked up a bass guitar and started rumbling away on the African sounds I recognized from groups like Ladysmith Black Mambazo. My eyes perked up, I found the key, and for 15 minutes we got the place rocking. It was like no other group I've ever played with before. The congregation jumped to their feet and formed line dances all around the church. It was the kind of music I thought I'd be hearing the whole time I was in Africa, full of power and spirit—it made me transcend to a different place. After the service I asked the band leader why we didn't play more of that style of music. "Brother Tom," he smiled, "when Jesus is in our hearts, how can we not rejoice?!" I'm guessing that if the American Catholics played like that, they might be able to keep a few more people in the pews. Not me, mind you, as I'm long gone, but lots more than they do.

The next week Gifty booked me for a tour of the Pentecostal hospital not far from Adenta. I spoke with several patients and two doctors who were planning on opening Dr. Ntumy's new physical therapy ward. Although the physical therapy and occupational therapy standards in Ghana are as high as any on Earth, there were no rehabilitation doctors in Ghana—or anywhere else in sub-Saharan Africa. My job for the IRF was to document the state of rehab medicine in Ghana, but it was a bit like documenting the state of cricket in South Dakota. There just wasn't much to document. Instead, I focused the film on the disability community, a decision which would lead to us winning an international film competition.

For all her help, the only thing Gifty asked of me was to give a lecture to her physical therapy students. I've lectured on disability all over the US and Asia and the class response is universal. They've been taught anatomy, physiology, and best practices, but they haven't heard how everyday life works for paras and quads. Like most of my talks, I got through two or three slides, someone asked a pertinent question, and the rest of the hour was taken up with responses to my answer and the other questions it brought up. It may not have been super professional, but it was the Socratic method at its best.

Unfortunately, while my experiences got deeper and the filming more intense, the caster wheel on my chair had nearly disintegrated. Just like in Dharamsala, I carried a brick in my backpack to support my chair where the wheel was missing. In the States, I only transfer two or three times a day, but on the road I'm constantly in and out of taxis, transport vans, and cars. On busy days with Gifty, I was transferring a dozen times. In Dharamsala my chair was well-balanced on three wheels, but this newer model relied heavily on the two front wheels. I spent almost my entire time in Accra moving in a wheelie or being supported by a brick where there used to be a wheel. Gifty knew of a welder she thought could affix my wheel to the frame, but it didn't work out so well. We drove to his shop where I showed him the collection of nuts and bolts that held the wheel in place. I had to sit in the car while he sparked up his torch and banged on my chair. When he came back, he had a frown on his face and a bunch of melted metal goo in his hands. Not only had the weld failed, but my wheelchair was all but ruined.

Gifty had scheduled a trip for me to head north to visit two more hospitals, but without a functional wheelchair, I told her I didn't think I could make the trip. She scratched her head and told me she had a solution! She was going to give me a new chair for the trip. Paras get quite attached to our chairs and I'd seen the chairs the other paras were using in Accra. They were super-heavy nurse-pusher chairs with loose, floppy foot pedals. At first I said it would be impossible, but she gave me a stern look and said, "Hey—when are you coming back to Ghana?! You need to take my wheelchair!"

Like in every practical matter, she was 100 percent correct. I hopped into the new chair and it was, as I'd predicted, heavy and difficult for transfers. But, unlike mine, it functioned. I had to stop being a chair baby and go see the rest of Ghana.

Ever since I'd arrived, people told me I had to head north of Ghana to see the real Africa. In low-resource environments, most cities are dirty and dusty while the countryside can be magical. My original idea of taking a bus to the northern city of Tamale proved impractical, though. It's a 30-hour trip that in recent years had been menaced by bandits who took everything— including the bus—and left the passengers stranded. Lately, the police had been escorting 100 cars at a time through the jungle and they moved them along in a slow caravan. Instead of riding through the jungle, you were stuck in a 30-hour traffic jam.

So armed with a new chair, I set about booking a flight to Tamale. Booking the flight was not as simple as going online and buying a seat. I had to go to the airport and find out which carrier would take someone in a wheelchair. Antrak, the first airline I spoke with, flat-out refused because they didn't own an airplane lift. Starbow, the next company, also refused, but Gifty pressed them, saying it was against the Ghanaians with Disabilities Act. They asked me if I would be flying with a doctor (a very common request for disabled persons in Africa and Asia), at which I scoffed, and Gifty stepped in to assure them I was quite healthy. They allowed me to buy a ticket, but they told me I had to climb up the stairs of the plane by myself.

When I showed up for the flight, I saw the lift that puts disabled passengers on jumbo jets parked just outside the gate. When I asked why we didn't use it, I was told it was owned by the big airlines and it would cost $300 a flight to use. I climbed up the stairs on my butt and slid along the floor of the plane to the first open seat in coach. Thank God I had good elastic in my sweatpants.

Tamale Airport doubles as an Air Force base and has virtually no services. I had to bump down the stairs of the plane on my butt, but at least my chair was waiting for me at the bottom. It was much quicker than most airports handle it.

My contact in Tamale was Dr. Dziffa Ahadzi, a resident at the Tamale Teaching Hospital. I grabbed a cab into town and met her while she was giving an exam to an elderly patient. She gave me an extensive tour of the "old" hospital, which was in its last days. A brand-new and very impressive 2,000-bed hospital would be opening in less than a week. Everywhere in the hospital complex was accessible, so I rolled around exploring while Dr. Ahadzi attended to other patients and students.

After a few hours I realized I hadn't had any chair issues—something that had been a constant strain for me since my arrival in Shkodër. Not only was the chair riding smoothly, but Tamale had very little traffic and the roads were well maintained and dry. For the first time since leaving France a month earlier, I actually did a workout.

The next morning, I was on the Tamale Teaching Hospital's lecture itin-erary and spoke to 70 medical students about Andy's dream of bringing rehab doctors to sub-Saharan Africa. I then went into a practical talk about what happens when you are the victim of a spinal cord injury. Again, they assumed losing your legs was the worst part of SCI and were dumbfounded when I told them the most devastating effects to the patient were the loss of bowel, bladder, and sexual function. In the States, I would finish these talks with slides from India or Turkey, but here, I opted for slides about American and French disability sports, which the medical students loved.

After lunch I spoke to a dedicated group of physical therapists, then went on rounds with doctors who were checking on the most recent SCI patients. This is always tough for me because I've repressed the horror of my days in the thoracic brace. I don't sugarcoat anything for new patients, but I stay as positive as I can. Hopefully, if I am able to come all the way to Africa in a wheelchair, they can make life work back in their village.

After the busy day in Tamale, I met my next contact, John Alo, the director of the Garu Community-Based Rehabilitation Centre (GCBRC). In the morning, John Alo drove me four hours to Garu, a village of 15,000 people located ten kilometers south of Burkina Faso and ten kilometers west of Togo, up in the far northeast corner of Ghana.

As we headed further north, the villages changed from cement brick buildings to hamlets made of circular red-clay huts with thatch roofs. Women dressed in blazing, nearly psychedelic traditional African dress car-ried goods in baskets on their heads. The village streets were lined with shops selling everything from TV remotes to truck parts to dresses to cell phones.

Almost all of these stores can sell you a small bag of cold water and there is usually a table where you can sit down, relax, and gossip.

When we arrived in Garu, Mr. Alo took me to the guest house operated by GCBRC. Garu was the most remote location I'd ever been to, so I assumed I would be relegated to a sweaty bunk room, far from an accessible toilet. But the GCBRC took disability advocacy very seriously and they painstakingly made their guest house 100 percent accessible. Everything from the ramp to the bathroom to the shower proved no obstacle to me at all. On top of that they had a 50-inch flat screen hooked up to a satellite dish with 40 channels, including a 24-hour soccer channel. My room had a huge double bed encased in a mosquito net. Malaria is prevalent in the north and most of the bites come at night while people were asleep. Contrary to myth, Ghanaian mosquitos are not gigantic, aggressive winged demons with 8-inch-long stingers. Rather, they are small and soft and you barely feel them or their bites, which makes them much deadlier. Also, the skin's reaction to the bites lasts only a few hours, so it is very possible to be bitten without ever knowing it.

I had time to kill before going to a meeting of the Garu Society of Disabled Persons, so I went into the neighborhood to shoot standups. A person in a wheelchair is not an oddity here, but a big white guy in a wheelchair talking to a camera will draw quite a bit of attention. While I was shooting against a thatched roof house, 50 blue-uniformed 3rd graders stopped to figure out who had invaded their village. I turned off my camera, looked at them with a big smile and yelled, "Hello!"

This was the signal for them to rush over and assume control of my chair. In seconds I was being whisked away, with the kids chanting anything I said. If I said, "One, two, three," they would in turn scream, "One, two, three!" If I howled like a wolf, they would howl like a wolf. I got them to sing "Go Johnny Go!" as well as "Roll Away the Dew!" Mr. Alo and his assistant Isaac were returning from their morning rounds when they came across me being escorted to the children's school, where the kids wanted to show me to their teacher. Mr. Alo pulled up to me in his truck, and with a big smile said, "Well, I guess you found your way to the clinic." Unbeknownst to me, the clinic was right across the main road from the school. He then said something in the local language to the kids who dispersed and went back to their classroom. He told me I may be one of only three or four white people they see all year—and certainly the first white person they've ever seen in a wheelchair.

Later in the afternoon Mr. Alo took me to a meeting of the Garu Society of Disabled Persons, where I was invited to speak. I told them about my film, but I was much more interested in hearing about their issues. Disability equipment is a big problem, but most of them had solved their issues with crutches and hand bikes. The majority of them suffered from birth defects, not spinal cord injury. They could manage short distances on crutches but used hand bikes for getting around town. I saw more than a dozen hand bikes in this small community—all thanks to the work of the GCBRC.

The depth of the Garu Society of Persons with Disabilities blew me away. This group, in the most remote part of the country, was tied to the national organization and was receiving 2 percent of the annual local government budget that the Ghanaian Persons with Disability Act guarantees them. The money is spent on education and mobility, providing most of them with not only a job, but a way to get there and back. Their leader is a blind schoolteacher who has also won two terms in the local assembly. That was quite an accomplishment for a blind man, but they seemed to be even more proud of the fact he has two wives who, they were quick to point out, are not disabled! Cultural changes come slowly. I'll take the disability advancement for now and leave the polygamy and women's rights issues up to some other group.

At sundown, I went back to the guest house to turn in early. Rural Ghanaians are very early risers. 5 a.m. is the norm and it is not unusual to schedule 6 a.m. events.

The next morning we made it to the GCBRC, where I spoke to the staff about the film and how they could help me. We came up with a plan, then

I went on rounds with John Alo's right hand man, Isaac, and two GCBRC employees. They took me all over the region to interview persons with disabilities who have been helped by the GCBRC. I

Remote standup in Garu, Ghana.

interviewed students, street vendors, farmers, and garment workers. All had moderate to severe disabilities, and all were earning a living.

The most impressive case was an elderly woman who was less than three-feet tall. Her daughter suffered from the same congenital condition and up until five years ago they only made enough money off their small farm to feed themselves. But with a microcredit loan from the GCBRC they bought sewing equipment and started making dresses. Neither of them were tall enough to take measurements, so they sized up clients with their naked eye, cut fabric, and sewed. Their technique and quality were beyond reproach. They were not only making big profits—they had more orders than they could fill.

The two-day stay in Garu was way too short. Of all the places I'd visited since leaving Oregon, Garu was the MOST accessible. Since everything was on the ground floor, I could get into every house, business, school, and government building. Before I left Accra, I had been afraid I would need lots of help to get around, but, in fact, it was in Garu where I was most independent.

Mr. Alo and I drove the four hours back to Tamale, stopping off at his parents' house for tea and sandwiches. Instead of taking the main road, John told me he had a shortcut that avoided the big crowded villages during rush hour. We turned off on a dirt road and spent an hour driving through corn and melon fields. Occasionally we passed through tiny hamlets where young children locked eyes with me and screamed for their parents. John told me it was very possible I was the first white man they'd ever seen.

Back in Accra, after having climbed on and off of another plane on my butt, I was facing my last few days in Ghana. Somehow, I was able to keep my camera charged most of the trip and had hours of video to sift through. There were a few times in Garu where I'd run out of juice, but I was packing a small shoot-and-click camera that could shoot ten minutes at a time. It was kind of embarrassing to be announced as a photojournalist and then pull out a toy camera, but a lot of what I shot with it made it into the final film. If I had been shooting in America, it would have looked cheesy. But audiences give you a lot of leeway when you are shooting in the middle of Africa.

My last interview was with Gifty, and I was never so proud to have someone on film. She not only set up my entire trip, she saved me with the loaner wheelchair. I never would have been able to travel up north without it, and those scenes would be the most important part of my film. As hard as she works and as important as her mission is, she never goes more than a few minutes without a big belly laugh. If I'd had to pay someone of her competence, the film would never have even gotten off the drawing board. But after four weeks of Gifty guiding and taking care of me, my laptop was bursting with incredible footage.

The Sunday before I left Ghana, I was invited to watch a football (soccer) match between the best players in Africa and a group of "World Stars" who came from the best leagues in Europe, Asia, and South America. It was at the 40,000-seat Accra Sports Stadium in the heart of downtown Accra. I arrived late and it took the entire first half for me to find the handicap entrance to the stadium. Eventually a group of ushers told me there was no accessible entrance and I would have to sit on the pitch. They rolled me down a steep ramp used by event trucks, where I found more than a dozen of my friends from the GSPD.

We danced with drummers the entire game, then exited the stadium in a wheelers conga line, drifting into the streets of Accra. I was able to keep one hand on my camera and another on my chair as the line wove in and out of post-game traffic. People cheered us on and stopped traffic to make a path for us. Even though this was an exhibition game, the ambiance outside the stadium was similar to many World Cup Football matches I've attended. When the sun set, I had to hop into a cab and say goodbye to my Ghanaian wheeling brothers and sisters, hoping we would one day cross paths again. I was never so proud to be included in a group in all my life.

The next morning, the wind blew out of my sails. As I sat at my Internet cafe checking emails and Facebook, I felt a nagging spasm around my torso. At one point it got so severe I had to back away from the table and look down at my legs. And that's where the next phase of my travel nightmare

Photobombed by a Black Star jester at Accra Stadium.

began. My jeans were soaked with urine. I'd been taking what is called a prophylactic dose of antibiotics ever since arriving in Africa: 250 mg of ciprofloxacin daily with dinner. The day of the football match, I saw I was down to my last four pills and, seeing as I hadn't had any troubles since leaving Oregon, I decided I'd stop taking them and save those pills for an emergency.

What I hadn't realized is I'd taken on a bug during my stay in Africa and those pills had been fighting it the entire time. Now, with less than 24 hours before an Accra-to-Beijing flight, the bugs were winning, and I had a massive urinary tract infection. And those bugs had beaten my cipro, one of the strongest antibiotics on Earth.

I'd prepared for such an occasion by packing a half-dozen adult diapers, but that wasn't going to make my flight pleasant. When I arrived at the Kotoka airport with a fresh diaper and a bag of clean catheters, I was praying nothing would go wrong and I could just get the 36-hour transit over with. But there were storms over the Sahara, forcing my first leg to Cairo to be delayed five hours. When I got on the new plane, I was seated as far back on the plane as possible, among a large contingent of Chinese miners who were continuing to Beijing. As soon as the flight took off, my legs began to spasm and they stayed clenched the entire way to Egypt.

The flight was a stunner as it skimmed the South Sahara then followed the Nile all the way from Thebes, past the Great Pyramids into Cairo. But the five-hour delay guaranteed we'd missed our connection, and everyone scrambled to get rebooked. Before I could deal with a new flight, I had to find a bathroom to change my diaper and clean myself up. I'd never been so stressed out on a flight in my life, but my delay ended up being a blessing. When I showed up at the Emirates Air customer service, they said coach seats were taken and I would be forced to fly (gulp!) first class.

It was the luckiest travel snafu I've ever had. Instead of being jammed into the back of a plane with my legs screaming for relief, I was prone in a cushy, wide chair that reclined fully and was located just a few feet from the bathroom. A flight attendant assured me that anytime I wanted to go to the bathroom, he would get me an aisle chair and I could use the gigantic first-class restroom. Instead of trying to dehydrate myself the entire flight, I could drink gallons of water to flush the infection and use the restroom whenever I needed. One would think that extra water would mean more diapers, but the opposite occurs. It dilutes the infection, causing much less irritation to the bladder and less incontinence. It also cooled me down, as I'd developed a fever since arriving at Kotoka 12 hours earlier.

I flew to Shanghai, then took a puddle jumper to Beijing. When I arrived, I was rested and my fever had subsided. All passengers arriving in China from Africa go through a thermal detector to look for sick passengers. By the time I arrived in Shanghai, it was as if I'd been relaxing in a spa for 14 hours.

After collecting my gear (bag, cameras, computer, guitar, chair, and chair bag), I grabbed a taxi and arrived at our hotel on Olympic Green in Beijing. It was midnight but I just had a full night's sleep on the plane. I snuck into the room, pulled out my computer, and listened to a Brewers game on the WiFi. It felt almost like I was home.

I hadn't put too much thought into Beijing, as it was the final stop on an 8-month, 40,000-mile trip. I was thinking more about getting home and editing the video. But Beijing ended up being every bit as exciting as if I'd taken a solo trip to China and nowhere else. Andy and I hosted a very successful IRF meeting, where I got to see the Bangladeshi doctors whom I'd met on the very first days of the trip. They hadn't seen my film of the Bangladesh conference and two of them teared up upon seeing it. As a filmmaker, it doesn't get much better than that.

The conference also offered some incredible day trips to the Forbidden City, the Beijing Summer Palace, and, of course, the Great Wall. Since I needed to film Andy's take on Ghana rehab medicine, I used the Great Wall as a spectacular backdrop. I was also able to interview Dr. Pestelli, the Italian doctor who set up my trip to Albania.

But the kicker of the trip occurred on the final day of the conference. Seven months earlier at the conference in Dhaka, the Bangladeshi doctors had held a talent show with doctors providing the entertainment. It shouldn't surprise me there are a number of doctors with amazing musical gifts, but seeing them come out from behind their professorial masks and perform took me aback. I got to play a few tunes and Andy even joined me onstage playing his blues harp, which he's gotten pretty damn good at over the years.

The Chinese delegation to the Bangladesh conference loved the idea and incorporated it into their closing day in Beijing. Andy and I hadn't seen each other all day and he wasn't sure if I'd gotten the message that there was a talent show. But Pestelli had told me the day before. I was ready to pull an oldie but goodie out of my bag.

The Chinese set up a large professional stage and hired two TV personalities to host the event. One of them was a short and, based on the fact that nobody laughed at his jokes, not-so-funny comedian. The female presenter, on the other hand, was a stone-cold fox. The ballroom was packed full of the world's finest rehab physicians as well as a few would-be clowns (me). When it was my turn to play, I found Andy, who lifted me onto the stage (no ramp at a rehab doctor's meeting?) and plugged in my guitar.

The female presenter said a few words in Mandarin, then asked me what song I was going to play. "I'm going to play a song by the greatest band in the world," I said. "They're called The Who."

With that I dug into an acoustic version of "Won't Get Fooled Again," which I'm sure would not have passed any of the Chinese censors had it been presented beforehand. I looked around the room and noticed plenty of foreign doctors grinning at my choice of song.

I finished it with the requisite triple power chord and got a rousing ovation from the crowd, 90 percent of whom had no idea what I'd just played. I looked over at Andy, who knew exactly what I pulled off, and he had an extra wry twist in his smile. The presenter came back on and we did a quick four-line skit to introduce the next act. I rolled off the stage feeling I'd done Mr. Townshend proud. I don't think even he has played "Won't Get Fooled Again" in downtown Beijing.

Forty weeks and more than 40,000 miles since leaving Portland, I arrived back in the United States. It was time to open the computer and make movies.

Glam standup at the Great Wall outside of Beijing.

• • • • • • • • • • • • •

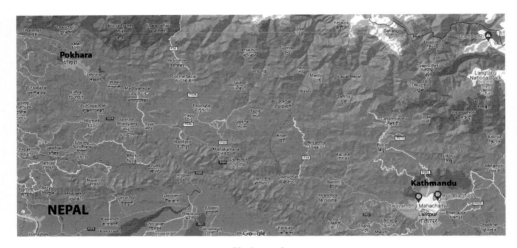

Kathmandu

Yes, I'm Goin' to Kathmandu!

The effects of the huge trip were both astounding and devastating. When I returned, I holed up at my parents' house in Wisconsin and, with the help of my sister Barb and my buddy Toys (who drove to Charlottesville with me on the first phase of the trip), produced two IRF documentaries: one on Albania and another on Ghana. Andy was coming through Wisconsin just as I was finishing, so my sister Nari and her husband Mark hosted a screening party in their backyard. The audience assumed the films were about the difficulties of traveling in a wheelchair in these countries, but after seeing the films, the conversation turned to the disability communities in Albania and Ghana. As a filmmaker, when my disability disappears into the work I'm doing, I feel like I've done my job.

We submitted an abridged version of the Ghana film to the Consortium of Universities for Global Health international film competition and the film won first prize in the "Advancements in Global Health" category.

After making these films I had enough resume fodder to get hired as a news producer for a small TV station in Eugene, Oregon. A few weeks later, Hélène came in from France to try living in America. With spring on the horizon in 2014, I thought I was seeing how the rest of my life would play out…but it all fell apart.

Two months after she arrived, Hélène told me she didn't think she could make it in the United States. This crushed me, because we never even got the chance to live in Portland, the most progressive city in the US and the entire basis of my social network. We'd been stuck in Eugene, where I didn't know a soul and was working a job I hated. She had nothing to do all day and when I came home from the television station, I was so exhausted I didn't have the energy to do much more than watch a movie and go to bed.

Hélène returned to France and the very next week I was called into the principal's office at the TV station. Although TV news production was a journalism job, it was a horrible fit for me. I was responsible for making 300 decisions a day and any errors, whether they made the broadcast or not, were written up and filed for potential dismissal. I was getting better and better every day, but the station had one news producer too many. After three months of trial by fire, I was canned.

I began to look for work back in Portland and took to the hand cycle to clear my head. I spent all day on the Internet looking for jobs, then headed out into the Willamette Valley on the bike just before rush hour. I was piling up miles and looking for another big city marathon to train for when my biking career came to a screeching halt.

I was sitting on my couch after dinner and reached for my sock to pull my left leg up onto the cushions. As I tugged on the sock, something in my shoulder snapped and I screamed out in pain. I couldn't transfer back into my chair, so I spent the night on the couch and waited to see how it felt in the morning. When I woke, I tried to put a little pressure on my arm, but it wouldn't take it. I called my neighbor, Anne, who got me some ice and aspirin. I spent the day binge-watching *Breaking Bad* and by the time Anne came home from work, the pain had subsided enough for the two of us to get me back into my chair.

Over the next few days, the pain subsided and my shoulder felt normal again. Two weeks later, I braved the hand cycle and had no lasting effects from the tweak. But less than a dozen rides later I transferred from the bike to my chair and received another painful ping that took me out of the game for another few weeks. I recovered, but never got back on my bike. My shoulder was a permanent source of pain and I stopped working out.

In the space of three months, I went from being physically fit, having a full-time job and a life partner, to being a worthless blob on the couch. I dumped my apartment in Eugene and moved back in with my sister Sue in Corvallis. For the next nine months, I withered in a numbing funk as I put on weight, looked for jobs, and occasionally scored tiny contracts with my web, print, and copywriting services.

The only source of pride I had was doing occasional work for the IRF and helping my brother Andy start Haig et al., a rehab medicine consulting firm. The contracts he was going for were intensive, big dollar, long-term service arrangements. Up until the beginning of 2015, he'd only scored smaller evaluation contracts. But persistence paid off: in March he scored a major deal with Aurora, one of the major health care providers in Wisconsin. Aurora had accumulated multiple hospital systems and needed a group to come in and design new system-wide policies on physical and occupational therapy. Since Andy was a full-time professor at Michigan, he could only attend occasional meetings. He needed someone to monitor the progress of the burgeoning Aurora Rehab Medicine group. As an award-winning journalist in medical rehabilitation, I was the perfect candidate. I just had to move back to Milwaukee for a few months.

Although the work was overwhelming in its scope, it was incredibly rewarding. For the first time in over a year I felt like I was back on the starting team. Then during the middle of the contract, a horrible event on the other side of the world put me on the all-star squad.

On April 25, an 8.1 magnitude earthquake fifty miles northwest of Kathmandu rocked Nepal, sending the country into turmoil. While catastrophic events are shocking to most people, they are like Gotham's bat signal to the IRF doctors. While groups like the Red Cross and Doctors without Borders will rush into the affected areas doing extractions and acute surgery, the IRF's members will stay on hand and take care of the long-term medical effects.

First, we needed to see if our friends were safe; most importantly, the family of Dr. Raju Dhakal, the Nepalese physiatrist Andy and I befriended two years earlier in Dhaka. Raju sent out a post on Facebook saying he and his wife Sheela were safe in Dhaka, but he had no idea how affected their families were back in Kathmandu. The medical staff at Bangabandhu Sheikh Mujib Medical University, where we'd held our conference two years earlier, went into emergency mode, collecting supplies and booking flights to Tribhuvan International Airport in Kathmandu.

We asked Raju what we could do, and he responded, "Send money." A common misconception about disaster situations is that they need food and clothing, when the thing they need most is money. Most of the supplies sent after disasters end up in massive warehouses experts call "The Second Disaster." It takes an army of people to administer the goods, when those people are needed elsewhere. The food rots and the supplies don't get delivered. The most effective way to help with disaster relief is to send money to authorized agencies.

When we set up the IRF, we created a fundraising clause in our charter that let us raise tax-deductible funds for disaster relief. While Andy was finishing our Aurora contract, I started a social and traditional media campaign to raise funds. We combined with colleagues in Australia and the UK to collect nearly $25,000, not a penny of which was spent on overhead.

When Raju got to Kathmandu, he made his way through the rubble to the Spinal Injury Rehabilitation Center (SIRC) just over the eastern ridge of the Kathmandu Valley. Although the SIRC is a modern, comprehensive rehabilitation hospital, it was not equipped to handle the 100 new spinal cord patients who arrived in the space of a few days. The 50-bed facility was already 90 percent full, so the new patients were undergoing acute care in Pakistani army tents set up in the parking lot.

The first month of my rehab had been the worst period of my life—and I was in a cushy hospital. Many of these patients had not only lost the use of their bodies, they'd lost family members, their jobs and their homes. Many of those homes had fallen on them, causing the spinal cord injuries. Less than three weeks later, as the chaos began to subside, another major earthquake hit the region, resulting in even more spinal cord injuries, often to first responders still working in the affected areas.

Andy and I were in the last days of our contract when I asked Raju if there was anything else we could do. Donor fatigue had set in, so there was no more money to be collected. Raju told me he'd never seen so much devastation and depression in his life. As much as he soldiered on and got through the day, it was hard to pick up anyone's spirits.

"It would be great if you could come here, man," he told me on a Skype conversation. "Just to show people there's life after a spinal cord injury."

"Then that's what I'll do!" I said. "Just say when!"

Since the country was a total mess, it wouldn't be a good idea to come immediately. I also had some commitments in the States that wouldn't allow me to leave for several months. But I told him I was on my way. We just had to wait for the right time.

There was another problem I needed to take care of before I left. I was in the worst shape of my life. The most important thing I tell wheelers about traveling in Asia is you need to be in great shape. You're going to push miles and miles up steep hills on unfinished roads, often carrying much more gear than you would at home. Due to my shoulder problem, I hadn't exercised in over a year. I was 20 pounds overweight, I had no stamina, and my shoulder was still in a lot of pain. I'd gotten an MRI confirming a rotator cuff tear, but one that was too small to operate on. If I was going to pull four months in the Himalayas, I was going to have to get in shape. For the first time since breaking my back, I returned to an old friend. I went to the pool.

Getting back into the pool was one of the scariest things I'd ever done. I'd only gone swimming a handful of times since breaking my back and I didn't like it one bit. People assume divers swim for training, but none of us do. We run, cycle, lift weights, jump trampoline, but nobody swims. Now it was the pool or nothing.

Before heading back to Oregon, I stopped at my brother Bagus' house in Denver and asked him if we could go to the pool. He lent me a big baggy suit (the last suit I'd put on was a tight Euro-Speedo) and I rolled onto the pool deck looking for the granny-slow swim lane.

Bagus held the back of my chair and I flopped into the pool making a whale-like body splash. For the first half of my life, my entire focus was getting into a pool without making a splash. A big splash might be an embarrassment to some, but to me it was an abhorrent rejection of who I was. I had to ignore the shame and go about the business of putting my body back together.

And so started the long, slow haul back to health and conditioning. When I got back to Oregon, I had to buy a swimming suit, something I hadn't done since high school. As a diver, I was good enough that I always got my suits for free. The next step was to join the public pool a mile from my house. As a bike rider, I'd scoffed at people who paid for fitness clubs. All I ever had to do to stay in shape was keep my tires full. But now I was plopping down $150 bucks for a three-month membership. I pulled on my suit and rolled my disgusting, white, flabby corpse through the crowded outdoor pool deck. I asked one of the lifeguards to hold my chair while I flopped into one of the adult swim lanes. Off I went on a Sisyphean elementary backstroke workout.

After a month of backstroke, I began working in one lap of freestyle for every ten laps of backstroke. Two months into training I upped my laps from 40 to 50. By the third month, I'd gotten off my back and swam the whole workout on my stomach. By the time Christmas rolled around, I was swimming five to six miles a week and I could see my ribs again. I called Raju. It was time to go to Nepal.

In February 2016, I arrived at the Tribhuvan airport armed with two cameras, a computer, a microphone, two solid tripods, and enough cords, wires, and data cards to keep me going strong for four months in Kathmandu. I was going to be filming as often as I could, and I didn't want any of the digital or electronic nightmares from the mega-trip to derail this effort.

I was scooped up at the airport by a van from the SIRC that took me far from the center of Kathmandu to a bustling neighborhood in the new suburb of Suryabinayak. I had spent a week in Kathmandu in 1991, but the city I was driving through bore no resemblance to the one I'd visited. The city I left in '92 had almost no motorized transport except for buses and construction vehicles. Everyone either walked, rode a bike, or took a bicycle rickshaw. That city was quiet and welcoming, whereas this new Kathmandu was noisy, aggressive and, above all, filthy.

I've lived in my share of hyper-polluted towns. Taipei was so bad your snot turned black. 1991 Delhi smelled so foul you could catch a disease just by breathing the air. Two years earlier I'd suffered through the dense smog of Beijing, often listed as having the worst air quality in the world. But Kathmandu, a town I once referred to as the "Coolest Big City on Earth," had jumped into pollution first place. The air was unbreathable, the streets were lined with burning garbage piles, and the rivers were choked with rotting detritus. It made me want to cry.

The van driver slithered up the main road through Suryabinayak, passing by dozens of tiny bodegas selling everything from shoes and bananas to mobile phones and raw meat. The men were mostly dressed in dark slacks and open shirts or the traditional Daura-Suruwal, a white cotton shirt and pants with a suit coat. The women wore brilliantly patterned parsis, flowing dresses usually accompanied by large shawls. The young people, on the other hand, wore nearly the same clothes one would find in Portland. Fashion globalization had hit Nepal. And, of course, everyone had a cell phone.

I was greeted at my host family's house by Fiona Stephens, whom I'd met a few years earlier at an IRF gathering in San Juan, Puerto Rico. Fiona is the international queen of spinal cord nurses, having worked in every corner of the world and making a specialty of disaster relief. She lived in Haiti when the 2010 earthquake hit, so she was a natural to help the SIRC wade through its unwanted growth.

Fiona showed me to my room and introduced me to my new family, who would soon become as close as any relatives I've ever had. Although the country had been ransacked by political upheavals and environmental Armageddon, the Nepalese overwhelmingly accepted foreigners. Having spent quite a bit of time in Asia, I am often disappointed by the social distance locals keep from Westerners. In Dharamsala, I couldn't even get my Indian co-workers to stop calling me "sir."

But that was not the case here. My new family consisted of university professors Sangeeta (Mom) and Rajendra (Dad) Kayastha and their beautiful, triple-smart daughters, Nishta and Nikita. They welcomed me into the house with a huge meal of rice and dal, then finished it off with a bottle of their homemade "wine," which was actually jet-fuel whiskey. The family lived in the upper levels of a four-story brick tower, while Fiona and I had large rooms on the ground floor. From time to time a few other foreigners stayed in the other two bottom-floor rooms, but for the most part, it was the six of us.

A 50-yard path from the main road to the front door proved really challenging in the mud, but Rajendra built a ramp from the ground up to the door, making the house accessible. He also rigged a smaller ramp from the hallway up the single step to the bathroom, making it accessible as well. The thing I worried about most when traveling in Asia was finding accessible housing and bathrooms. I hadn't yet begun my jetlag, and my biggest problems were already in the rearview mirror.

The growth of Kathmandu had been so rapid (500,000 in 1990 to 3.5 million in 2016) that electricity service had not been able to keep up. Rolling blackouts and poor Internet service were ubiquitous. I only had a few hours of electricity after work, so I slept and rose with the sun; asleep at 9 p.m. and awake at 5:30 a.m.

Although Raju asked me to be a peer counselor, I thought it would be better to show patients a paraplegic could do more than just talk about disability. I spoke with the managing director of the SIRC and proposed a plan to shoot physical therapy, occupational therapy, and nursing videos in Nepalese. The SIRC could send them to clinics in the far reaches of the country, obviating the need for hours of rough travel by staff. After interviewing the heads of each department, we came up with a list of 25 subjects we could cover. I set out on a comprehensive mission to document the crucial functions of the SIRC.

Although I had buy-in from the hospital, I was on my own to make it work. I needed a full-time translator who could help me edit the Nepalese. The hospital gave me an assistant one day a week, but I needed much more help.

Six weeks after I started my project, I only had three videos in the can. At the onset, the project garnered a lot of excitement and attention, but I had to get approval from the director to post any of my finished videos online. Since the hospital project was slow, I hooked up with other disability groups in Kathmandu and produced side projects. The first was for the "Asia Try" movement, a gathering of more than 300 wheelers from a dozen countries. The wheelers split up into five groups, with each group starting a peaceful

Accidental run-in with former Nepalese Prime Minister, Madhav Kumar Nepal.

protest march from different villages on the outskirts of the Kathmandu Valley. Over the course of three days, the groups made their way into a large festival park in the center of Kathmandu. I caught up with one group at the SIRC and wheeled with them for two days until we joined the other groups at the big party. I shot video and stills along the way and cobbled together a promo video the group still uses.

The next project led to the most thrilling day I've ever had as a filmmaker. Deepak KC is a great friend of Raju's and was Nepal's only licensed architect in a wheelchair. After the earthquake, Deepak had been commissioned to redesign the National Disabled Table Tennis Center that had been reduced to rubble by the earthquakes. I ran into him just a few days before he had scheduled a grand reopening that would be attended by a few hundred people, including some high-level UN diplomats. Deepak had worked around the clock for a year but had one bullet point he couldn't check off. The committee wanted him to prepare a video presentation for the ceremony. Almost apologetically, he asked if I could help.

Since work at the hospital was at a standstill, I moved into a room in the same disability complex as the center and began putting the video together. Deepak had still photos from the original catastrophe, through each step of the remodel. I plugged them into my video editor, then spent a full day filming his workers as they put on the final touches at the table tennis center.

On the morning of the opening, I found Deepak and showed him my edit of the project. He corrected a few errors and gave me some better slides to use. With less than an hour before showtime, I went back to make final edits.

I was serving double duty at the opening. Deepak also asked if I could play some music while people were arriving. After I returned from Dharamsala, I had given myself a 50th birthday present: I bought a 44-key Yamaha piano from Craigslist and set out to teach myself how to play. After four years of practicing nearly every day, I was ready to get up onstage.

As the dignitaries, wheelers, and friends of the club filtered in, I played every song in my abridged piano repertoire. When Deepak was ready to start the presentation, I finished my last tune and got a warm reception from the crowd. I didn't think anyone was paying attention, but they were. The UN Ambassador for Sport thanked me, as did a few other dignitaries. I have a feeling a lot of the applause had to do with playing from a wheelchair at a wheelchair event, but I thought I played well enough, so I took the compliment and hustled offstage for Act II.

Nepalese people *love* big formal presentations, and if you attend a ceremony, you are in for a long afternoon of speeches and honors. After more than a dozen dignitaries spoke and awards were handed out to nearly every volunteer who picked up a paint brush, it was time to show the video.

Deepak introduced me, and after I acknowledged the dignitaries (obligatory!), I started the three-minute video. The opening section was a compilation of stills from the earthquake, showing the initial devastation. I used dramatic piano music to set the tone but switched to upbeat Nepali sarangi music while images of the reconstruction moved across the screen.

For the transition from the old still images to the fresh color video of the brand-new club, I used an up-tempo rock change from the Grateful Dead's "Eyes of the World" (the Bm-A bounce for any of you Deadheads). The images went from static to dynamic, black and white to color. The volume picked up a bit and the house exploded with cheers!

The crowd yelled as if the Nepalese football team had just scored a goal. It was so loud I got goosebumps. I leaned over to give Deepak a giant hug and his smile was wider than the Himalayas. This wasn't a bucket-list moment; this was an "I never in my life thought anything like this would ever happen!" moment. I ended up doing several outside projects, but none of those releases came close to the immediate and gratifying response of the table tennis center opening.

While the outside projects were a blast to put together, the hospital project—the main reason I was shooting in Nepal—had become stagnant. It was difficult to schedule therapists and patients and explain to them what I was doing. It got so frustrating at one point I considered going home.

But then, from out of the blue, a miracle happened in the form of Rownika Shrestha. Rownika's father, a paraplegic, had come to the SIRC after spending nearly twenty years sequestered in the family's inaccessible house. Rownika's sister was getting married, and the family insisted her father come to rehab so he would be healthy enough to participate in the week-long Newari wedding ceremony.

The worst rule of the SIRC is that each patient must have a family member stay with them at the hospital. They want to teach the family how to care for the SCI patient, but in the end, it discourages the patient from getting fully healthy. The rule was counterproductive, but it did give me a production assistant.

Rownika had just finished university and was studying for a comprehensive final in July. Because her father only needed her a few hours a day, she was bored to tears at the SIRC. I'd started working behind the reception desk because it had the best WiFi reception at the SIRC. Rownika always saw me working on my laptop and one day she told me she was bored and wanted to learn how to build web pages. I was looking for a break from my frustrating production project and gladly agreed. But the Internet connection at the SIRC was so weak, we couldn't even upload files to a server. Again, super frustrated with yet another project, I asked her if she wanted to learn how to edit video.

"Sure!" she said. "That sounds like much more fun anyway!"

And thus, Rownika joined the ranks of Gifty in Ghana and Linda in Albania as top-notch production assistants. By the end of my stay, she had learned so much I credited her as a co-producer for the project. I'd already shot a lot of footage that had been left unedited because I don't speak a lick of Nepalese. I showed Rownika how to chop out bad video, as well as how to sync up multiple tracks of video and audio. In just three days she became proficient enough to edit all the raw footage. All I had to do was add the bells and whistles. The next day I'd scheduled a film shoot with the occupational therapy department and gave her a brief lesson on how to work the cameras, the tripods, and the microphone. Again, after just a few minor corrections, she picked up everything.

Within two weeks of Rownika joining me, we converted five weeks of backlogged video into several finished training films. As Rownika gained confidence and the rest of the hospital staff recognized she was a part of the team, our production schedule went into overdrive. My checklist, which had gone dormant for a few weeks, was now back in action. Every day we either shot a new video or edited what we'd shot the day before. Eventually, Rownika even began taking control of the film shoots.

At the same time, we were laughing ourselves silly. We were working with therapists, nurses, and patients—not professional actors. It may have been mean, but sometimes the gaffes were just too funny. There were constant "wardrobe malfunctions" and elderly patients seemed to have no problem wheeling right into the middle of a set to get a better look at what we were doing. We also came from two completely different cultures and not a day went by without one of us looking at the other and saying, "What the hell are you talking about!" and then laughing uncontrollably about it.

Break in filming the Kathmandu wheelchair basketball league with
production assistant, Rownika Shrestha.

Having fun at your job is contrary to the serious Nepalese work ethic,
and it drew the ire of some in upper management. I was called into one of the
director's offices and told Rownika could no longer assist me, because it was
taking too much time from her duties as her father's caretaker. I let her go for
a day, and then asked them if she could help on just one more project because
she'd already started it. They begrudgingly agreed, and Rownika came back
for good, just as if they'd never said anything in the first place. Basically, they
were jealous. Rownika was as beautiful as any fashion model and this did not
sit well with them, even though all she did was crank out high-quality work
without a hint of ego.

Although it took seven weeks to get the hospital project on solid ground,
with Rownika in place it was firing on all cylinders. I went from being frustrated with nothing to do to being frustrated because the end of the day
came too quickly. As the weeks went by, I made more and more friends at the
hospital and became close with the other employees who were in wheelchairs.
Several of them lived in the northeastern suburb of Jorpati, along with many
other people with disabilities. It's close to a large complex with a hospital, a
vocational skills center, a school (Raju and Deepak's school), the table tennis
center, and two large assisted-living quarters.

The SIRC bus began and ended each day in Jorpati. On days when there was little traffic it was 60 minutes each way, but on days with traffic it could be a three-hour one-way trip. When I wanted to spend the weekend in Jorpati with my friends, I could rent a room in the "Green Building" and wait for the SIRC bus to pick us up on Sunday morning. (Sunday is a working day in Nepal.) The Green Building was where my friend Krishna lived, and unfortunately it was a slum. The bathrooms were smelly with broken-down plumbing and the showers were filthy—often full of excrement that wouldn't be cleaned for days.

The Green Building was an inhumane solution to housing Nepal's disabled community, but it was a better solution than living in the remote villages where there were no services at all. The SIRC had sent many patients back to their villages, but the survival rate for them was dismal. They were most likely to be put in an inaccessible room, and their families would have to construct make-shift toilets that turned their one- or two-room houses into open sewers. Patients were sent home with the necessary soft bedding to keep them from getting bedsores, but those mattresses got wet and became degraded. Many patients developed terrible sores, often dying less than two years after being released. Although the dire survival statistics were kept under wraps at the SIRC, the patients knew them and feared being returned to their villages, even though it was the only life they had ever known.

Although the living conditions in the Green Building were abysmal, there were some excellent social advantages to living in Jorpati. An active sports community provided opportunities to play basketball and cricket, run track events, or even swim. Once I found out there was a swimming pool in Jorpati, I began swimming every Saturday morning. I became friends with Laxmi Kunwar, the only woman on the Nepalese Paralympic swim team. Although Laxmi was on the team, she had very poor technique. I worked with her on strokes and turns until she was a para-swimming machine. I met with the head of the Paralympic committee, and he appointed me head swimming coach. But when it came time to pay for a trip to Rio for me to attend the 2016 Olympic games, the committee became very quiet. Eventually they sent only two athletes and seven committee members. And there was nothing those committee members did that an athlete representative couldn't have handled.

As incredible as my homestay family and co-workers were, living in Kathmandu was the roughest stay I'd ever experienced in a wheelchair; even rougher than Dharamsala. Although the burn incident in Dharamsala was harrowing, daily life there was amazing. But living in the constant pollution and frustrations of Kathmandu was overwhelming, and I needed to get some fresh air.

Just a few weeks into my stay I'd met Sita KC, a star of the Nepali disability movement. Sita had been bugging me for months to visit her home in Pokhara, a six-hour drive from Kathmandu. Just as the video project was ending, Sita was passing through Kathmandu on her way home from a trip to Thailand. I caught up with her the day before she returned, and we then shared a car from the Thamel district in central Kathmandu to her home in Pokhara.

I'd been to Pokhara on my trip through Nepal in 1991, and it left me with the most stunning image my brain has ever been able to process. Pokhara is the home of the mountain god Machapuchare. The locals call it the fishtail mountain because of its double peaks, which soar 24,000 feet above the low-lying city. (Kathmandu is 4,600 feet above sea level, but Pokhara is only at 2,700 feet.) Although one of the lower peaks of the Annapurna Range, Machapuchare is an imposing geological structure that has long been the symbol of Nepalese beauty. If you are looking at a travel book about Nepal, most likely Machapuchare is on the cover. Calling it a mountain god is not hyperbole either. The locals revere it as sacred, and no human being is allowed anywhere near its summit.

In 1991 I hiked to the top of Sarangkot, a foothill on the north side of Pokhara. It was a testy two-hour climb, almost entirely on stairs carved out by locals wanting to make easy access to the summit for travelers. It was cloudy at the beginning of the hike, and I'd been shadowed by the hill the entire length of the climb. But when I got to the summit, the fog had burned off, revealing the massive mountain god dominating several terrace-farmed river valleys. I was not only out of breath from the climb, I was pulverized by the majesty of the most jaw-dropping landscape I'd ever seen.

Twenty-five years later—and this time in a wheelchair—I returned to Pokhara. I'd planned my Nepal trip to end in July to avoid the monsoon season, but the 2016 downpours arrived six weeks early. I was hoping to catch a glimpse of the mountain god, but according to the locals, I would be lucky just to see some of the snow fields on its neck.

We arrived in Pokhara, and Sita showed me to my room in her completely accessible complex. She and her husband Noshi, a Japanese physical therapist who often visited the SIRC, lived on the ground floors of adjoining four-story houses. They converted both ground floors into accessible dwellings and rented out rooms to help pay the bills. The couple lived with their four-year-old daughter, a cook, a student, and an older Japanese man who had been caring for Sita since her accident when she was only 13 years old. Sita also had a legion of friends who would pop in, stay for dinner, and often grab a room to crash for the night…or a few days. I discovered I'd been welcomed into yet another exceedingly generous Nepalese family.

While I unpacked my bag and showered, Sita yelled for me to hurry outside. I rolled into the courtyard to see the clouds give way to a dark pink sunset on my old friend, Machapuchare. I hadn't been in town for two hours when the mountain shooed away the mist to welcome me back after all these years. From this distance, Machapuchare resembled its distant Oregon cousin, Mt. Hood, albeit 10,000 feet higher. The clouds quickly closed in, but that short glimpse was much more than I'd been led to believe I would see.

Over the next few days, Sita and her friends took me around Pokhara, which was the cleanest city I had seen in South Asia. Unless there are some hidden gems in Sri Lanka or south India, no city in the region is anywhere near as pristine as Pokhara. There was no trash on the streets, garbage containers were regularly emptied, and the air was clean. I began to cough up the residue my lungs had been gathering from four months in the incinerator of Kathmandu.

We had two goals in our meanderings. I wanted to film the local rehab hospital and I wanted to find swimming pools so I could get some relief from the oppressive humidity. Sita had worked at the Pokhara Rehabilitation Center and knew the staff well. We visited the campus, which was a series of open dorms and physical therapy rooms with plenty of grass and gardens in between. Their staff was as well-educated and competent as the crew at the SIRC.

After spending an hour filming and conducting interviews, it occurred to me I could have done my entire project in the paradise of Pokhara instead of Kathmandu. While I could never forget the welcoming generosity of my family or the tight camaraderie of the SIRC peer counselors, I could have spent four months in a good mood instead of four months wearing a mask to work.

One day of shooting at the hospital was enough for me. I was on vacation and wanted to see if I could remember anything from 1991. At that time, Pokhara was just a few tiny guest houses and coffee shops. The city has since exploded to 400,000 residents with an annual tourist draw of a quarter million. The main drag straddles Phewa Lake, where there are dozens of restaurants and bars. On the far side of the lake are some upscale resorts, but much of the southern edge is pristine mountain shoreline reflecting bright tropical flora and the occasional Buddhist temple. Western travelers used to debate what is the true Shangri-La—Kathmandu or Lhasa. The correct answer is Pokhara.

One day Sita gathered two friends, and we ventured northwest out of town to discover the Penguin Pool, a six-lane, 25-meter pool on the banks of the Seti Gandaki river. The drive along the river was spectacular, and I nearly jumped out of my seat when I saw the glistening pool situated at the base of steep, wooded Himalayan foothills. Unfortunately, the pool was inaccessible with several steps leading up to the deck as well as down to the pool. I could see it would be rough getting to the pool, but I also saw several dozen young men who could help out.

But my enthusiasm wasn't shared by the three women in my party. They were terrified to go near the pool. When I asked why, they revealed a dark secret of Nepal. Sita said the women didn't want to get in the pool because they knew they would be harassed, if not attacked, by the young men. She told me the reason women never go swimming alone is Nepal, as it turns out, has a bit of a "rapey" culture.

I told them we didn't have to stay (even though I was dying to jump in!), but with the two of us in wheelchairs, it looked like we were from a hospital, so they might just leave us alone. I asked the lifeguards to help me down to the pool deck. Once there, I flopped in and began carving out a lane amidst a pasta bowl of humanity. The shock of seeing a paraplegic doing laps was enough for them to give me space to swim. Soon Sita and her two friends ventured down to the deck. I swam over to them and motioned to the lifeguards the women were with me.

Sita's friends lifted her into the pool, and when she flopped in, her face exploded with joy. It was 89 degrees with 100 percent humidity, so she had been dying to get in. We splashed around like little kids for an hour. Earlier in the week, I'd taught Sita how to breathe while doing the front crawl, and she was stunned by how far she could swim without stopping. Swimming the front crawl in a public pool seems like a small thing, but she was being super brave. Just five years earlier, the thought of a Nepalese woman with a spinal cord injury swimming in a public pool would have been unthinkable—and possibly illegal. People assumed wheelers were too sick or contagious to swim in public pools.

Not far from the pool was an open-air restaurant right on the banks of the Seti Gandaki. We ordered a huge picnic dinner and kicked back to take in some of the most exotic tropical scenery on Earth. And then, as if I'd won the grand prize on a game show, the clouds parted and Machapuchare stepped out from behind her curtain and greeted us with her full dramatic presence.

I tried to take pictures and shoot video, but Machapuchare can't be absorbed by any kind of replication. The emotional tug of seeing the world's most beautiful geologic fixture can only be experienced firsthand. You have to suffer the trials and tribulations of living in Nepal to know how exceptional the experience is. If a landslide would have thrown me into the Seti Gandaki and taken me away from this life, I would have felt I'd done the Bridge to Venice proud.

●　●　●　●　●　●　●　●　●　●　●　●

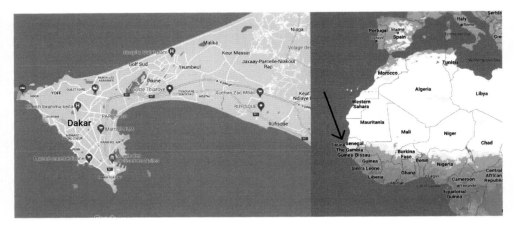

Dakar, Senegal

Out of Africa

The big takeaway from my Nepal experience was the look on the faces of the patients and my co-workers at the SIRC on filming days. The SIRC offered vocational programs, but they were mostly handicraft projects and computer training. All very good programs, although nothing the patients looked forward to.

But when we rolled out the cameras and asked for volunteer actors, everyone's faces lit up. When I showed my co-workers how to edit video, their brains would go into overdrive thinking of projects.

I'd only been back in Oregon for a few weeks when the idea hit me: Video production is the best vocational rehabilitation tool ever invented. I had a new calling in life. I was going to teach video production to disabled kids. Seeing the light bulbs turn on over the heads of the Nepalese wheelers when we went on video was a profound experience, and I felt compelled to exploit it. I just had to figure out where to go and how to finance it.

The "where" part came early in the process. I had met Badou and Sophie Faye during the 1998 World Cup in France. They were tight with my friend Pat, who stayed in France for decades after I left. I'd connected with them several times over the years, and we always clicked. Badou is a Senegalese national and Sophie grew up in a British-French household. In 2014 they moved from Paris to Badou's hometown of Dakar, Senegal, along with their two daughters. I threatened that someday I would darken their doorstep, and now the time had come.

In 2018, Badou put me in touch with Dakar's premiere disability school, the Centre Talibou Dabo (CTD) in Dakar's Grand Yoff neighborhood. I wrote to the headmaster, Madembo Sao, and planted the seeds for "Cinema Dakar." The idea was to raise enough money to pay for computers, cameras, a plane ticket, and living expenses so I could teach video production to young kids with disabilities.

It was a perfect project for the IRF. I set a $5,000 budget and spent two years filling out grant applications. I worked for hours completing forms and detailing my budget. It was tedious and frustrating work, but each time I finished the paperwork, I was sure I was going to win the grant. My idea was great, I had buy-in from the CTD, and I left no stone unturned when filling out the applications.

But as the months went on and the rejections piled up, I began to lose faith. On the side, I'd built up a fun life in Corvallis. I was in great shape, swimming five to six miles a week at the Osborn Aquatic Center. I convinced Osborn to hire me as its diving coach and I was making great progress with the student athletes. I got picked up to play guitar with a local blues-rock band, The Burdens, and that led to a super fun social life in the Corvallis hippie music scene.

I joined a Tuesday morning French conversation club that led to the revival of a long-dormant passion—I started acting again! My friend Jodi Altendorf, a lifelong thespian from the French group, told me about the Corvallis Readers Theater. It's a group of actors who don't have the time to mount full productions, so they put on plays with scripts in their hands. They construct minimal sets, then dress in full costume and act out the scenes. When done properly, it comes off just like a normal play.

To my great surprise, I won the lead in my first attempt at real acting. This wasn't a dive show comedy or a college skit show. It was a real production with experienced actors. Wini Kovacic, the star of my first play, *My Old Lady*, had been onstage for more than 60 years. I spent hours rehearsing my role of Matthais Gold, an American loser who had just inherited an apartment building in Paris. I was going off book by the end of rehearsals, but I wasn't going to take the stage without my script to back me up! We sold out three shows, and the crowds loved every minute of it.

Over the next year I was cast in two more plays, *Foxfire* and *On the Verge*. In those productions I was able to play guitar and piano and even sing. The grade-school nun who kicked me out of music class because my voice was so bad would be turning in her grave! The nicest thing about these roles was, aside from some staging issues, the wheelchair was an absolute non-factor. Obviously, people realized I was in a chair, but just a few minutes into each performance, the disability aspect disappeared into the character. It would be nice if all theater companies and film directors realized this.

I was having success cobbling together a life, but I was beyond frustrated trying to raise money for my project. I was constantly hearing what a great idea Cinema Dakar was, only to be rejected over email a few months after submitting a grant application. Finally, it occurred to me: If I wanted to make this project a reality, I was going to have to raise the money myself.

I started raising cash through public speaking. Jon Leys, an old high school cross-country teammate, hired Andy and me to speak at an awards banquet at Oakland University in Detroit. I booked a gig at the University of Rochester and did some talks to local Corvallis organizations—including my Tuesday morning French group.

I earned enough money to get by in Africa, so I made my reservation to go. Now I needed equipment for the kids. I announced on Facebook that Cinema Dakar was going to happen, and then magically, money and technology started coming in. Donations began coming through the IRF website as well as a GoFundMe page. Friends from all over America gave me their unused GoPro cameras and camcorders. The week before I left for Dakar, musician friends gathered in Milwaukee for a four-band benefit concert that raised more than enough money for a semester's worth of food and rent. So while huge organizations with millions of dollars had nothing to do with Cinema Dakar, my friends made it a reality with cash to spare.

On December 10, 2019, I took off for Africa, packed with two laptops, three camcorders, seven GoPros and enough cables, SD cards, and batteries to start a small shop. I was headed to Dakar, but my first stop was a five-day stopover in Addis Ababa, Ethiopia. Andy had been training doctors in Africa for decades, and three of his proteges were building the first PM&R program in Ethiopia. After a comfortable 14-hour flight, I landed at Bole International Airport and stepped foot in the oldest civilization on Earth.

Most people know Ethiopia from the pictures of the famines that led to the Live Aid concerts. They envision starving kids with flies buzzing about their eyes. Although it has had its share of problems, modern Ethiopia is a vibrant, progressive country leading the emergence of the new Africa.

Addis Ababa has an electric pace to it, with contemporary buildings and late model cars. Businesswomen and men are impeccably dressed and hurry about town, always on their cell phones. The city hosts the African Union, so there are more diplomats in Addis Ababa than in any other city in Africa. The country was in a festive mood the day after I arrived because Prime Minister Abiy Ahmed had just been awarded the Nobel Peace Prize for negotiating peace in the decades-long conflict with neighboring Eritrea.

Andy's colleagues Drs. Tesfaye Berme, Sisay Gizaw, and Tilahun Desta picked me up at the hotel and took me to the Macedonians Humanitarian Association (MHA) enclave. It's home to Ethiopia's most disadvantaged population—the disabled homeless. While the doctors saw patients on their voluntary rounds, I filmed and talked to any resident who could speak English. All of the residents had been living on the streets, many with severe disabilities, until they found a home with the MHA. Although they were housed in large bunkhouses, their rooms were clean; they were well fed, and they had access to doctors, physical therapists, and even prosthetic craftsmen and wheelchair builders.

As we were driving around Addis, I noticed that, compared to other major cities in Africa and Asia, it was incredibly clean. Dr. Berme explained the government had hired an army of unemployed people to sweep the streets every morning. The next day, on our early trip to the teaching hospital, I saw hundreds of people sweeping streets, washing down bus stops, and maintaining the gardens in the boulevards.

When we arrived at the Addis Ababa Teaching Hospital I sat in on a class where medical students presented cases in English, with critiques by the doctors. Then it was my turn. I gave a 45-minute talk on SCI and fielded questions from a shy group of second-year medical students. It wasn't until I said, "Hey—don't you all have questions about sex?" that they laughed and opened up a bit.

What started out being a very productive day came to a screeching and embarrassing halt. I was pushing hard up a steep ramp when my bowels gave way to the first of several bouts of diarrhea I would experience over the next four months. Fortunately, I come equipped for such instances with a change of clothes and a diaper, but this bout was particularly aggressive.

I got cleaned up in a hospital shower and was able to film some of the PT ward when the diarrhea attacked again. I had to call it a day. They put down plastic and loaded me into a hospital car that took me to my hotel. I ended up spending the next 48 hours in a weird, hallucinatory, feverish funk that broke the night before I left. Unfortunately, my plans to visit the wheelchair basketball team and several rehab facilities had to be canceled. In the end, I was able to have a nice farewell dinner before leaving. But not without vowing to return. The new Ethiopia is endlessly fascinating.

• • • • • • • • • • • • •

Two years after I came up with the idea for Cinema Dakar, I found myself circling over the peninsula of Dakar, getting ready to land at Blaise Diagne International Airport. Once on the ground, I deplaned and prepared my paperwork to explain why I was showing up with a truckload of electronics I had no intention of selling.

For weeks I'd been worried about how I was going to pass through customs without paying a tariff on the $5,000 worth of gear I was bringing into the country. I had my Centre Talibou Dabo (CTD) letter of invitation and a printout on IRF letterhead explaining the project. Before I had a chance to explain myself, the customs agent stamped my passport and waved me through without a second glance. I guess I'm not as menacing as I thought.

In minutes I was coasting along a manicured highway that could have passed for the French autoroute. The airport is more than an hour outside the city, and what I didn't know while flying down the freeway at 70 mph is I wouldn't reach half that speed again the entire time I spent in Dakar—not until four months later, when I would find myself sprinting back to Blaise Diagne in a panic.

As the sun set, I arrived at the outskirts of Dakar, and my pace slowed to the normal plodding tempo of the town. Even though it was after dark, the sidewalks were full, and people gathered on rooftops, in parks and in front of stores. We circled around to SICAP Baobab, my neighborhood for the next four unforgettable months. Cinema Dakar was set to run for five months, and halfway through I was ready to extend my stay indefinitely. But there ended up being…complications.

Badou and Sophie greeted me in front of their house, and we had a good laugh about the fact that I came through with my promise to show up on their doorstep. Unfortunately, the WiFi in their house only worked on the second floor, so I was carried up two flights of stairs to get the new Cinema Dakar computer acclimated to Senegal. I'd purchased it before leaving but didn't want to open it up in the US and have to reconfigure it in Senegal. I dialed all the language settings to French and let Google figure out I was no longer in America.

Aside from wanting to hang out with Badou and Sophie, the main reason I picked Senegal was I wanted to re-immerse myself in a francophone environment. I hadn't taught in French since I taught baseball at the College des Avenières in 1991. I usually keep my internal dialogue in French, and I always set my computer software to French. I'd geared up for the challenge, but you never know what kids will throw at you.

Badou's mother had an open room on the ground floor in her spacious house, and it could not have been more convenient for me. I had an accessible toilet and shower and three workers who cooked, cleaned, and even ran to the store for me. The neighborhood was only three miles from the Centre and, in the other direction, two miles from Dakar's Piscine Olympique (Olympic Pool), where I spent my days off.

Before the winter term started (they call it "winter," but it was 85 degrees every day) I had a meeting with my new boss, Madame Touré. I told her I was 100 percent available to teach any students at any level on subjects from web production to guitar, but my focus would be on the video production class. For that, I needed to have the best of the best students. I was willing to do the entire project as an after-school extracurricular program if that worked best.

When I showed up for my first day of class, I came equipped with the new computer, the bag of cameras, and all the tripods, cords, and data cards necessary to make videos.

I had ten students, so I bought each of them a small reporter's notebook and got ready to greet them with an inspirational speech about journalism and the power of video production. Outside of trade schools and universities, this class was not offered at any school in Senegal. Disability be damned! Together we were going to put the Centre Talibou Dabo on the map!

But there was a big problem. As I began to give my rousing speech, it occurred to me only a few of the students understood me. They spoke the native Wolof language, and although much of their schooling had been in French, only a few could respond in French.

I changed course and asked them one at a time to tell me their names, ages and neighborhoods. It was then I realized the severe limitations I faced. Only one of the ten could accomplish that simple task. Either they couldn't speak French, or they had speech or cognitive disabilities preventing them from communicating clearly. I passed one of the small reporter's notebooks around and asked everyone to write their name and age. In addition to the language and cognitive issues, many of them had physical limitations preventing them from holding my pen.

Only five of the ten could write their names. I remember the first lesson taught to me by Glenn Johnson, the head of the broadcasting team at Washington State: Good television stems from good writing! None of these kids could even type out a sentence on a computer. I didn't get the "best of the best" as I'd asked for. I got the high school students from all over the city the other schools had given up on.

Before leaving the States, I envisioned getting aggressive wheelchair athletes and award-winning students who would hop on the equipment and crank out story after story for a weekly newscast. Instead, I was facing a group of students that posed nothing but obstacles. I left the CTD wondering if I'd made a huge mistake. On that first day, I never thought in a million years they could produce a single minute of video. But oh, what little faith I had!

I returned to Baobab and explained the situation to Sophie and Badou. They could see the look of defeat in my eyes, and this was only my first day. But Sophie, always an optimist, had a great opportunity that turned out to be the jewel of the entire trip.

Sophie volunteered with an educational program at the nearby Centre Hospitalier de l'Ordre de Malte, or CHOM. The Order of Malta is one of the oldest medical organizations in the world. It was founded in Jerusalem almost a millennium ago to care for pilgrims coming to the Holy Lands. Its mission now is to take care of the poorest of the poor; the neediest of the needy.

In Dakar that meant the lepers. CHOM was the number one leprosy hospital in Western Africa. CHOM has resident patients who spend months at a time with very little to do. Nadine Germain, the wife of CHOM director Michel Germain, organized educational programs in literacy, geography, English—any subject she could find a teacher for. Sophie had been tutoring in both French and English and thought the video production idea would work great for the patients, most of whom were young adults.

The next day I showed up at CHOM with my cameras and computers and met Abdou Ndao, an eloquent resident patient who talked my ear off and had no end of ideas for short films. Along with other volunteers and patients, we came up with the idea to do a video resume of the entire hospital. We would interview the heads of all the departments, the main doctors, and even the director, Michel.

We wrote down all our interview ideas on the huge blackboard and within just a few sessions we had mapped out our project for the next four months. Regardless of how disastrous the actual Cinema Dakar project had turned out to be, if we could complete the CHOM project, it would save the entire enterprise.

So now my schedule was set. I would power through my teaching days at the CTD, then drive over to CHOM on Monday and Wednesday afternoons to set up interviews with medical professionals. Sophie employed an old family friend, Laye, as her driver. I didn't start class at the CTD until 10 a.m., so our schedules synched up, and I hired him as well.

Four members of the CHOM video team taking a break from filming.

Laye and I became fast friends, and I spent more time with him than with anyone else in Dakar. Dakar traffic features a confusing range of obstacles to negotiate, from motorcycles to late-model cars to horse-drawn carts to the ubiquitous and psychedelically painted minibuses that serve as the city's mass transit. In addition, the foot traffic spans from well-dressed businesspeople and blue-uniformed school kids to street vendors and a fair number of disabled beggars.

If anyone broke one of the many unwritten rules of Dakar traffic, Laye would blast on the horn and unleash a mouthful. We were never in much of a hurry, so I didn't get his frustration. Eventually I chimed in, pointing out dreadful drivers and shaking my head in solidarity and disgust, when actually I thought the whole thing was hilarious.

While difficult, the days at CTD were not a complete bust. Aside from my struggling video class, I was teaching beginner computer to 30 grade-school students. The CTD technology center had six old Windows computers, so I taught groups of six students at a time. I plugged my laptop into a big screen TV and taught them rudimentary skills in Word, Excel, and Internet.

After lectures, I'd unleash them into the computer bank, where they would forget everything, and I'd have to give each student the same lesson one at a time. The room was small, and many of the kids were in wheelchairs, so it was a super-tight squeeze. Once the kids were in front of their screens, I heard a nonstop chorus of, "Mr. Tom—aidez-moi!" (Mr. Tom, help me!) It was a bit frustrating, but in the end, I got a pretty good workout from it. And when a kid learned how to plot a spreadsheet or copy a picture from the Internet into their Word doc, it was incredibly rewarding.

Friday was music day, when I would bring my guitar and bang out songs after class. The Centre had a brand-new piano in one of the classrooms, and I would roll up to it and try to play, but before long some kid had to bang on the high or low notes while I was playing.

It was chaotic and unorganized, but the kids loved it. Most of the time I would play with a gathering of 20 or more students crammed so close I couldn't even reach my tuner. But if I came up with a catchy tune, they would sing it loud, and the chorus would continue as they were loaded into their buses and driven out of the compound.

I had Tuesdays and Thursdays free, but I spent most of my days off editing video in bed with my laptop propped up on a pillow.

At 2:30 those days, I slapped on my swimming suit and rolled two miles through Dakar traffic to the pool. The Piscine Olympique is the finest pool in Western Africa, and on many days I had the entire 50-meter, 10-lane pool to myself. It was sunny and glorious, and I never loved swimming so much in my entire life.

On the way home, I rode a different street every day, until I had my whole section of town, which was quite a labyrinth, mapped out. Since I was a white guy in a wheelchair, I tended to make a scene, but I took advantage of it. I said hello to anyone I made eye contact with and never hesitated to get in a conversation if it was in the offing.

Reaching back to tweak a GoPro with the video team at the Centre Talibou Dabo.

If I ban into a soccer or basketball game, I'd relax with a water bottle and take it in. A pub, the Oburo, had opened along my route, so on Fridays I'd stop in to grab a pint and watch the TV news. (I didn't have a television.) Before going home, I'd hang out at a local bottle shop that had outdoor tables where 50-somethings played a bridge-like card game. I made a lot of friends, but the game was so confusing that even after three months of studying it, I never understood how to play. I could make it back from the pool in 20 minutes if I needed to, but on Fridays, it usually took a couple hours.

All this time, though, I'd been frustrated with the video production class at the CTD. It was my main reason for being in Dakar, but I didn't know how I was going to make it work. And then it occurred to me: let the equipment do the teaching, not me. These kids weren't dumb, they just hadn't been given the opportunity to shine. Although I didn't have any single student who could perform all the facets of video production, between the 10 of them, there was a combined skill set to pull it off.

After the first few weeks, I gave up trying to teach journalism or story-telling and simply showed them how to work the equipment. They began by shooting rudimentary videos that I would put up on the big screen and critique. I showed them how to use a tripod. I showed them how to use two cameras on the same shoot. I demonstrated how GoPros were great when you were moving, but the camcorder was better when standing still. I showed them how to use the Zoom microphone, and how to upload video from their phones. I showed them how to frame a shot.

And to my great surprise, it worked! The kids had all sorts of ideas, and the school was a treasure trove of subjects. A few students began taking leadership roles, and soon enough, they were taking the initiative to shoot projects by themselves.

I would be in the computer lab teaching my other classes when a core group of video students would politely interrupt and point to my bag that housed all the equipment. Once I was confident they knew what they were doing, I would nod, then they would grab the cameras and go shoot. One day I left my computer class only to find five of them in an adjacent class-room doing a three-camera interview with one of the teachers. It was all in Wolof, but that just meant the students had to do all the editing them-selves.

The main leader of my crew was an illiterate yet super-smart 16-year-old named Mustapha Ba. Mustapha could not read or write, and his French was sketchy at best. But after seeing me put together a few videos from scratch, he got it. His mind raced with possibilities, and he constantly asked me for the cameras.

Editing the videos, however, proved another challenge. After the first month we had shot hours of video, but I was the only person who knew how to edit. Video editing requires hours of hands-on experience, so I plugged my laptop into the huge monitor and showed them how to take the SD cards from the cameras and load them into the computer. Due to their disabilities, only a few of them had the manual dexterity to perform this task, so it was slow going.

Once the cards were in the computer, I showed them how to bring the video snippets into the software so we could place them on a timeline and start editing. For some students this was way beyond their computer competence, but Mustapha ate this up and was able to replicate almost every task I performed after only one try. Since we had one computer with the editing software, time on the laptop was at a premium. I had to use it often to teach the other classes, but Mustapha hung around me like a vulture. Every time he saw the laptop idle, he pounced on it and meticulously edited his pieces.

Another bright spot on the team was Moussa Sow. Moussa came to CTD from a small village in Guinea. Although he was a fluent French speaker, he had a severe vocalization disability that hindered every facet of his life. It was incredibly difficult for him to express himself, but it was obvious he was a very intelligent kid. He also had mobility issues preventing him from walking fluidly or holding a camera motionless. On top of that, his manual dexterity was so restricted that it took him minutes just to type a sentence on the computer. But this wasn't a newsroom, and we weren't in any hurry.

Because of his speaking disability, it took a few weeks for me to realize how smart he was, but eventually I figured it out. Before we would get down to work, I would fire up the Internet and give them a quick geography lesson or a look at current events. Moussa always knew the subjects and had interesting questions to ask. It just took a long time for him to get the words out and for me to understand him.

But once I got his groove, I made him king of the GoPros and he loved it. I could set him up with the head mount or the chest mount, and he scoured the campus shooting every class, every department, the cafeteria, the sport courts—EVERYTHING! Even though his dexterity issues made it difficult to edit on the laptop, he understood the entire process, and given enough time, he came up with some really nice pieces.

The one big skill the kids lacked was oral presentation. None of my 10 students was capable of getting up in front of the camera and reading a script in French. So I started plucking some of the better grade-school students from my computer classes as presenters. My two superstar announcers were 7th graders Celestine Antoinette and Aissatou Kebe. It took me a while to convince them they would be great presenters, but after the first time they saw themselves on the big screen, they were hooked. And they were GOOD!

Another student, Auguste Tendeng, emerged from the pack and caught fire as an editor. Before I knew it, my ragtag team of castaways from the Dakar education system was operating the first K-12 video production unit in the country! And the rest of the school took notice. Two months into my project, every student in the school wanted in. Before I got to Dakar, I knew this would happen. I just thought it would come from an elite team of students, not a crew of students that other schools threw away.

I began to indoctrinate some of my brighter computer students into the dark magic of video production, and even some of my youngest kids took to it. I had a small platoon of cameramen, and with CTD festivals coming up, we had plenty of work to do.

The school held an all-day open house for the International Finance Corporation and another all-school assembly for a visit from the Senegalese Minister of Health. My crew was out in force. The only problem: We had hours and hours of video to edit from each event. It took more time to catalog the video snippets than it did to edit down the final pieces.

Three months into my stay in Dakar I was running not one but two incredible video production projects. As I predicted (and told my donors before leaving!) the projects were changing the lives of the participants and creating content that made both CHOM and CTD extremely proud. The content was coming from their own students, and they got it all for free. Cinema Dakar was a raging success, and we still had a month to go to finish our projects.

And then one Friday, it all came tumbling down. I had just finished my afternoon workout at the pool and stopped in at the Oburo to watch the news on the big-screen TV. I had a pint in my hand when the minister of education announced that due to COVID-19, all schools would be closing for at least three weeks. I had heard of the virus that was wreaking havoc in Italy and Iran, but in Senegal there were only four cases. I thought it was a giant overreaction. I'd never been more wrong in my life.

My plane home was leaving in four weeks, so I held on to hope that I would at least be able to finish the final projects before I left. Like nearly everyone at this point, I had no idea how upside down the world would become.

A week later, I was in my room when, in the space of two hours, my entire existence changed. I saw a news report from US Secretary of State Mike Pompeo urging all Americans living abroad to go back to the United States. He announced he was bringing all non-essential embassy personnel back to the States. An hour later, Senegalese President Macky Sall addressed the nation, saying he was closing Blaise Daigne International Airport until the crisis subsided.

It was the definition of a catch-22: I had to leave, but I was not permitted to leave. In the morning, Laye took me to the US embassy, where I threw up my hands and asked what I should do. They said they had no orders and that I should just make sure I was on the embassy email list to receive further instructions.

I returned to the car, unnerved by their lack of action. The embassy asks all US citizens living abroad to register in case of emergency. Well, this WAS an emergency, and they had no plans in place. I was furious, but I had to evaluate my situation. I wasn't hurt, there wasn't a war going on and I lived in an incredibly comfortable house with trusted long-standing friends. The airport was scheduled to reopen on April 17—oddly enough, the day of my exit flight. But I had no confidence they would hold to that date.

The next morning, Saturday, March 21, I was in my pajamas scanning Facebook when my phone rang from an unknown Senegalese number. I answered in French, but the voice on the other side was in English. This was odd, because I hadn't had more than a handful of conversations in English since I arrived.

An American announced herself as the station chief at the embassy and told me a plane was leaving at 3:15 that afternoon. If I wanted to be on it, I had to stop off at the embassy, purchase a $1,900 ticket, then get to the airport, which in Dakar traffic was more than 90 minutes away. She also said if I didn't get on that flight, there was no guarantee I could leave Dakar for the next several months.

I was shocked, but there was no time for panic. I called Laye, who dropped what he was doing and ran right over. I called Sophie and Badou, who came downstairs and helped me pack. The entire time I was holding back tears: these people had become my family, but due to social distancing I was leaving without even a goodbye hug.

As Laye packed my bags into the car, I waved goodbye to Badou's mother and the three staff workers who also lived in the compound. Everyone was on the verge of tears, but there was no time—I had to go!

Laye rushed me to the embassy, where I had been 24 hours earlier. Once my paperwork was approved, I hopped back into the car with Laye, and we were off to the airport. Dakar traffic was experiencing a "bouchon," as the French call it—a stopped-up wine cork. We were stuck in standstill traffic with the local hawkers knocking on our windows. But now, instead of selling Chinese electronics, they were all selling hand sanitizer!

Eventually we got out of Dakar and onto the open road to the airport. The autoroute was empty, so we made it to the flight with an hour to spare. There was only one flight leaving the Blaise Daigne airport that day, and that was the embassy charter to Washington, DC. Laye assembled my wheelchair one last time, and I handed him the laptop for the CTD. I had transfered all my files onto an external hard drive on the way to the airport. It all began to feel like a Jason Bourne movie.

Once inside the airport, I presented my paperwork at the gate, to which they responded, "I'm sorry sir, you're not on the list." Again, I showed them my paperwork, from the embassy, but they insisted I wasn't on their list.

I was in a state of total exasperation, when a calm voice came up behind me and said, "Tom, do you remember me?"

I'd been in Senegal since December, and I'd been meeting scores of people every day. The face looked vaguely familiar, and then it hit me. This was Tulinabo Mushingi—the US AMBASSADOR!

"Yes, Mr. Ambassador!" I replied, "So great to see you, even under these difficult circumstances. By the way, I have paperwork, but they say I'm not on the list?"

"Don't worry," he said. "You're on our list. You'll be on that plane. Your friend David called me this morning. I told him I'd make sure you would get out."

My "friend David" is David Schenker, who had been the US State Department Assistant Secretary of Near Eastern Affairs. David grew up with Adam Freifeld, the same Adam Freifeld I'd played softball with for four years in Portland and who had hosted me for the New York Marathon.

I'd met David years ago, but Adam was still in close touch with him. Adam heard about my plight through Facebook and reached out to David, who made a call to the embassy. Although it is still good practice to register with the embassy, it is much better to know somebody in the State Department.

My first meeting with Ambassador Tulinabo Mushingi, months before Covid hit.

After a five-hour wait, the final list from the embassy was confirmed and I was on the flight. I was loaded into a catering cart that lifted me up to the flight deck, from which I rolled onto the plane. They had left the first seat open for me.

Just like that, the two years of planning, fundraising, and eventual successes of Cinema Dakar was over. I never got to say goodbye to my students, and we left hours of unproduced video projects on the laptop. I was able to leave the video equipment and the magic laptop with the editing software, but I have no idea if they'll ever get to use it. There was no cheering as the plane took off. I was sitting with 250 people who were as devastated as I was. We loved Dakar, loved what we were doing, and we felt absolutely victimized by an invisible enemy.

• • • • • • • • • • • •

EPILOGUE

The return to America was harsh for a number of reasons. The full effect of COVID-19 had not hit Senegal when I'd left. Although institutions had started to close, restaurants were still open and the streets were still buzzing. There were only a dozen cases in the entire country, so I thought it was a bit of overkill.

But by the time I got to America, things were in complete lockdown. Dulles Airport was nearly empty, and I was able to buy a one-way flight to Milwaukee for less than $100. Mask-wearing wasn't yet a thing, but nearly every business was closed, and nobody was leaving their homes for any reason except grocery shopping or hospital visits.

My parents had been exposed to COVID-19 right before I came home and were in quarantine at the house. My sister Barb picked me up at the airport and took me directly to a hotel two miles away from them. I stayed there for ten days, living on microwave meals and beer dropped off by my brother-in-law Dan.

On the tenth day, I made it to my childhood home on Fairfield Court and saw my mom was still in bed. I wasn't going to wake her, but by 1 p.m. I thought it might be good to see if she was okay. I asked her if she wanted lunch, and she complained bitterly that her body ached and she just didn't feel like getting up. My dad and I let her sleep some more, but by late in the afternoon I went back in to see how she was doing. Begrudgingly, she agreed to get up, but 10 minutes later I went back to see she was again asleep. She tried again to wake for dinner, but only managed to sit up and complain about the food.

Within an hour, she passed away. She had not been healthy for quite a while and had signed a do-not-resuscitate order the last time she had home health care. My sister Barb and my dad were there. As she passed, we held her hand and sang old family songs from our road trips as kids. Soon afterwards, my sister Nari and her husband Mark arrived. Luckily for us there was a nurse on hand who had come by to talk to us about hospice care. When she saw my mom in her last stages, she just looked at us and said, "Okay you guys…this is it. This is how it happens…"

And just like that, the woman who had raised seven kids and visited seventy countries in the last fifteen years of her life left us. Over the next 18 months, the pandemic would evolve into the worst event of the young 21st century, but for us, it never got worse than those first weeks.

So I came home with my Africa project in shambles, a raging pandemic, complete isolation and a virtual funeral to plan for my mom. We were allowed to have only seven people present at the grave-side ceremony for a woman who had hundreds of friends and relatives. I returned home with my dad, where we held the first of thousands of Zoom calls. This one had thirteen screens. I remember snapping a screenshot thinking, "Nobody's going to believe this—thirteen screens!" Within the week it was the only way anyone communicated.

As the pandemic raged on, it gave me the chance to finish writing this tome. One lucky day I got an email from Linda Bathgate at Washington State University Press telling me she had agreed to publish the manuscript. I was over the moon and decided it was time to go back to Oregon.

Three months after leaving Dakar, I showed up back at my sister's house in Corvallis. Although my job as the diving coach at the Osborn Aquatic Center was on hold, the pool was allowed to open, giving me some sort of cadence to my day. I took up a couple of volunteer virtual teaching jobs, and my brother Andy and I began cobbling together the future of the IRF with a new executive director, Miriam Chen.

But I'd drained all of my funding sources doing the Africa trip, and America was in a state of complete donor fatigue during the pandemic. There was just too much uncertainty in our future to start spending money on new programs.

I began job hunting, and after a long search, scored a job with the Portland Bureau of Transportation as a communications specialist. It's a wonderful work atmosphere with a group of Portland do-gooders doing their best to rebuild a city devastated by the pandemic, street demonstrations, and wildfires. But it's our town and we're gonna rebuild it better than ever. And yes, "We're Keeping it WEIRD!"

I'm so grateful to be living in the most beautiful part of our country and am very proud to point out where I live when I am communicating with my friends from past lives. People complain about Facebook, often with good reason, but it has kept me in touch with so many people who have made my life so much richer.

There's the CASA, with whom I communicate daily. They need to be individually acknowledged as they have been the sounding board of my life: Gizard, Bagus, Goother, Greeble, Ox, Boomer, MOM, Toys, Lance, Devin, Johnny B, Andy, and Dave. And although we're a men's club, we would go nowhere without the support of our cadre of women: Zoe, Sissy, Shawn, Betsy, Lisa, Sharon, Brigit, Linda, Laura, Karen, and Jayne. We still get together as often as we can to play music and pretend we can solve world problems—if only they would listen to us!

There are my Diving Illini teammates who never cease to amaze me by being both accomplished and well-grounded at the same time: Brian, Tom, Matt, Barb, Piercy, Karen, Michelle, Jen, Sue, Ann-Marie, Kristine, Jonesy, Magda, Arthur, Susan, Andy and, of course, Fred and Sandy (honorable mention to the revelers at the Chateau Relaxeau and the Don't Ease Me Inn!). Keith Potter and Robin Duffy are responsible for turning the light on in my world and exposing me to possibilities I could never imagine. It's all their fault!

My World Wide Production teammates took huge chances with their lives while everyone else settled into normal careers. There are too many to name, but I'll give a special shout out to Robert, Jen, John, Roger, Rachel, Ann-Marie, Minnow, Jerry, Richard, Jean-Marie, Phillippe and Jean-Pierre. You made my time in France a dream.

The town of Harderwijk took me in and makes me smile on every occasion I have to revisit.

Pat…Besides your unconditional friendship and all the adventures we've experienced, you told me I could speak French if I worked at it. It wasn't an impossible dream—it just takes time and effort. Watching you exist in a francophone world was the greatest motivation of my life. It made my time in Les Avenières glorious; it made my rehab in Les Avenières possible. It solidified my international street cred. It allowed me to teach in Senegal. It means everything.

Tout le monde—et je veux dire TOUT LE MONDE de la belle époque aux Avenières. Des ouvriers de Walibi et meme les commerçants le long de la rue principale—le spectacle équestre! En particulier les familles Couty, Fabbris et Vermaut et tous les amis de nos cercles. Je suis tellement reconnaissante pour vous tous et pour notre expérience partagée.

To my Adidas cohorts—You're all pretty much certifiable, but I think you'll make it if you follow the Golden Rule: WWJ(ay Edwards)D.

Keeping it in Pullman, this book goes absolutely nowhere without Linda Bathgate, Caryn Lawton, and the crew at Basalt Books for believing in the project and getting this tome in print after dozens had rejected it. You all did so much work and always with a positive and productive attitude. I'm forever in your debt.

Jim Schley and Gary Garner, who have more professional credentials than I can print here, reviewed my contract at an industry and legal level and scoffed at my offers to remunerate them.

I would not have been able to write the second half of this book without the help of the physicians, nurses and therapists associated with the International Rehabilitation Forum. Dr. Germano Pestilli got me to Albania, Dr. Taslim Udin got me to Bangladesh (with the help of Devendra Peer!), Dr. Raju Dhakal got me to Nepal (with Fi Stephens!), and Dr. Gifty Gnyante got me to Ghana. So many others helped me with filming, editing, carrying gear …just too many volunteers to count!

I want to thank the Faye family in Dakar and the Kayastha family in Kathmandu for housing, feeding, and tolerating me on my last two trips.

My core friends in Portland have gotten the short end of the stick in this book, as so much of it occurs when I've been out of town. Chris, Kate, Paul, Katie, Jeff, Dianne, Aaron, Anne, Jim, Julie, Bill, Chelsey, Adam, Victoria, John, Rachel, Leigh, Paolo, Rachel, Esteban, Jolynn, Nora, Pete, Patrick, Jamie, and the Hassenbergs, Woodburys, and Fogartys. Not to forget the originals: Sean, Laura, Banker, Michele, Eddie, Cathy, Troy, Marnie, Todd, Karen, Matt, Jess, Julie, Greg, Derrick, and Toby, as well as the expats, Bill, Kelly, Adam, Greg, and Kevin—along with your kids and animals. For the past 30 years, you guys have been my rock and I look forward to growing old with you. And we'll always keep Grizzy with us along that journey.

Super special recognition to my amazing friends that made my time in Corvallis exciting and productive. I was an actor, a diving coach, a blues musician, and a weekly French speaker. It took a lot of effort for every member of those communities, and I cherish all of you who joined me on those adventures. And then there's my neighbors up on Crest Place. It's probably the best neighborhood you could ever imagine. It's composed of some of the most accomplished academics in the country and their offspring, who run roughshod through the forest with reckless abandon. It's definitely the coolest neighborhood I've lived in since Fairfield Court.

To my nieces and nephews: Patrick, Molly, Kelly, Tim, Megan, Tashi, William, Tucker, and Tristan. I don't know if I've ever told you this, but you guys kept me alive during my darkest times in rehab. It would have been so easy to check out back then—and I really wanted to. But knowing an uncle offed himself would wreck your lives. I couldn't do it and you guys kept me going.

And then there's SABLTDJ—Susie, Andy, Barb, Laurie (Nari), Tom, Dan, John (Bagus) as well as the victims we've roped in: Brigit, Dan, Mark, Zoe, and Sissy. After 60+ years, most big families have suffered irreconcilable differences, but it seems the older we get, the more we rely on each other. We've all worked with each other on projects both personally and professionally and that only seems to be increasing with time.

On this project specifically, I have to laud the editing strengths of Dan and Barb for making me appear a far-stronger writer than I actually am. And my life goes nowhere without the support of my sister Sue, our nation's most prized ornithologist (look it up—she's the most decorated American ornithologist of all time!), who housed me in between all the later trips.

And finally, there's Mom and Dad. What a whirlwind. I don't know how you kept it together when at some points you had five kids in college or four of us living abroad at the same time. It's unfathomable. While we don't always agree, there has always been the respect we've had for the way you two lived your lives. It was honest, hard-working, accomplished—and for the most part, FUN! And we're all going to do our best to live up to those morals as long as we walk (or WHEEL!) this Earth.